J. W. Ebsworth

Choyce Drollery

songs & sonnets

J. W. Ebsworth

Choyce Drollery
songs & sonnets

ISBN/EAN: 9783337265533

Printed in Europe, USA, Canada, Australia, Japan

Cover: Foto ©Thomas Meinert / pixelio.de

More available books at **www.hansebooks.com**

Choyce
DROLLERY:
SONGS & SONNETS.
BEING

*A Collection of Divers Excellent
Pieces of Poetry,*

OF SEVERAL EMINENT AUTHORS.

Now First Reprinted from the Edition of 1656.

TO WHICH ARE ADDED THE EXTRA SONGS OF

MERRY DROLLERY, 1661,

AND AN

ANTIDOTE AGAINST MELANCHOLY, 1661.

EDITED,

With Special Introductions, and Appendices of Notes,
Illustrations, Emendations of Text, &c.,

BY J. WOODFALL EBSWORTH, M.A., CANTAB.

BOSTON, LINCOLNSHIRE:
Printed by *Robert Roberts*, Strait Bar-Gate.
M,DCCCLXXVI.

TO THOSE

STUDENTS OF ART,

AMONG WHOM HE FOUND

Friendship and Enthusiasm;

BEFORE HE LEFT THEM,

WINNERS OF UNSULLIED FAME,

AND SOUGHT IN A QUIET NOOK

CONTENT, INSTEAD OF RENOWN:

THESE

"DROLLERIES OF THE RESTORATION"

ARE BY THE EDITOR

DEDICATED.

CONTENTS.

	PAGE
DEDICATION	V
PRELUDE	ix
INTRODUCTION TO "CHOICE DROLLERY, 1656"	xi
§ 1. HOW CHOICE DROLLERY WAS INHIBITED	xi
2. THE TWO COURTS IN 1656	xix
3. SONGS OF LOVE AND WAR . . .	xxvi
4. CONCLUSION: THE PASTORALS . .	xxxiii
ORIGINAL "ADDRESS TO THE READER," 1856	
"CHOYCE DROLLERY," 1656	1
TABLE OF FIRST LINES TO DITTO . .	101
INTRODUCTION TO "ANTIDOTE AGAINST MELANCHOLY," 1661	
§ 1. REPRINT OF "ANTIDOTE"	105
2. INGREDIENTS OF "AN ANTIDOTE" . .	108
ORIGINAL ADDRESS "TO THE READER," 1661.	111
,, CONTENTS (ENLARGED) . . .	112
"ANTIDOTE AGAINST MELANCHOLY," 1661 .	113

	PAGE
EDITORIAL POSTSCRIPT TO DITTO: § 1. ON THE "AUTHOR" OF THE ANTIDOTE. 2. ARTHUR O' BRADLEY	161
"WESTMINSTER DROLLERIES," EDITION 1674: EXTRA SONGS.	177
"MERRY DROLLERY," 1661:	
PART 1. EXTRA SONGS	195
,, 2. DITTO	233
APPENDIX OF NOTES, &c., ARRANGED IN FOUR PARTS:	
1. "CHOICE DROLLERY"	259
2. "ANTIDOTE AGAINST MELANCHOLY"	305
3. "WESTMINSTER DROLLERY," 1671-4	333
4. § 1. "MERRY DROLLERY," 1661	345
2. ADDITIONAL NOTES TO "M. D.," 1670	371
3. SESSIONS OF POETS	405
4. TABLES OF FIRST LINES	411
FINALE	423

PRELUDE.

Not dim and shadowy, like a world of dreams,
We summon back the past Cromwellian time,
Raised from the dead by invocative rhyme,
   Albeit this no Booke of Magick seems :

Now,—while few questions of the fleeting hour
Cease to perplex, or task th' unwilling mind,—
Lest party-strife our better-Reason blind
   To the dread evils waiting still on Power.

We see Old England torn by civil wars,
Oppress'd by gloomy zealots—men whose chain
More galled because of Regicidal stain,
   Hiding from view all honourable scars :

We see how those who raved for Liberty,
Claiming the Law's protection 'gainst the King,
Trampled themselves on Law, and strove to bring
   On their own nation tenfold Slavery.

So that with iron hand, with eagle eye,
Stout Oliver Protector scarce could keep
The troubled land in awe; while mutterings deep
   Threatened to swell the later rallying cry.

Well had he probed the hollow friends who stood
Distrustful of him, though their tongues spoke praise ;
Well read their fears, that interposed delays
   To rob him of his meed for toil and blood.

X.

A few brief years of such uneasy strife,
While foreign shores and ocean own his sway;
Then fades the lonely Conqueror away,
   Amid success, weary betimes of life.

So passing, kingly in his soul, uncrown'd,
With dark forebodings of th' approaching storm,
He leaves the spoil at mercy of the swarm
   Of beasts unclean and vultures gathering round.

For soon from grasp of Richard Cromwell slips
Semblance of power he ne'er had strength to hold;
And wolves each other tear, who tore the fold,
   While lurid twilight mocks the State's eclipse.

Then, from divided counsels, bitter snarls,
Deceit and broken fealty, selfish aim—
Where promptitude and courage win the game,—
   Self-scattered fall they; and up mounts
              KING CHARLES.

June 1st, 1876.   J. W. E.

EDITORIAL
INTRODUCTION
TO
CHOICE DROLLERY:
1656.

Charles.—" They say he is already in the forest of Arden, and a many merry men with him; and there they live like the old Robin Hood of England. They say many young gentlemen flock to him every day, and fleet the time carelessly, as they did in the golden world." *(As You Like It,* Act i. sc. 1.)

§ 1. *CHOYCE DROLLERY* INHIBITED.

E may be sure the memory of many a Cavalier went back to that sweetest of all Pastorals, Shakespeare's Comedy of "As You Like It," while he clutched to his breast the precious little volume of *Choyce Drollery, Songs and Sonnets,* which was newly published in the year 1656. He sought a covert amid the yellowing fronds of fern, in some old park that had not yet been wholly confiscated by the usurping Commonwealth; where, under the broad shadow of a beech-tree, with the squirrel

watching him curiously from above, and timid fawns sniffing at him suspiciously a few yards distant, he might again yield himself to the enjoyment of reading "heroick Drayton's" *Dowsabell,* the love-tale beginning with the magic words " Farre in the Forest of Arden "—an invocative name which summoned to his view the Rosalind whose praise was carved on many a tree. He also, be it remembered, had "a banished Lord;" even then remote from his native Court, associating with "co-mates and brothers in exile"—somewhat different in mood from Amiens or the melancholy Jacques; and, alas! not devoid of feminine companions. Enough resemblance was in the situation for a fanciful enthusiasm to lend enchantment to the name of Arden (p. 73), and recall scenes of shepherd-life with Celia, the songs that echoed " Under the greenwood-tree;" without needing the additional spell of seeing " Ingenious Shakespeare" mentioned among "the Time-Poets" on the fifth page of *Choyce Drollery.*

Not easily was the book obtained; every copy at that time being hunted after, and destroyed when found, by ruthless minions of the Commonwealth. A Parliamentary injunction had been passed against it. Commands were given for it to be burnt by the hangman. Few copies escaped, when spies and informers were numerous, and fines were levied upon those who had secreted it. Greedy eyes, active fingers, were after the *Choyce Drollery*. Any fortunate possessor, even in those early days, knew well that he grasped a treasure which few persons save himself could boast. Therefore it is not strange, two hundred and twenty years having rolled away since then, that the book has grown to be among the rarest of the *Drolleries*. Probably not six perfect copies remain in the world. The British Museum holds not one. We congratulate ourselves on restoring it now to students, for many parts of it possess historical value, besides poetic grace; and the whole work forms an interesting relic of those troubled times.

Unlike our other *Drolleries*, reproduced *verbatim et literatim* in this series, we here find little describing the last days of Cromwell and the Commonwealth; except one graphic picture of a despoiled West-Countryman (p. 57), complaining against both Roundheads and "Cabbaleroes." The poems were not only composed before hopes revived of speedy Restoration for the fugitive from Worcester-fight and Boscobel; they were, in great part, written before the Civil Wars began. Few of them, perhaps, were previously in print (the title-page asserts that *none* had been so, but we know this to be false). Publishers made such statements audaciously, then as now, and forced truth to limp behind them without chance of overtaking. By far the greater number belonged to an early date in the reign of the murdered King, chiefly about the year 1637; two, at the least, were written in the time of James I. (viz., p. 40, a contemporary poem on the Gunpowder Plot of 1605; and, p. 10, the Ballad on King James I.), if not also the still earlier one, on the Defeat of the Scots at Muscleborough Field; which is probably corrupted from an original so remote as the reign of Edward VI. "Dowsabell" was certainly among the *Pastorals* of 1593, and "Down lay the Shepherd's swain" (p. 65) bears token of belonging to an age when the Virgin Queen held sway. These facts guide to an understanding of the charm held by *Choyce Drollery* for adherents of the Monarchy; and of its obnoxiousness in the sight of the Parliament that had slain their King. It was not because of any exceptional immorality in this *Choyce Drollery* that it became denounced; although such might be declared in proclamations. Other books of the same year offended worse against morals : for example, the earliest edition known to us of *Wit and Drollery*, with the extremely "free" *facetiæ* of *Sportive Wit, or Lusty Drollery* (both works issued in 1656), held infinitely more to shock proprieties and call for repression. The *Musarum Deliciæ* of Sir J[ohn] M[ennis] and Dr. J[ames] S[mith], in the same year, 1656, cannot be held blameless. Yet the hatred shewn towards *Choyce Drollery* far exceeded all the rancour against these bolder sinners, or the previous year's delightful miscellany of merriment and true poetry, the *Wit's Interpreter* of industrious J[ohn] C[otgrave]; to whom, despite multitudinous typographical errors, we owe thanks, both for *Wit's Interpreter* and for the wilderness of dramatic beauties, his *Wit's Treasury:* bearing the same date of 1655.

It was not because of sins against taste and public or private morals, (although, we admit, it has some few of these, sufficient to afford a pretext for persecutors, who would have been equally bitter had it possessed virginal purity:) but in consequence of other and more dangerous ingredients, that *Choyce Drollery* aroused such a storm. Not disgust, but fear of its influence in reviving loyalty, prompted the order of its extermination. Readers at this later day, might easily fail to notice all that stirred the loyal sentiments of chivalric devotion, and consequently made the fierce Fifth-Monarchy men hate the small volume worse than the *Apocrypha* or *Ikon Basilike*. Herein was to be found the clever "Jack of Lent's" account of loyal preparations made in London to receive the newly-wedded Queen, Henrietta Maria, when she came from France, in 1625, escorted by the Duke of Buckingham, who compromised her sister by his rash attentions: Buckingham, whom King Charles loved so well that the favouritism shook his throne, even after Felton's dagger in 1628 had rid the land of the despotic courtier. Here, also, a more grievous offence to the Regicides, was still recorded in austere grandeur of verse, from no common hireling pen, but of some scholar like unto Henry King, of Chichester, the loyal "New-Year's Wish" (p. 48) presented to King Charles at the beginning of 1638, when the North was already in rebellion: wherein men read, what at that time had not been deemed profanity or blasphemy, the praise and faithful service of some hearts who held their monarch only second to their Saviour. Referring to their hope that the personal approach of the King might cure the evils of the disturbed realm, it is written :—

> "You, like our sacred and indulgent Lord,
>   When the too-stout Apostle drew his sword,
>   When he mistooke some secrets of the cause,
>   And in his furious zeale disdained the Lawes,
>   Forgetting true Religion doth lye
>   On prayers, not swords against authority:
>   You, like our substitute of horrid fate,
>   That are next Him we most should imitate,
>   Shall like to Him rebuke with wiser breath,
>   Such furious zeale, but not reveng'd with death.
>   Like him, the wound that's giv'n you strait shall heal
>   Then calm by precept such mistaking zeal."

INTRODUCTION. xvii.

Here was a sincere, unflinching recognition of Divine Right, such as the faction in power could not possibly abide. Even the culpable weakness and ingratitude of Charles, in abandoning Strafford, Laud, and other champions to their unscrupulous destroyers, had not made true-hearted Cavaliers falter in their faith to him. As the best of moralists declares :—

" Love is not love
Which alters when it alteration finds,
Or bends with the remover to remove."

These loyal sentiments being embodied in print within our *Choyce Drollery*, suitable to sustain the fealty of the defeated Cavaliers to the successor of the " Royal Martyr," it was evident that the Restoration must be merely a question of time. " If it be now, 'tis not to come; if it be not to come, it will be now; if it be not now, *yet it will come: the readiness is all !*"

To more than one of those who had sat in the ill-constituted and miscalled High Court of Justice, during the closing days of 1648-9, there must have been, ever and anon, as the years rolled by, a shuddering recollection of the words written anew upon the wall in characters of living fire. They had shown themselves familiar, in one sense much too familiar, with the phraseology but not the teaching of Scripture. To them the *Mene, Mene, Tekel Upharsin* needed no

Daniel come to judgment for interpretation. The Banquet was not yet over; the subjugated people, whom they had seduced from their allegiance by a dream of winning freedom from exactions, were still sullenly submissive; the desecrated cups and challices of the Church they had despoiled, believing it overthrown for ever, had been, in many cases, melted down for plunder,—in others, sold as common merchandize: and yet no thunder heard. But, however defiantly they might bear themselves, however resolute to crush down every attempt at revolt against their own authority, the men in power could not disguise from one another that there were heavings of the earth on which they trod, coming from no reverberations of their footsteps, but telling of hollowness and insecurity below. They were already suspicious among themselves, no longer hiding personal spites and jealousies, the separate ambition of uncongenial factions, which had only united for a season against the monarchy and hierarchy, but now began to fall asunder, mutually envenomed and intolerant. Presbyterian, Independent, and Nondescript-Enthusiast, while combined together of late, had been acknowledged as a power invincible, a Three-fold Cord that bound the helpless Victim to an already bloody altar. The strands of it were now unwinding, and there scarcely needed much prophetic wisdom to discern that one by one they could soon be broken.

To us, from these considerations, there is intense attraction in the *Choyce Drollery*, since it so narrowly escaped from flames to which it had been judicially condemned.

§ 2.—THE TWO COURTS, IN 1656.

AT this date many a banished or self-exiled Royalist, dwelling in the Low Countries, but whose heart remained in England, drew a melancholy contrast between the remembered past of Whitehall and the gloomy present. With honest Touchstone, he could say, "Now am I in Arden! the more fool I. When I was at home I was in a better place; but travellers must be content."

Meanwhile, in the beloved Warwickshire glades, herds of swine were routing noisily for acorns, dropped amid withered leaves under branches of the Royal Oaks. They were watched by boys, whose chins would not be past the first callow down of promissory beards when Restoration-day should come with shouts of welcome throughout the land.

In 1656 our Charles Stuart was at Bruges, now and then making a visit to Cologne, often getting into difficulties through the misconduct of his unruly followers, and already quite enslaved by Dalilahs, syrens against whom his own shrewd sense was powerless to defend him. For amusement he read his favourite

French or Italian authors, not seldom took long walks, and indulged himself in field sports:

"*A merry monarch, scandalous and poor.*"

For he was only scantily supplied with money, which chiefly came from France, but if he had possessed the purse of Fortunatus it could barely have sufficed to meet demands from those who lived upon him. A year before, the Lady Byron had been spoken of as being his seventeenth Mistress abroad, and there was no deficiency of candidates for any vacant place within his heart. Sooth to say, the place was never vacant, for it yielded at all times unlimited accommodation to every beauty. Music and dances absorbed much of his attention. So long as the faces around him showed signs of happiness, he did not seriously afflict himself because he was in exile, and a little out at elbows.

Such was the "Banished Duke" in his Belgian Court; poor substitute for the Forest of Ardennes, not far distant. By all accounts, he felt "the penalty of Adam, the season's difference," and in no way relished the discomfort. He did not smile and say,

"This is no flattery: these are counsellors
That feelingly persuade me what I am."

For, in truth, he much preferred avoiding such counsel, and relished flattery too well to part with it on cheap terms. He never considered the "rural life more sweet than that of painted pomp," and, if all tales of Cromwell's machinations be held true, Charles by no means found the home of exile "more free from peril than the envious court." On the other hand, his own proclamation, dated 3rd May, 1654, offering an annuity of five hundred pounds, a Colonelcy and Knighthood, to any person who should destroy the Usurper ("a certain mechanic fellow, by name Oliver Cromwell!"), took from him all moral right of complaint against reprisals: unless, as we half-believe, this proclamation were one of the many forgeries. As to any sweetness in "the uses of Adversity," Charles might have pleaded, with a laugh, that he had known sufficient of them already to be cloyed with it.

The men around him were of similar opinion. A few, indeed, like Cowley and Crashaw, were loyal hearts, whose devotion was best shown in times of difficulty. Not many proved of such sound metal, but there lived some "faithful found among the faithless"; and

"He that can endure
To follow with allegiance a fallen lord,
Does conquer him that did his master conquer,
And earns a place in the story."

The Ladies of the party scarcely cared for anything beyond self-adornment, rivalry, languid day-dreams of future greatness, and the encouragement of gallantry.

There was not one among them who for a moment can bear comparison with the Protector's daughter, Elizabeth Claypole—perhaps the loveliest female character of all recorded in those years. Everything concerning her speaks in praise. She was the good angel of the house. Her father loved her, with something approaching reverence, and feared to forfeit her conscientious approval more than the support of his companions in arms. In worship she shrank from the profane familiarity of the Sectaries, and devotedly held by the Church of England. She is recorded to have always used her powerful influence in behalf of the defeated Cavaliers, to obtain mercy and forbearance. Her name was whispered, with blessing implored upon it, in the prayers of many whom she alone had saved from death.* No personal ambition, no foolish pride and ostentation marked her short career. The searching glare of Court publicity could betray no flaw in her conduct or disposition; for the

* ELIZABETH CROMWELL.—A contemporary writes, "How many of the Royalist prisoners got she not freed? How many did she not save from death whom the Laws had condemned? How many persecuted Christians hath she not snatched out of the hands of the tormentors; quite contrary unto that [daughter of] Herodias who could do anything with her [step] father? She

heart was sound within, her religion was devoid of all hypocrisy. Her Christian purity was too clearly stainless for detraction to dare raise one murmur. She is said to have warmly pleaded in behalf of Doctor Hewit, who died upon the scaffold with his Royalist companion, Sir Harry Slingsby, the 8th of June, 1658 (although she rejoiced in the defeat of their plot, as her extant letter proves). Cromwell resisted her solicitations, urged to obduracy by his more ruthless Ironsides, who called for terror to be stricken into the minds of all reactionists by wholesale slaughter of conspirators. Soon after this she faded. It was currently reported and believed that on her death-bed, amid the agonies and fever-fits, she bemoaned the blood that had been shed, and spoke reproaches to

imployed her Prayers even with Tears to spare such men whose ill fortune had designed them to suffer," &c. (S. Carrington's *History of the Life and Death of His most Serene Highness OLIVER, Late Lord Protector.* 1659. p. 264.)

Elizabeth Cromwell, here contrasted with Salome, more resembled the Celia of *As you Like It*, in that she, through prizing truth and justice, showed loving care of those whom her father treated as enemies.

By the way, our initial-letter W. on opening page 11 (representing Salome receiving from the Σπεκουλάτωρ, sent by Herod, the head of S. John the Baptist)—is copied from the Address to the Reader prefixed to Part II. of *Merry Drollery*, 1661. *Vide postea*, p. 232.

Our initial letters in M.D., C., pp. 3, 5, are in *fac simile* of the original.

the father whom she loved, so that his conscience smote him, and the remembrance stayed with him for ever.* She was only twenty-nine when at Hampton Court she died, on the 6th of August, 1658. Less than a month afterwards stout Oliver's heart broke. Something had gone from him, which no amount of power and authority could counter-balance. He was not a man to breathe his deeper sorrows into the ear of those political adventurers or sanctified enthusiasts whose glib tongues could rattle off the words of con-

* Cromwell "seemed much afflicted at the death of his Friend the Earl of *Warwick;* with whom he had a fast friendship, though neither their humours, nor their natures, were like. And the Heir of that House, who had married his youngest Daughter [Frances], died about the same time [or, rather, two months earlier]; so that all his relation to, or confidence in that Family was at an end; the other branches of it abhorring his Alliance. His domestick delights were lessened every day; he plainly discovered that his son [in-law, who had married Mary Cromwell,] Falconbridge's heart was set upon an Interest destructive to his, and grew to hate him perfectly. *But that which chiefly broke his Peace was the death of his daughter [Elizabeth] Claypole;* who had been always his greatest joy, and who, in her sickness, which was of a nature the Physicians knew not how to deal with, had several Conferences with him, which exceedingly perplexed him. Though no body was near enough to hear the particulars, yet her often mentioning, in the pains she endured, the blood her Father had spilt, made people conclude, that she had presented his worst Actions to his consideration. And though he never made the least show of remorse for any of those Actions, it is very certain, that *either what she said, or her death,* affected him wonderfully." (Clarendon's *Hist. of the Rebellion.* Book xv., p. 647, edit. 1720.)

solation. While she was slowly dying he had still tried to grapple with his serious duties, as though undisturbed. Her prayers and her remonstrances had been powerless of late to make him swerve. But now, when she was gone, the hollow mockery of what power remained stood revealed to him plainly; and the Rest that was so near is not unlikely to have been the boon he most desired. It came to him upon his fatal day, his anniversary of still recurring success and happy fortune; came, as is well known, on September 3rd, 1658. The Destinies had nothing better left to give him, so they brought him death. What could be more welcome? Very few of these who reach the summit of ambition, as of those other who most lamentably failed, and became bankrupt of every hope, can feel much sadness when the messenger is seen who comes to lead them hence,—from a world wherein the jugglers' tricks have all grown wearisome, and where the tawdry pomp or glare cannot disguise the sadness of Life's masquerade.

> "Naught's had—all's spent,
> When our desire is got without content:
> 'Tis safer to be that which we destroy,
> Than by destruction dwell in doubtful joy."

§ 3.—Songs of Love and War.

It was still 1656, of which we write (the year of *Choyce Drollery* and *Parnassus Biceps*, of *Wit and Drollery* and of *Sportive Wit*); not 1658: but shadows of the coming end were to be seen. Already it was evident that Cromwell sate not firmly on the throne, uncrowned, indeed, but holding power of sovereignty. His health was no longer what it had been of old. The iron constitution was breaking up. Yet was he only nine months older than the century. In September his new Parliament met; if it can be called a Parliament in any sense, restricted and coerced alike from a free choice and from free speech, pledged beforehand to be servile to him, and holding a brief tenure of mock authority under his favour. They might declare his person sacred, and prohibit mention of Charles Stuart, whose regal title they denounced. But few cared what was said or done by such a knot of praters. More important was the renewed quarrel with Spain; and all parties rejoiced when gallant Blake and Montague fell in with eight Spanish ships off Cadiz, captured two of them and stranded others. There had been no love for that rival fleet since the Invincible Armada made its boast in 1588; but what had happened in "Bloody Mary's" reign, after her union with Philip, and the later cruelties wrought under Alva against the patriots of the

Netherlands, increased the national hatred. We see one trace of this renewed desire for naval warfare in the appearance of the Armada Ballad, "In eighty-eight ere I was born," on page 38 of our *Choyce Drollery:* the earliest copy of it we have met in print. Some supposed connection of Spanish priestcraft with the Gunpowder Plot of 1605 (Guido Faux and several of the Jesuits being so accredited from the Low Country wars), may have caused the early poem on this subject to be placed immediately following.

But the chief interest of the book, for its admirers, lay not in temporary allusions to the current politics and gossip. Furnishing these were numerous pamphlets, more or less venomous, circulating stealthily, despite all watchfulness and penalties. Next year, 1657, "Killing no Murder" would come down, as if showered from the skies; but although hundreds wished that somebody else might ·act on the suggestions, already urged before this seditious tract appeared, not one volunteer felt called upon to immolate himself to certain death on the instant by standing forward as the required assassin. Cautious thinkers held it better to bide their time, and await the natural progress of events, allowing all the enemies of Charles and Monarchy to quarrel and consume each other. Probably the bulk of country farmers and their labourers cared not one jot how things fell out, so long as they were left without exorbitant oppression; always excepting those who dwelt where recently the hoof of war-horse trod, and whose fields and villages bore still the trace of havoc. Otherwise, the interference with the Maypole dance, and such innocent rural sports, by the grim enemies to social revelry, was felt to be a heavier sorrow than the slaughter of their King.* So long as wares were sold, and profits gained, Town-traders held few sentiments of favour towards either camp. It was (owing to the parsimony of Parliament, and his continual need of supplies to be obtained without their sanction,) the frequency of his exactions, the ship-money, the forced loans, and the uncertainty of ever gaining a repayment, which had turned many hearts against King Charles I., in his long years of difficulty, before shouts arose of "Privilege." But for the cost of wasteful revels at Court, with gifts to favourites, the expense of foreign or domestic wars, there would have been no popular complaint against tyranny. Citizens care little about questions of Divine Right and Supremacy, *pro* or *con*, so long as they are left

* John Cleveland wrote a satirical address to Mr. Hammond, the Puritan preacher of Beudley, who had exerted himself "for the Pulling down of the Maypole." It begins, in mock praise, "The mighty zeal which thou hast put on," &c.; and is printed in *Parnassus Biceps*, 1656, p. 18; and among "*J. Cleveland Revived: Poems*," 1662, p. 96.

unfettered from growing rich, and are not called on to disgorge the wealth they swallowed ravenously, perhaps also dishonestly. Some remembrance of this fact possessed the Cavaliers, even before George Monk came to burst the city gates and chains. The Restoration confirmed the same opinion, and the later comedies spoke manifold contempt against time-serving traders; who cheated gallant men of money and land, but in requital were treated like Acteon.

Although, in 1656, disquiet was general, amid contemporary records we may seek far before we meet a franker and more manly statement of the honest Englishman's opinion, despising every phase of trickery in word, deed, or visage, than the poem found in *Choyce Drollery*, p. 85,—"The Doctor's Touchstone." There were, doubtless, many whose creed it stated rightly. A nation that could feel thus, would not long delay to pluck the mask from sanctimonious hypocrites, and drag "The Gang" from out their saddle.

Here, too, are the love-songs of a race of Poets who had known the glories of Whitehall before its desecration. Here are the courtly praises of such beauties as the Lady Elizabeth Dormer, 1st Countess of Carnarvon, who, while she held her infant in her arms, in 1642, was no less fascinating than she had been in her virgin bloom. The airy trifling, dallying with conceits in verse, that spoke of a refinement and graceful idlesse more than passionate warmth, gave us these relics of such men as Thomas Carew, who died in 1638, before the Court dissolved into a Camp. Some of them recal the strains of dramatists, whose only actresses had been Ladies of high birth, condescending to adorn the Masques in palaces, winning applause from royal hands and voices. These, moreover, were "Songs and Sonnets" which the best musicians had laboured skilfully to clothe anew with melody: Poems already breathing their own music, as they do still, when lutes and virginals are broken, and the composer's score has long been turned into gun-wadding.

What sweetness and true pathos are found among them, readers can study once more. The opening poem, by Davenant, is especially beautiful, where a Lover comforts himself with a thought of dying in his Lady's presence, and being mourned thereafter by her, so that she shall deck his grave with tears, and, loving it, must come and join him there :—

"Yet we hereafter shall be found
By Destiny's right placing,
Making, like Flowers, Love under ground,
Whose roots are still embracing."*

* Here the thought is enveloped amid tender fancies. Compare the more passionate and solemn earnestness of the loyal church-

Seeing, alongside of these tender pleadings from the worshipper of Beauty, some few pieces where the taint of foulness now awakens our disgust, we might feel wonder at the contrast in the same volume, and the taste of the original collector, were not such feeling of wonder long ago exhausted. Queen Elizabeth sate out the performance of *Love's Labour's Lost* (if tradition is to be believed), and was not shocked at some free expressions in that otherwise delightful play;—words and inuendoes, let us own, which were a little unsuited to a Virgin Queen. Again, if another tradition be trustworthy, she herself commissioned the comedy of *Merry Wives of Windsor* to be written and acted, in order that she might see Falstaffe in

man, Henry King, Bishop of Chichester, in his poem of *The Exequy*, addressed "To his never-to-be-forgotten Friend," wherein he says:—

> "Sleep on, my Love, in thy cold bed,
> Never to be disquieted!
> My last good-night! Thou wilt not wake,
> Till I thy fate shall overtake;
> Till age, or grief, or sickness, must
> Marry my body to that dust
> It so much loves; and fill the room
> My heart keeps empty in thy Tomb.
> *Stay for me there; I will not faile*
> *To meet thee in that hollow Vale.*
> And think not much of my delay;
> I am already on the way,
> And follow thee with all the speed
> Desire can make, or sorrows breed," &c.

love: but after that Eastcheap Boar's-Head Tavern scene, with rollicking Doll Tear-sheet, in the Second Part of *Henry IV.*, surely her sedate Majesty might have been prepared to look for something very different from the proprieties of "Religious Courtship" or the refinements of Platonic affection in the Knight, who, having "more flesh than other men," pleads this as an excuse for his also having more frailty.

Suppose we own at once, that there is a great deal of falsehood and mock-modesty in the talk which ever anon meets us, the Puritanical squeamishness of each extremely moral (undetected) Tartuffe, acting as Aristarchus; who cannot, one might think, be quite ignorant of what is current in the newspaper-literature of our own time.* The fact is this, people now-a-days keep their dishes of spiced meat and their Barmecide show-fasts separate. They sip the limpid spring before company, and keep hidden behind a

---

* For special reasons, the Editor felt it nearly impossible to avoid the omission of a few letters in one of the most objectionable of these pieces, the twelfth in order, of *Choyce Drollery*. He mentions this at once, because he holds to his confirmed opinion that in Reprints of scarce and valuable historical memorials *no tampering with the original is permissible*. (But see Appendix, Part IV. and pp. 230, 288.) He incurs blame from judicious antiquaries by even this small and acknowledged violation of exactitude. Probably, he might have given pleasure to the general public if he had omitted much more, not thirty letters only, but entire poems or songs; as the books deserved in punishment.

curtain the forbidden wine of Xeres, quietly iced, for private drinking. Our ancestors took a taste of both together, and without blushing. Their cup of nectar had some "allaying Tyber" to abate "the thirst complaint." They did not label their books "Moral and Theological, for the public Ken," or "Vice, *sub rosa*, for our locked-cabinet!" *Parlons d'autres choses, Messieurs, s'il vous plâit.*

§ 4.—ON THE PASTORALS.

THERE were good reasons for Court and country being associated ideas, if only in contrast. Thus Touchstone states, when drolling with Colin, as to a Pastoral employment:—"Truly, shepherd in respect of itself it is a good life; but in respect it is not in the Court, it is tedious." The large proportion of pastoral songs and poems in *Choyce Drollery* is one other noticeable characteristic. Even as Utopian schemes, with dreams of an unrealized Republic where laws may be equally administered, and cultivation given to all highest arts or sciences, are found to be most popular in times of discontent and tyranny, when no en-

But he leaves others to produce expurgated editions, suitable for unlearned triflers. Any reader can here erase from the Reprint what offends his individual taste (as we know that Ann, Countess of Strafford, cut out the poem of "Woman" from our copy of Dryden's *Miscellany Poems*, Pt. 6, 1709). *No Editor has any business to thus mutilate every printed copy.*

couragement for hope appears in what the acting government is doing; even so, amid luxurious times, with artificial tastes predominant, there is always a tendency to dream of pastoral simplicity, and to sing or paint the joys of rural life. In the voluptuous languor of Miladi's own *boudoir*, amid scented fumes of pastiles and flowers, hung round with curtains brought from Eastern palaces, Watteau, Greuze, Boucher, and Bachelier were employed to paint delicious panels of bare-feeted shepherdesses, herding their flocks with ribbon-knotted crooks and bursting bodices; while goatherd-swains, in satin breeches and rosetted pumps, languish at their side, and tell of tender passion through a rustic pipe. The contrast of a wimpling brook, birds twittering on the spray, and daintiest hint of hay-forks or of reaping-hooks, enhanced with piquancy, no doubt, the every-day delights of fashionable wantonness. And as it was in such later times with courtiers of *La belle France* surrounding Louis XV., so in the reign of either Charles of England—the Revolution Furies crept nearer unperceived.

Recurrence to Pastorals in *Choyce Drollery* is simply in accordance with a natural tendency of baffled Cavaliers, to look back again to all that had distinguished the earlier days of their dead monarch, before Puritanism had become rampant. Even Milton, in his youthful "Lycidas," 1637, showed love for such Idyllic transformation of actual life into a Pastoral Eclogue. (A bitter spring of hatred against the Church was even then allowed to pollute the clear rill of Helicon: in him thereafter that Marah never turned to sweetness.) Some of these Pastorals remain undiscovered elsewhere. But there can be no mistaking the impression left upon them by the opening years of the seventeenth, if not more truly the close of the sixteenth, century. Dull, plodding critics have sneered at Pastorals, and wielded their sledge-hammers against the Dresden-china Shepherdesses, as though they struck down Dagon from his pedestal. What then? Are we forbidden to enjoy, because their taste is not consulted? ———

> "Fools from their folly 'tis hopeless to stay!
> Mules will be mules, by the law of their mulishness;
> Then be advised, and leave fools to their foolishness,
> What from an ass can be got but a bray?"

Always will there be some smiling *virtuosi*, here or elsewhere, who can prize the unreal toys, and thank us for retrieving from dusty oblivion a few more of these early Pastorals. When too discordantly the factions jar around us, and denounce every one of moderate opinions or quiet habits, because he is unwilling to become enslaved as a partisan, and fight under the banner that he deems disgraced by falsehood and intolerance, despite its ostentatious blazon of "Liberation" or "Equality," it is not easy, even for such as "the melancholy Cowley," to escape into his solitude without a slanderous mockery from those who hunger for division of the spoil. Recluse philosophers of science or of literature, men like Sir Thomas Browne, pursue their labour unremittingly, and keep apart from politics; but even for this abstinence harsh measure is dealt to them by contemporaries and posterity whom they labour to enrich. It is well, no doubt, that we should be convinced as to which side the truth is on, and fight for that unto the death. Woe to the recreant who shrinks from hazarding everything in life, and life itself, defending what he holds to be the Right. Yet there are times when, as in 1656, the fight has gone against our cause, and no further gain seems promised by waging single-handedly a warfare against the triumphant multitude. Patience, my child, and wait the inevitable turn of the already quivering balance! —such is Wisdom's counsel. Butler knew the truth of Cavalier loyalty:—

> " For though out-numbered, overthrown,
> And by the fate of war run down,
> Their Duty never was defeated,
> Nor from their oaths and faith retreated :
> For Loyalty is still the same
> Whether it lose or win the game;

True as the dial to the sun,
Although it be not shone upon."

Some partizans may find a paltry pleasure in dealing stealthy stabs, or buffoons' sarcasms, against the foes they could not fairly conquer. Some hold a silent dignified reserve, and give no sign of what they hope or fear. But for another, and large class, there will be solace in the dreams of earlier days, such as the Poets loved to sing about a Golden Pastoral Age. Those who best learnt to tell its beauty were men unto whom Fortune seldom offered gifts, as though it were she envied them for having better treasure in their birthright of imagination. The dull, harsh, and uncongenial time intensified their visions: even as Hogarth's "Distressed Poet"—amid the squalour of his garret, with his gentle uncomplaining wife dunned for a milk-score—revels in description of Potosi's mines, and, while he writes in poverty, can feign himself possessor of uncounted riches. Such power of self-forgetfulness was grasped by the "Time-Poets," of whom our little book keeps memorable record.

So be it, Cavaliers of 1656. Though Oliver's troopers and a hated Parliament are still in the ascendant, let your thoughts find repose awhile, your hopes regain bright colouring, remembering the plaints of one despairing shepherd, from whom his *Chloris* fled; or of that other, "sober and demure," whose mistress had herself to blame, through freedoms being borne too far. We, also, love to seek a refuge from the exorbitant demands of myriad-handed interference with Church and State; so we come back to you, as you sit awhile in peace under the aged trees, remote from revellers and spies, "Farre in the Forest of Arden"—O take us thither!—reading of happy lovers in the pages of *Choyce Drollery*. Since their latest words are of our favourite Fletcher, let our invocation also be from him, in his own melodious verse :—

"How sweet these solitary places are! how wantonly
  The wind blows through the leaves, and courts and
    plays with 'em!
Will you sit down, and sleep? The heat invites you.
Hark, how yon purling stream dances and murmurs;
The birds sing softly too. Pray take your rest, Sir."

J. W. E.

September 2nd, 1875.

Choyce Drollery :
Songs & Sonnets.

Choyce
DROLLERY:
SONGS & SONNETS.
BEING
A Collection of divers excellent pieces of Poetry,
OF
Severall eminent Authors.

Never before printed.

LONDON,
Printed by *J. G.* for *Robert Pollard*, at the
Ben. Johnson's head behind the Exchange, and *John Sweeting*, at the
Angel in Popes-Head Alley.
1656.

To the READER.

Courteous Reader,

Hy grateful reception of our first Collection hath induced us to a second essay of the same nature; which, as we are confident, it is not inferioure to the former in worth, so we assure our selves, upon thy already experimented Candor, that it shall at least equall it in its fortunate acceptation. We serve up these Delicates

[To the Reader: 1656.]

cates by frugall Messes, as aiming at thy Satisfaction, not Saciety. But our designe being more upon thy judgement, than patience, more to delight thee, than to detain thee in the portall of a tedious, and seldome-read Epistle; we draw this displeasing Curtain, that intercepts thy (by this time) gravid, and almost teeming fancy, and subscribe,

R. P.

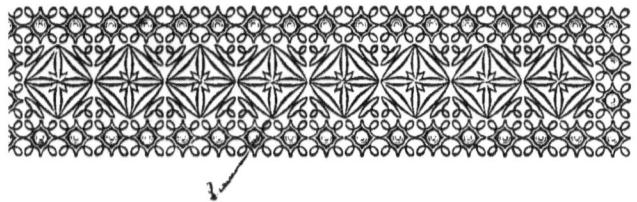

Choice
DROLLERY:
SONGS
AND
SONNETS.

The broken Heart.

1.

Deare Love let me this evening dye,
  Oh smile not to prevent it,
But use this opportunity,
Or we shall both repent it:
Frown quickly then, and break my heart,
That so my way of dying
May, though my life were full of smart,
Be worth the worlds envying.

2

Some striving knowledge to refine,
Consume themselves with thinking,
And some who friendship seale in wine
Are kindly kill'd with drinking:
And some are rackt on th' Indian coast,
Thither by gain invited,
Some are in smoke of battailes lost,
Whom Drummes not Lutes delighted.

3.

Alas how poorely these depart,
Their graves still unattended,
Who dies not of a broken heart,
Is not in death commended.
His memory is ever sweet,
All praise and pity moving,
Who kindly at his Mistresse feet
Doth dye with over-loving.

4.

And now thou frown'st, and now I dye,
My corps by Lovers follow'd,
Which streight shall by dead lovers lye,
For that ground's onely hollow'd : [hallow'd]
If Priest take't ill I have a grave,
My death not well approving,
The Poets my estate shall have
To teach them th' art of loving.

And

5.
And now let Lovers ring their bells,
For thy poore youth departed ;
Which every Lover els excels,
That is not broken hearted.
My grave with flowers let virgins strow,
For if thy teares fall neare them,
They'l so excell in scent and shew,
Thy selfe wilt shortly weare them.

6.
Such Flowers how much will *Flora* prise,
That's on a Lover growing,
And watred with his Mistris eyes,
With pity overflowing?
A grave so deckt, well, though thou art [? will]
Yet fearfull to come nigh me,
Provoke thee straight to break thy heart,
And lie down boldly by me.

7.
Then every where shall all bells ring,
Whilst all to blacknesse turning,
All torches burn, and all quires sing,
As Nature's self were mourning.
Yet we hereafter shall be found
By Destiny's right placing,
Making like Flowers, Love under ground,
Whose Roots are still embracing.

Of a Woman that died for love of a Man.

Nor Love nor Fate dare I accuse,
    Because my Love did me refuse:
But oh! mine own unworthinesse,
That durst presume so mickle blisse;
Too mickle 'twere for me to love
A thing so like the God above,
An Angels face, a Saint-like voice,
Were too divine for humane choyce.

Oh had I wisely given my heart,
For to have lov'd him, but in part,
Save onely to have lov'd his face
For any one peculiar grace,
A foot, or leg, or lip, or eye,
I might have liv'd, where now I dye.
But I that striv'd all these to chuse,
Am now condemned all to lose.

You rurall Gods that guard the plains,
And chast'neth unjust disdains;
Oh do not censure him him for this,
It was my error, and not his.
This onely boon of thee I crave,
To fix these lines upon my grave,
With *Icarus* I soare[d] too high,
For which (alas) I fall and dye.

Songs and Sonnets. 5

On the
TIME-POETS.

One night the great *Apollo* pleas'd with *Ben*,
Made the odde number of the Muses ten;
The fluent *Fletcher*, *Beaumont* rich in sense,
In Complement and Courtships quintessence;
Ingenious *Shakespeare*, *Massinger* that knowes
The strength of Plot to write in verse and prose:
Whose easie Pegassus will amble ore
Some threescore miles of Fancy in an houre;
Cloud-grapling *Chapman*, whose Aerial minde
Soares at Philosophy, and strikes it blinde;
Danbourn [*Dabourn*] I had forgot, and let it be,
He dy'd Amphibion by the Ministry;
Silvester, *Bartas*, whose translatique part
Twinn'd, or was elder to our Laureat:
Divine composing *Quarles*, whose lines aspire
The April of all Poesy in May,   [*Tho. May.*]

Who

Who makes our English speak *Pharsalia;*
Sands metamorphos'd so into another　　[Sandys]
We know not *Sands* and *Ovid* from each other;
He that so well on *Scotus* play'd the Man,
The famous *Diggs*, or *Leonard Claudian;*
The pithy *Daniel*, whose salt lines afford
A weighty sentence in each little word;
Heroick *Draiton, Withers*, smart in Rime,
The very Poet-Beadles of the Time:
Panns pastoral *Brown*, whose infant Muse did squeak
At eighteen yeares, better than others speak:
Shirley the morning-child, the Muses bred,
And sent him born with bayes upon his head:
Deep in a dump *Iohn Ford* alone was got
With folded armes and melancholly hat;
The squibbing *Middleton*, and *Haywood* sage,
Th' Apologetick Atlas of the Stage;
Well of the Golden age he could intreat,
But little of the Mettal he could get;
Three-score sweet Babes he fashion'd from the lump,
For he was Christ'ned in *Parnassus* pump;
The Muses Gossip to *Aurora's* bed,
And ever since that time his face was red.
Thus through the horrour of infernall deeps,
With equal pace each of them softly creeps,
And being dark they had *Alectors* torch,　　[Alecto's]
And that made *Churchyard* follow from his Porch,
Poor, ragged, torn, & tackt, alack, alack
You'd think his clothes were pinn'd upon his back.

The whole frame hung with pins, to mend which clothes,
In mirth they sent him to old Father Prose;
Of these sad Poets this way ran the stream,
And *Decker* followed after in a dream;
Rounce, Robble, Hobble, he that writ so high big [;]
Basse for a Ballad, *John Shank* for a Jig: [*Wm.* Basse.]
Sent by *Ben Jonson,* as some Authors say,
Broom went before and kindly swept the way:
Old *Chaucer* welcomes them unto the Green,
And *Spencer* brings them to the fairy Queen;
The finger they present, and she in grace
Transform'd it to a May-pole, 'bout which trace
Her skipping servants, that do nightly sing,
And dance about the same a Fayrie Ring.

The Vow-breaker.

When first the Magick of thine eye
    Usurpt upon my liberty,
Triumphing in my hearts spoyle, thou
Didst lock up thine in such a vow:
When I prove false, may the bright day
Be govern'd by the Moones pale ray,
(As I too well remember) this
Thou saidst, and seald'st it with a kisse.

Oh heavens! and could so soon that tye
Relent in sad apostacy?
Could all thy Oaths and mortgag'd trust,
Banish like Letters form'd in dust,   [? vanish]
Which the next wind scatters? take heed,
Take heed Revolter; know this deed
Hath wrong'd the world, which will fare worse
By thy example, than thy curse.

Hide that false brow in mists; thy shame
Ne're see light more, but the dimme flame
Of Funerall-lamps; thus sit and moane,
And learn to keep thy guilt at home;
Give it no vent, for if agen
Thy love or vowes betray more men,
At length I feare thy perjur'd breath
Will blow out day, and waken death.

The Sympathie.

IF at this time I am derided,
   And you please to laugh at me,
Know I am not unprovided
   Every way to answer thee,
   Love, or hate, what ere it be,

Never Twinns so nearly met
   As thou and I in our affection,
When thou weepst my eyes are wet,
   That thou lik'st is my election,
   I am in the same subjection.

In one center we are both,
   Both our lives the same way tending,
Do thou refuse, and I shall loath,
   As thy eyes, so mine are bending,
   Either storm or calm portending.

I am carelesse if despised,
   For I can contemn again;
How can I be then surprised,
   Or with sorrow, or with pain,
   When I can both love & disdain?

The Red Head and the White.

1.

COme my White head, let our Muses
   Vent no spleen against abuses,
Nor scoffe at monstrous signes i' th' nose,
Signes in the Teeth, or in the Toes,
Nor what now delights us most,
The sign of signes upon the post.
    For other matter we are sped,
    And our signe shall be i' th' head.

2.   [White Head's ANSWER.]

Oh! *Will: Rufus*, who would passe,
Unlesse he were a captious Asse;
The Head of all the parts is best,
And hath more senses then the rest.
This subject then in our defence
Will clear our Poem of non-sense.
    Besides, you know, what ere we read,
    We use to bring it to a head.

Why there's no other part we can
Stile Monarch o're this Isle of man:
'Tis that that weareth Nature's crown,
'Tis this doth smile, 'tis this doth frown,
O what a prize and triumph 'twere,
To make this King our Subject here:
    Believ't, tis true what we have sed,
    In this we hit the naile o' th' head.

2.   [W. H.'s ANSWER.]

Your nails upon my head Sir, Why?
How do you thus to villifie
The King of Parts, 'mongst all the rest,
Or if no king, methinks at least,
To mine you should give no offence,
That weares the badge of Innocence;
    Those blowes would far more justly light
    On thy red scull, for mine is white.

1.

Come on yfaith, that was well sed,
A pretty boy, hold up thy head,
Or hang it down, and blush apace,
And make it like mines native grace.
There's ne're a Bung-hole in the town
But in the working puts thine down,
    A byle that's drawing to a head
    Looks white like thine, but mine is red.
Poore

2.   [W. H.'s ANSWER.]

Poore foole, 'twas shame did first invent
The colour of thy Ornament,
And therefore thou art much too blame
To boast of that which is thy shame;
The Roman Prince that Poppeys topt,
Did shew such Red heads should be cropt:
    And still the Turks for poyson smite
    Such Ruddy skulls, but mine is white.

1.

The Indians paint their Devils so,
And 'tis a hated mark we know,
For never any aim aright
That do not strive to hit the white:
The Eagle threw her shell-fish down,
To crack in pieces such a crown:
    Alas, a stinking onions head
    Is white like thine, but mine is red.

2.   [White's]

Red like to a blood-shot eye,
Provoking all that see 't to cry:
For shame nere vaunt thy colours thus
Since 'tis an eye-sore unto us;
Those locks I'd swear, did I not know't,
Were threds of some red petticoat;
    No Bedlams oaker'd armes afright
    So much as thine, but mine is white.
                      Now

I.

Now if thou'lt blaze thy armes Ile shew't,
My head doth love no petticoat,
My face on one side is as faire
As on the other is my haire,
So that I bear by Herauld's rules,
Party per pale Argent and Gules.
    Then laugh not 'cause my hair is red,
    Ile swear that mine's a noble head.

I.   [2. White Head's Reply.]

The Scutcheon of my field doth beare
One onely field, and that is rare,
For then methinks that thine should yeild,
Since mine long since hath won the field;
Besides, all the notes that be,
White is the note of Chastity,
    So that without all feare or dread,
    Ile swear that mine's a maidenhead.

I.

There's no Camelion red like me,
Nor white, perhaps, thou'lt say, like thee;
Why then that mine is farre above
Thy haire, by statute I can prove;
What ever there doth seem divine
Is added to a Rubrick line,
    Which whosoever hath but read,
    Will grant that mine's a lawful head.
                     Yet

2.   [White Head.]

Yet adde what thou maist, which by yeares,
Crosses, troubles, cares and feares, ;
For that kind nature gave to me
In youth a white head, as you see,
At which, though age it selfe repine,
It ne're shall change a haire of mine ;
    And all shall say when I am am dead,
    I onely had a constant head.

1.

Yes faith, in that Ile condescend,
That our dissention here may end,
Though heads be alwaies by the eares,
Yet ours shall be more noble peeres :
For I avouch since I began,
Under a colour all was done.
    Then let us mix the White and Red,
    And both shall make a beauteous head.

1.

We mind our heads man all this time[,]
And beat them both about this rime ;
And I confesse what gave offence
Was but a haires difference.
And that went too as I dare sweare
In both of us against the haire ;
    Then joyntly now for what is said
    Lets crave a pardon from our head.

Son-

SONNET.

SHall I think because some clouds
   The beauty of my Mistris shrouds,
To look after another Star?
Those to *Cynthia* servants are;
May the stars when I doe sue,
In their anger shoot me through;
Shall I shrink at stormes of rain,
Or be driven back again,
Or ignoble like a worm,
Be a slave unto a storm?
Pity he should ever tast
The Spring that feareth Winters blast;
Fortune and Malice then combine,
Spight of either I am thine;
And to be sure keep thou my heart,
And let them wound my worser part,
Which could they kill, yet should I bee
Alive again, when pleaseth thee.

On the Flower-de-luce in Oxford.

A Stranger coming to the town,
   Went to the *Flower-de-luce*,
A place that seem'd in outward shew
   For honest men to use;

And finding all things common there,
   That tended to delight,
By chance upon the French disease
   It was his hap to light.

And lest that other men should fare
   As he had done before,
As he went forth he wrote this down
   Upon the utmost doore.

All you that hither chance to come,
   Mark well ere you be in,
The *Frenchmens* arms are signs without
   Of *Frenchmens* harms within.

[*ALDOBRANDINO*,] *Jack*

ALDOBRANDINO, a fat Cardinal.

Never was humane soule so overgrown,
    With an unreasonable Cargazon
Of flesh, as *Aldobrandine*, whom to pack,
No girdle serv'd lesse than the zodiack:
So thick a Giant, that he now was come
To be accounted an eighth hill in *Rome*,
And as the learn'd *Tostatus* kept his age,
Writing for every day he liv'd a page;
So he no lesse voluminous then that
Added each day a leaf, but 'twas of fat.

    The choicest beauty that had been devis'd
By Nature, was by her parents sacrific'd
Up to this Monster, upon whom to try,
If as increase, he could, too, multiply.

    Oh how I tremble lest the tender maid
Should dye like a young infant over-laid!
For when this Chaos would pretend to move
And arch his back for the strong act of Love,
He fals as soon orethrown with his own weight,
And with his ruines doth the Princesse fright.
She lovely Martyr) there lyes stew'd and prest,
Like flesh under the tarr'd saddle drest,
And seemes to those that look on them in bed,
Larded with him, rather than married.

Oft did he cry, but still in vain [,] to force
His fatnesse [,] powerfuller then a divorce :
No herbs, no midwives profit here, nor can
Of his great belly free the teeming man.
What though he drink the vinegars most fine,
They do not wast his fleshy Apennine ;
His paunch like some huge Istmos runs between
The amarous Seas, and lets them not be seen ;
Yet a new *Dedalus* invented how
This Bull with his *Pasiphae* might plow.

    Have you those artificial torments known,
With which long sunken Galeos are thrown
Again on Sea, or the dead Galia
Was rais'd that once behinde St. *Peters* lay :
By the same rules he this same engine made,
With silken cords in nimble pullies laid ;
And when his Genius prompteth his slow part
To works of Nature, which he helps with Art :
First he intangles in those woven bands,
His groveling weight, and ready to commands,
The sworn Prinadas of his bed, the Aids
Of Loves Camp, necessary Chambermaids ;
Each runs to her known tackling, hasts to hoyse,
And in just distance of the urging voyce,
Exhorts the labour till he smiling rise
To the beds roof, and wonders how he flies.

    Thence as the eager Falcon having spy'd
Fowl at the brook, or by the Rivers side,
Hangs in the middle Region of the aire,
So hovers he, and plains above his faire :
                                               Blest

    Blest *Icarus* first melted at those beames,
That he might after fall into those streames,
And there allaying his delicious flame,
In that sweet Ocean propogate his name.
    Unable longer to delay, he calls
To be let down, and in short measure falls
Toward his Mistresse, that without her smock
Lies naked as *Andromeda* at the Rock,
And through the Skies see her wing'd *Perseus* strike
Though for his bulk, more that sea-monster like.
    Mean time the Nurse, who as the most discreet,
Stood governing the motions at the feet,
And ballanc'd his descent, lest that amisse
He fell too fast, or that way more than this;
Steeres the Prow of the pensile Gallease,
Right on Loves Harbour the Nymph lets him pass
Over the Chains, & 'tween the double Fort
Of her incastled knees, which guard the Port.
    The Burs as she had learnt still diligent,
Now girt him backwards, now him forwards bent;
Like those that levell'd in tough Cordage, teach
The mural Ram, and guide it to the Breach.

Jack of Lent's Ballat.

[On the welcoming of Queen Henrietta Maria, 1625].

1.

L Ist you Nobles, and attend,
For here's a Ballat newly penn'd
  I took it up in *Kent*,
If any ask who made the same,
To him I say the authors name
  Is honest *Jack of Lent*.

2.

But ere I farther passe along,
Or let you know more of my Song,
  I wish the doores were lockt,
For if there be so base a Groom,
As one informes me in this room,
  The Fidlers may be knockt.

3.

T́is true, he had, I dare protest,
No kind of malice in his brest,
  But Knaves are dangerous things;
And they of late are grown so bold,
They dare appeare in cloth of Gold,
  Even in the roomes of Kings.

But

4.

But hit or misse I will declare
The speeches at London and elsewhere,
  Concerning this design,
Amongst the Drunkards it is said,
They hope her dowry shall be paid
  In nought but Clarret wine.

5.

The Country Clowns when they repaire
Either to Market or to Faire,
  No sooner get their pots,
But straight they swear the time is come
That England must be over-run
  Betwixt the French and Scots.

6.

The Puritans that never fayle
'Gainst Kings and Magistrates to rayle,
  With impudence aver,
That verily, and in good sooth,
Some Antichrist, or pretty youth,
  Shall doubtlesse get of her.

7.

A holy Sister having hemm'd
And blown her nose, will say she dream'd,
  Or else a Spirit told her,
That they and all these holy seed,
To Amsterdam must go to breed,
  Ere they were twelve months older.

8.

And might but *Jack Alent* advise,
Those dreams of theirs should not prove lies,
  For as he greatly feares,
They will be prating night and day,
Till verily, by yea, and nay,
  They set's together by th' ears.

9.

The Romish Catholiques proclaim,
That *Gundemore*, though he be lame,
  Yet can he do some tricks;
At *Paris*, he the King shall show
A pre-contract made, as I know,
  Five hundred twenty six.

10.

But sure the State of *France* is wise,
And knowes that *Spain* vents naught but lies,
  For such is their Religion;
The Jesuits can with ease disgorge
From that their damn'd and hellish forge,
  Foule falshood by the Legion.

11.

But be it so, we will admit,
The State of *Spain* hath no more wit,
  Then to invent such tales,
Yet as great *Alexander* drew,
And cut the Gorgon Knot in two,
  So shall the Prince of Wales.

      The

12.

The reverend Bishops whisper too,
That now they shall have much adoe
   With Friers and with Monks,
And eke their wives do greatly feare
Those bald pate knaves will mak't appeare
   They are Canonical punks.

13.

At *Cambridge* and at *Oxford* eke,
They of this match like Schollers speak
   By figures and by tropes,
But as for the Supremacy,
The Body may King *James's* be,
   But sure the Head's the *Pope's*.

14.

A Puritan stept up and cries,
That he the major part denies,
   And though he Logick scorns,
Yet he by revelation knows
The Pope no part o' th' head-piece ows
   Except it be the horns.

15.

The learned in Astrologie,
That wander up and down the sky,
   And their discourse with stars, [there]
Foresee that some of this brave rout
That now goes faire and soundly out,
   Shall back return with scars.

16.
Professors of Astronomy,
That all the world knows, dare not lie
    With the Mathematicians,
Prognosticate this Somer shall
Bring with the pox the Devil and all,
    To Surgeons and Physitians.

17.
The Civil Lawyer laughs in's sleeve,
For he doth verily believe
    That after all these sports,
The Cit[i]zens will horn and grow,
And their ill-gotten goods will throw
    About their bawdy Courts.

18.
And those that do *Apollo* court,
And with the wanton Muses sport,
    Believe the time is come,
That Gallants will themselves addresse
To Masques & Playes, & Wantonnesse,
    More than to fife and drum.

19.
Such as in musique spend their dayes,
And study Songs and Roundelayes,
    Begin to cleare their throats,
For by some signes they do presage,
That this will prove a fidling age
    Fit for men of their coats.

                But

20.

But leaving Colleges and Schools,
To all those Clerks and learned Fools,
   Lets through the city range,
For there are Sconces made of Horn,
Foresee things long ere they be born,
   Which you'l perhaps think strange.

21.

The Major and Aldermen being met, [Mayor]
And at a Custard closely set
   Each in their rank and order,
The Major a question doth propound,
And that unanswer'd must go round,
   Till it comes to th' Recorder.

22.

For he's the Citys Oracle,
And which you'l think a Miracle,
   He hath their brains in keeping,
For when a Cause should be decreed,
He cries the bench are all agreed,
   When most of them are sleeping.

23.

A Sheriff at lower end o' th' board
Cries Masters all hear me a word,
   A bolt Ile onely shoot,
We shall have Executions store
Against some gallants now gone o're,
   Wherefore good brethren look to't.

24.

The rascall Sergeants fleering stand,
Wishing their Charter reacht the Strand,
  That they might there intrude ;
But since they are not yet content,
I wish that it to Tyburn went,
  So they might there conclude.

25.

An Alderman both grave and wise
Cries brethren all let me advise,
  Whilst wit is to be had,
That like good husbands we provide
Some speeches for the Lady bride,
  Before all men go mad.

26.

For by my faith if we may guesse
Of greater mischiefs by the lesse,
  I pray let this suffice,
If we but on men's backs do look,
And look into each tradesmans book
  You'l swear few men are wise.

27.

Some thred-bare Poet we will presse,
And for that day we will him dresse,
  At least in beaten Sattin,
And he shall tell her from this bench,
That though we understand no French,
  At *Pauls* she may hear Lattin.

        But

28.

But on this point they all demurre,
And each takes counsell of his furre
   That smells of Fox and Cony,
At last a Mayor in high disdain,
Swears he much scorns that in his reign
   Wit should be bought for mony.

29.

For by this Sack I mean to drink,
I would not have my Soveraign think
   for twenty thousand Crownes,
That I his Lord Lieutenant here,
And you my brethren should appear
   Such errant witlesse Clownes.

30.

No, no, I have it in my head,
Devises that shall strike it dead,
   And make proud *Paris* say
That little *London* hath a Mayor
Can entertain their Lady faire,
   As well as ere did they.

31.

S. *Georges* Church shall be the place
Where first I mean to meet her grace,
   And there St. George shall be
Mounted upon a dapple gray,
And gaping wide shall seem to say,
   Welcome St. *Dennis* to me,
      From

32.

From thence in order two by two
As we to *Pauls* are us'd to goe,
   To th' Bridge we will convey her,
And there upon the top o' th' gate,
Where now stands many a Rascal's pate,
   I mean to place a player.

33.

And to the Princess he shall cry,
May't please your Grace, cast up your eye
   And see these heads of Traytors;
Thus will the city serve all those
That to your Highnesse shall prove foes,
   For they to Knaves are haters.

34.

Down Fishstreet hill a Whale shall shoot,
And meet her at the Bridges foot,
   And forth of his mouth so wide a
Shall *Jonas* peep, and say, for fish,
As good as your sweet-heart can wish,
   You shall have hence each Friday.

35.

At Grace-church corner there shall stand
A troop of Graces hand in hand,
   And they to her shall say,
Your Grace of *France* is welcome hither,
'Tis merry when Graces meet together,
   I pray keep on your way.

          At

36.

At the Exchange shall placed be,
In ugly shapes those sisters three
      That give to each their fate,
And *Spaine's Infanta* shall stand by
Wringing their hands, and thus shall cry,
      I do repent too late.

37.

There we a paire of gloves will give,
And pray her Highnesse long may live
      On her white hands to wear them;
And though they have a *Spanish* scent,
The givers have no ill intent,
      Wherefore she need not feare them.

38.

Nor shall the Conduits now run Claret,
Perhaps the *Frenchman* cares not for it,
      They have at home so much,
No, I will make the boy to pisse
No worse then purest Hypocris,
      Her Grace ne're tasted such.

39.

About the Standard I think fit
Your wives, my brethren, all should sit,
      And eke our Lady Mayris,
Who shall present a cup of gold,
And say if we might be bold,
      We'l drink to all in *Paris*.

40.

In *Pauls* Church-yard we breath may take,
For they such huge long speeches make,
      Would tire any horse;
But there I'le put her grace in minde,
To cast her Princely head behind
      And view S. *Paul's* Crosse.

41.

Our Sergeants they shall go their way,
And for us at the Devil stay,
      I mean at Temple-barre,
And there of her we leave will take,
And say 'twas for King *Charls* his sake
      We went with her so farre.

42.

But fearing I have tir'd the eares,
Both of the Duke and all these Peeres,
      Ile be no more uncivill,
Ile leave the Mayor with both the Sheriffs,
With Sergeants, hanging at their sleeves,
      For this time at the Devill.

A SONG.

A Story strange I will you tell,
  But not so strange as true,
Of a woman that danc'd upon the ropes,
  And so did her husband too.
    With a dildo, dildo, dildo,
      With a dildo, dildo, dee,
    Some say 'twas a man, but it was a woman
      As plain report may see.

She first climb'd up the Ladder
  For to deceive men's hopes,
And with a long thing in her hand
  She tickled it on the ropes.
    With a dildo, dildo, dildo,
      With a dildo, dildo, dee,
    And to her came Knights and Gentlemen
      Of low and high degree.

She jerk'd them backward and foreward
  With a long thing in her hand,
And all the people that were in the yard,
  She made them for to stand.
    With a dildo, &c.

They

They cast up fleering eyes
   All under-neath her cloaths,
But they could see no thing,
   For she wore linnen hose.
        With a dildo, &c.

The Cuckold her husband caper'd
   When his head in the sack was in,
But grant that we may never fall
   When we dance in the sack of sin.
        With a dildo, &c.

And as they ever danc't
   In faire or rainy weather,
I wish they may be hang'd i' th' rope of Love,
   And so be cut down together.
        With a dildo, &c.

Upon a House of Office over a River, set on fire by a coale of TOBACCO.

OH fire, fire, fire, where?
   The usefull house o're Water cleare,
The most convenient in a shire,
   Which no body can deny,

The house of Office that old true blue
Sir-reverence so many knew [,]
You now may see turn'd fine new.   [? fire]
   Which no body, &c.

And to our great astonishment
Though burnt, yet stands to represent
Both mourner and the monument,
   Which no body, &c.

Ben Johnson's Vulcan would doe well,
Or the merry Blades who knacks did tell,
At firing *London Bridge* befell.
   Which no body, &c.

They'l say if I of thee should chant,
The matter smells, now out upon't ;
But they shall have a fit of fie on't.
   Which no body, &c.

And why not say a word or two
Of she that's just ? witness all who
Have ever been at thy Ho go,*   **Haut goust.*
   Which no body, &c.

Earth, Aire, and Water, she could not
Affront, till chollerick fire got
Predominant, then thou grew'st hot,
   Which no body, &c.

The present cause of all our wo,
But from Tobacco ashes, oh !
'Twas s.....n luck to perish so,
   Which no body, &c

'Tis fatall to be built on lakes,
As Sodom's fall example makes ;
But pity to the innocent jakes,
   Which no body, &c

Whose genius if I hit aright,
May be conceiv'd Hermophrodite,
To both sex common when they sh . . .
   Which no body, &c.

Of severall uses it hath store,
As Midwifes some do it implore,
But the issue comes at Postern door :
    Which no body, &c.

Retired mortalls out of feare,
Privily, even to a haire,
Did often do their business there,
    Which no body, &c.

For mens and womens secrets fit
No tale-teller, thongh privy to it,
And yet they went to't without feare or wit,
    Which no body, &c.

A Privy Chamber or prison'd roome,
And all that ever therein come
Uncover must, or bide the doome,
    Which no body, &c.

A Cabinet for richest geare
The choicest of the Ladys ware,
And pretious stones full many there.
    Which no body, &c.

And where in State sits noble duck,
Many esteem that use of nock,
The highest pleasure next to oc -
    Which no body, &c.

And yet the hose there down did goe,
The yielding smock came up also,
But still no Bawdy house I trow,
    Which no body, &c.

There nicest maid with naked r . . . ,
When straining hard had made her mump,
Did sit at ease and heare it p . . . . ,
    Which no body, &c.

Like the Dutch Skipper now may skit,
When in his sleeve he did do it,
She may skit free, but now plimp niet,
    Which no body, &c.

Those female folk that there did haunt,
To make their filled bellies gaunt,
And with that same the brook did launt,
    Which no body, &c.

Are driven now to do't on grasse,
And make a sallet for their A . . .
The world is come to a sweet passe,
    Which no body, &c.

Now farewell friend we held so deare,
Although thou help'st away with our cheare,
An open house-keeper all the yeare,
    Which no body, &c.

                                        The

The Phœnix in her perfumed flame,
Was so consum'd, and thou the same,
But the Aromaticks were to blame,
    Which no body, &c.

That Phœnix is but one thing twice,
Thy Patron nobler then may rise,
For who can tell what he'l devise?
    Which no body, &c.

Diana's Temple was not free,
Nor that world *Rome*, her Majesty
Smelt of the smoke, as well as thee,
    Which no body, &c.

And learned Clerks whom we admire,
Do say the world shall so expire,
Then when you sh . . remember fire.
    Which no body, &c.

Beware of fire when you scumber,
Though to sh . . fire were a wonder,
Yet lightning oft succeeds the thunder,
    Which no body, &c.

We must submit to what fate sends,
'Tis wholsome counsel to our friends,
Take heed of smoking at both ends,
    Which no body can deny.

Upon the Spanish Invasion in Eighty eight.

1.

IN *Eighty eight*, ere I was born,
As I do well remember a,
In *August* was a Fleet prepar'd
The month before *September* a.

2.

Lisbone, Cales and *Portugall*   [*Cales*, i.e. *Cadiz.*]
Toledo and *Grenada;*
They all did meet, & made a Fleet,
And call'd it their *Armada.*

3.

There dwelt a little man in *Spain*
That shot well in a gun a;
Don Pedro hight, as black a wight
As the Knight of the Sun a.

4.

King *Philip* made him Admirall,
And charg'd him not to stay a,
But to destroy both man and boy,
And then to come his way a.

He

5.

He had thirty thousand of his own,
But to do us more harm a,
He charg'd him not to fight alone,
But to joyn with the Prince of *Parma*.

6.

They say they brought provision much
As Biskets, Beans and Bacon,
Besides, two ships were laden with whips,
But I think they were mistaken.

7.

When they had sailed all along,
And anchored before *Dover*,
The English men did board them then,
And heav'd the Rascalls over.

8.

The queen she was at *Tilbury*,
What could you more desire a?
For whose sweet sake Sir *Francis Drake*
Did set the ships on fire a.

9.

Then let them neither brag nor boast,
For if they come again a,
Let them take heed they do not speed
As they did they know when a.

Upon the Gun-powder Plot.

1.

And will this wicked world never prove good?
Will Priests and Catholiques never prove true?
Shall *Catesby*, *Piercy* and *Rookwood*
Make all this famous Land to rue?
With putting us in such a feare,
   With huffing and snuffing and guni-powder,
   With a Ohone hononoreera tarrareera, tarrareero
                                                      (hone.

2.

'Gainst the fifth of *November*, Tuesday by name,
Peircy and *Catesby* a Plot did frame,
Anno one thousand six hundred and five,
In which long time no man alive
Did ever know, or heare the like,
Which to declare my heart growes sike.
    With a O hone, &c.

Under the Parliament-house men say
Great store of Powder they did lay,
Thirty six barrels, as is reported,
With many faggots ill consorted,
With barres of iron upon them all,
To bring us to a deadly fall.
    With a O hone, &c.

                                                     And

4.

And then came forth Sir *Thomas Knyvet*,
You filthy Rogue come out o' th' doore,
Or else I sweare by Gods trivet
Ile lay thee flatlong on the floore,
For putting us all in such a feare,
   With huffing and snuffing, &c.

5.

Then *Faux* out of the vault was taken
And carried before Sir *Francis Bacon*,
And was examined of the Act,
And strongly did confesse the Fact,
And swore he would put us in such a feare.
   With huffing, &c.

6.

Now see it is a miraculous thing,
To see how God hath preserv'd our King,
The Queen, the Prince, and his Sister dear,
And all the Lords, and every Peere,
And all the Land, and every shire,
   From huffing, &c.

7.

Now God preserve the Council wise,
That first found out this enterprise;
Not they, but my Lord *Monteagle*,
His Lady and her little Beagle,
His Ape, his Ass, and his great Beare,
   From huffing, and snuffing, and gunni-powder.

Other

[8.]
Other newes I heard moreover,
If all was true that's told to me,
Three Spanish ships landed at *Dover*,
Where they made great melody,
But the Hollanders drove them here and there,
With huffing, &c.

A CATCH.

DRink boyes, drink boyes, drink and doe not spare,
Troule away the bowl, and take no care.
So that we have meat and drink, and money and clothes
What care we, what care we how the world goes.

A pitiful Lamentation.

MY Mother hath sold away her Cock
    And all her brood of Chickins,
And hath bought her a new canvasse smock
And righted up the Kitchin.
And has brought me a Lockeram bond
With a v'lopping paire of breeches,
Thinking that *Jone* would have lov'd me alone,
But she hath serv'd me such yfiches.
Ise take a rope and drowne my selfe,
Ere Ist indure these losses:
Ise take a hatchet and hang my selfe
Ere Ist indure these crosses.
Or else Ile go to some beacon high,
Made of some good dry'd furzon [,]
And there Ile seeme in love to fry
Sing hoodle a doodle Cuddon.

A Woman with Child that desired a Son, which might prove a Preacher.

A Maiden of the *pure Society*,
   Pray'd with a passing piety
That since a learned man had o're-reacht her,
The child she went withall should prove [a]
   Preacher.
The time being come, and all the dangers past,
The Goodwife askt the Midwife
What God had sent at last.
Who answer'd her half in a laughter,
Quoth she the Son is prov'd a Daughter.
But be content, if God doth blesse the Baby,
She has a *Pulpit* where a *Preacher* may be.

The Maid of Tottenham.

1.

AS I went to *Totnam*
   Upon a Market-day,
There met I with a faire maid
Cloathed all in gray,
Her journey was to *London*
With Buttermilk and Whay,
    To fall down, down, derry down,
       down, down, derry down,
       derry, derry dina.

2.

God speed faire maid, quoth one,
You are well over-took;
With that she cast her head aside,
And gave to him a look.
She was as full of Leachery
As letters in a book.
    To fall down, &c.

3.

And as they walk'd together,
Even side by side,
The young man was aware
That her garter was unty'd,
For feare that she should lose it,
Aha, alack he cry'd,
Oh your garter that hangs down!
    Down, down, derry down, &c.
                      Quoth

4.

Quoth she [,] I do intreat you
For to take the pain
To do so much for me,
As to tye it up again.
That will I do sweet-heart, quoth he,
When I come on yonder plain.
    With a down, down, derry down, &c.

5.

And when they came upon the plain
Upon a pleasant green,
The fair maid spread her l...s abroad,
The young man fell between,
Such tying of a Garter
I think was never seen.
    To fall down, &c.

6.

When they had done their businesse,
And quickly done the deed,
He gave her kisses plenty,
Aed took her up with speed.
But what they did I know not,
But they were both agreed
    To fall down together, down
    Down, down, derry down,
    Down, down, derry dina.

                                                She

7.

She made to him low curtsies
And thankt him for his paine,
The young man is to High-gate gone [,]
The maid to *London* came
To sell off her commodity
She thought it for no shame.
    To fall downe, &c.

8.

When she had done her market,
And all her money told
To think upon the matter
It made her heart full cold [:]
But that which will away, quoth she,
Is very hard to hold.
    To fall down, &c.

9.

This tying of the Garter
Cost her her Maidenhead,
Quoth she it is no matter,
It stood me in small stead,
But often times it troubled me
As I lay in my bed.
    To fall down, &c.

*To the King on New-yeares
day, 1638.*

THis day inlarges every narrow mind,
   Makes the Poor bounteous, and the Miser kind ;
Poets that have not wealth in wisht excesse,
I hope may give like Priests, which is to blesse.
And sure in elder times the Poets were
Those Priests that told men how to hope and feare,
Though they most sensually did write and live,
Yet taught those blessings, which the Gods did give,
But you (my King) have purify'd our flame,
Made wit our virtue which was once our shame;
For by your own quick fires you made ours last,
Reform'd our numbers till our songs grew chast.
Farre more thou fam'd *Augustus* ere could doe
With's wisdome, (though it long continued too)
You have perform'd even in your Moon of age ;
Refin'd to Lectures, Playes, to Schooles a stage.
Such vertue got [,] why is your Poet lesse
A Priest then his who had a power to blesse?

                                             So

So hopefull is my rage that I begin
To shew that feare which strives to keep it in :
And what was meant a blessing soars so high
That it is now become a Prophesie.
Your selfe (our *Plannet* which renewes our year)
Shall so inlighten all, and every where,
That through the Mists of error men shall spy
In the dark North the way to Loyalty ;
Whilst with your intellectuall beames, you show
The knowing what they are that seeme to know.
You like our Sacred and indulgent Lord,
When the too-stout Apostle drew his sword,
When he mistooke some secrets of the cause,
And in his furious zeale disdain'd the Lawes,
Forgetting true Religion doth lye
On prayers, not swords against authority.
You like our substitute of horrid fate
That are next him we most should imitate,
Shall like to him rebuke with wiser breath,
Such furious zeale, but not reveng'd with death.
Like him the wound that's giv'n you strait shall heal,
Then calm by precept such mistaking zeal.

In praise of a deformed woman.
1.

I Love thee for thy curled haire,
   As red as any Fox,
Our forefathers did still commend
   The lovely golden locks.
Venus her self might comelier be,
   Yet hath no such variety.

2.

I love thee for thy squinting eyes,
  It breeds no jealousie,
For when thou do'st on others look,
  Methinks thou look'st on me,
    Venus her self, &c.

3.

I love thee for thy copper nose,
  Thy fortune's ne're the worse,
It shews the mettal in thy face
  Thou should'st have in thy purse,
    Venus her self, &c.

4.

I love thee for thy Chessenut skin,
  Thy inside's white to me,
That colour should be most approv'd,
  That will least changed be.
    Venus her self, &c.

5.

I love thee for thy splay mouth,
  For on that amarous close
There's room on either side to kisse,
  And ne're offend the nose.
    Venus her self, &c.

6.

I love thee for thy rotten gummes,
  In good time it may hap,
When other wives are costly fed,
  Ile keep thy chaps on pap.
    Venus her self, &c.

7.

I love thee for thy blobber lips,
    'Tis good thrift I suppose,
They're dripping-pans unto thy eyes,
    And save-alls to thy nose.
        Venus her self, &c.

8.

I love thee for thy huncht back,
    'Tis bow'd although not broken,
For I believe the Gods did send
    Me to Thee for a Token.
        Venus her self, &c.

9.

I love thee for thy pudding wast,
    If a Taylor thou do'st lack,
Thou need'st not send to *France* for one,
    Ile fit thee with a sack.
        Venus her self, &c.

10.

I love thee for thy lusty thighes
    For tressels thou maist boast,
Sweet-heart thou hast a water-mill,
    And these are the mill-posts.
        Venus her self, &c.

[11.] 10.

I love thee for thy splay feet,
    They're fooles that thee deride,
Women are alwaies most esteem'd,
    When their feet are most wide.
        Venus her self may comelier be, &c.

On a TINKER.

HE that a Tinker, a Tinker, a Tinker will be,
    Let him leave other Loves, and come follow me.
Though he travells all the day,
Yet he comes home still at night,
And dallies, dallies with his Doxie,
And dreames of delight.
His pot and his tost in the morning he takes,
And all the day long good musick he makes;
He wanders up and down to Wakes & to Fairs,
He casts his cap, and casts his cap at the Court
    and its cares;
And when to the town the Tinker doth come,
Oh, how the wanton wenches run,
Some bring him basons, and some bring him bowles,
All maids desire him to stop up their holes.
Prinkum Prankum is a fine dance, strong Ale is
    good in the winter,
And he that thrumms a wench upon a brass pot,
The child may prove a Tinker.
With tink goes the hammer, the skellit and the
    scummer,
Come bring me thy copper kettle,
For the Tinker, the Tinker, the merry merry Tinker
Oh, he's the man of mettle.

Upon his Mistris's black Eye-browes.

Hide, oh hide those lovely Browes,
   Cupid takes them for his bowes,
And from thence with winged dart
He lies pelting at my heart,
Nay, unheard-of wounds doth give,
Wounded in the heart I live ;
From their colour I descry,
Loves bowes are made of Ebony ;
Or their Sable seemes to say
They mourn for those their glances slay ;
Or their blacknesse doth arise
From the Sun-beams of your eyes,
Where *Apollo* seemes to sit,
As he's God of Day and Wit ;
Your piercing Rayes, so bright, and cleare,
Shewes his beamy Chariots there.
Then the black upon your brow,
Sayest wisdomes sable hue,   [? sagest]
Tells to every obvious eye,
There's his other Deity.
This too shewes him deeply wise,
To dwell there he left the skies ;

So pure a black could *Phœbus* burn,
He himself would *Negro* turn,
And for such a dresse would slight
His gorgeous attire of light;
Eclipses he would count a blisse,
Were there such a black as this:
Were Night's dusky mantle made
Of so glorious a shade,
The ruffling day she would out-vie
In costly dresse, and gallantry:
Were Hell's darknesse such a black,
For it the Saints would Heaven forsake;
So pure a black, that white from hence
Loses its name of innocence;
And the most spotlesse Ivory is
A very stain and blot to this:
So pure a black, that hence I guesse,
Black first became a holy dresse.
The Gods foreseeing this, did make
Their Priests array themselves in Black.

To my Lady of Carnarvon,
January 1.

I Dol of our Sex ! Envy of thine own !
 Whom not t' have seen, is never to have known,
What eyes are good for ; to have seen, not lov'd,
Is to be more, or lesse then man, unmov'd ;
Deigne to accept, what I i' th' name of all
Thy Servants pay to this dayes Festival,
Thanks for the old yeare, prayers for the new,
So may thy many dayes to come seeme few,
So may fresh springs in thy blew rivolets flow,
To make thy roses, and thy lillies grow.
So may all dressings still become thy face,
As if they grew there, or stole thence their grace.
So may thy bright eyes comfort with their rayes
Th' humble, and dazle those that boldly gaze :
So may thy sprightly motion, beauties best part,
Shew there is stock enough of life at heart.
So may thy warm snow never grow more cold,
So may they live to be, but not seem old.
So may thy Lord pay all, yet rest thy debtor,
And love no other, till he sees a better :

So may the new year crown the old yeares joy,
By giving us a Girle unto our Boy;
I' th' one the Fathers wit, and in the other
Let us admire the beauty of the Mother,
That so we may their severall pictures see,
Which now in one fair Medall joyned be:
Till then grow thus together, and howe're
You grow old in your selves, grow stil young here;
And let him, though he may resemble either,
Seem to be both in one, and singly neither.
Let Ladies wagers lay, whose chin is this,
Whose forehead that, whose lip, whose eye, then kiss
Away the difference, whilst he smiling lies,
To see his own shape dance in both your eyes.
Sweet Babe! my prayer shall end with thee,
(Oh may it prove a Prophecy !)
May all the channels in thy veynes
Expresse the severall noble straines,
From whence they flow; sweet *Sydney's* wit,
But not the sad, sweet fate of it;
The last great *Pembroke's* learning, sage
Burleigh's both wisdome and his age;
Thy Grandsires honest heart expresse
The *Veres* untainted noblenesse.
To these (if any thing there lacks)
Adde *Dormer* too, and *Molenax*.
Lastly, if for thee I can woo
Gods, and thy Godfathers grace too,
Together with thy Fathers Thrift:
Be thou thy Mothers New-years gift.

The Western Husband-man's
Complaint in the late Wars.

UDs bodykins! Chill work no more:
Dost think chill labour to be poor?
    No ich have more a do:
If of the world this be the trade,
That ich must break zo knaves be made,
    Ich will a blundering too.   [plundering]

Chill zel my cart and eke my plow,
And get a zword if ich know how,
    For ich mean to be right:
Chill learn to zwear, and drink, and roar,
And (Gallant leek) chill keep a whore,   [like]
    No matter who can vight.

God bless us! What a world is here,
It can ne're last another year,
    Vor ich can't be able to zoe:
Dost think that ever chad the art,
To plow the ground up with my cart,
    My beasts be all a go.

                                      But

But vurst a Warrant ich will get
From Master Captaine, that a vet
    Chill make a shrewd a do:
Vor then chave power in any place,
To steal a Horse without disgrace,
    And beat the owner too.

Ich had zix oxen tother day,
And them the Roundheads vetcht away,
    A mischiefe be their speed:
And chad zix horses left me whole,
And them the Cabbaleroes stole:
    Chee voor men be agreed.

Here ich doe labour, toyl and zweat,
And dure the cold, with dry and heat,
    And what dost think ich get?
Vaith just my labour vor my pains,
The garrisons have all the gains,
    Vor thither all's avet.

There goes my corne and beanes, and pease,
Ich doe not dare them to displease,
    They doe zo zwear and vapour:
When to the Governour ich doe come,
And pray him to discharge my zum,
    Chave nothing but a paper.

                         Uds

U'ds nigs dost think that paper will
Keep warme my back and belly fill?
  No, no, goe vange thy note:
If that another year my vield
No profit doe unto me yield,
  Ich may goe cut my throat.

When any money chove in store,
Then straight a warrant comes therefore,
  Or ich must blundred be:
And when chave shuffled out one pay,
Then comes another without delay,
  Was ever the leek azee? [like]

If all this be not grief enow,
They have a thing cald quarter too,
  O'ts a vengeance waster:
A pox upon't they call it vree, ["free quarters"]
Cham zure they make us zlaves to be,
  And every rogue our master.

The

The High-way man's Song.

I Keep my Horse, I keep my Whore,
  I take no Rents, yet am not poore,
I traverse all the land about,
And yet was born to never a foot;
With Partridge plump, and Woodcock fine,
I do at mid-night often dine;
And if my whore be not in case,
My Hostess daughter has her place.
The maids sit up, and watch their turnes,
If I stay long the Tapster mourns;
The Cook-maid has no mind to sin,
Though tempted by the Chamberlin;
But when I knock, O how they bustle;
The hostler yawns, the geldings justle;
If maid be sleep, oh how they curse her!
And all this comes of, *Deliver your purse sir*.

Against Fruition, &c.

THere is not half so warme a fire
  In the Fruition, as Desire.
When I have got the fruit of pain,
Possession makes me poore again,
Expected formes and shapes unknown,
Whet and make sharp tentation;
Sense is too niggardly for Bliss,
And payes me dully with what is;
But fancy's liberall, and gives all
That can within her vastnesse fall;
Vaile therefore still, while I divine
The Treasure of this hidden Mine,
And make Imagination tell
What wonders doth in Beauty dwell.

Upon Mr. Fullers *Booke*,
called Pisgah-sight.

Fuller of wish, than hope, methinks it is,
    For me to expect a fuller work than this,
Fuller of matter, fuller of rich sense,
Fuller of Art[,] fuller of Eloquence ;
Yet dare I not be bold, to intitle this
The fullest work ; the Author fuller is,
Who, though he empty not himself, can fill
Another fuller, yet continue still
Fuller himself, and so the Reader be
Alwayes in hope a fuller work to see.

On a Sheepherd that died
for Love.

1.

CLoris, now thou art fled away,
Aminta's Sheep are gone astray,
And all the joyes he took to see
His pretty Lambs run after thee.
　　Shee's gone, shee's gone, and he alway,
　　Sings nothing now but welladay.

2.

His Oaten pipe that in thy praise,
Was wont to play such roundelayes,
Is thrown away, and not a Swaine
Dares pipe or sing within this Plaine.
　　'Tis death for any now to say
　　One word to him, but welladay.

3.

The May-pole where thy little feet
So roundly did in measure meet,
Is broken down, and no content
Came near *Amintas* since you went.
　　All that ere I heard him say,
　　Was Cloris, Cloris, *welladay.*

4.

Upon those banks you us'd to tread,
He ever since hath laid his head,
And whisper'd there such pining wo,
That not one blade of grasse will grow.
    Oh Cloris, Cloris, *come away,*
    And hear Aminta's *welladay.*

5.

The embroyder'd scrip he us'd to weare
Neglected hangs, so does his haire.
His Crook is broke, Dog pining lyes,
And he himself nought doth but cryes,
    Oh Cloris, Cloris, *come away,*
    And hear, &c.

6.

His gray coat, and his slops of green,
When worn by him, were comely seen,
His tar-box too is thrown away,
There's no delight neer him must stay,
    But cries, oh Cloris *come away,*
    Aminta's *dying, welladay.*

*The Shepheards lamentation
for the losse of his Love.*

1.

DOwn lay the Shepheards Swain,
 So sober and demure,
Wishing for his wench again,
 So bonny and so pure.
 With his head on hillock low,
 And his armes on kembow;
And all for the losse of her Hy nonny nonny no.

2.

His teares fell as thin,
 As water from a Still,
His haire upon his chin,
 Grew like tyme upon a hill:
 His cherry cheeks were pale as snow,
 Testifying his mickle woe;   (no.
 And all was for the loss of her hy nonny nonny
         Sweet

F

3.

Sweet she was, as fond of love,
  As ever fettred Swaine;
Never such a bonny one
  Shall I enjoy again.
 Set ten thousand on a row,
  Ile forbid that any show
Ever the like of her, hy nonny nonny no.

4.

Fac'd she was of Filbard hew,
  And bosom'd like a Swanne:
Back't she was of bended yew,
  And wasted by a span.
 Haire she had as black as Crow,
  From the head unto the toe,
Down down, all over, hy nonny nonny no.

5.

With her Mantle tuck't up high,
  She foddered her Flocke,
So buckesome and alluringly,
  Her knee upheld her smock;
 So nimbly did she use to goe,
  So smooth she danc'd on tip-toe,
That all men were fond of her, hy nonny nonny no.

She

6.

She simpred like a Holy-day,
  And smiled like a Spring,
She pratled like a Popinjay,
  And like a Swallow sing.
  She tript it like a barren Doe,
  And strutted like a Gar-crowe:
Which made me so fond of her, hy, &c.

7.

To trip it on the merry Down,
  To dance the lively Hay,
To wrastle for a green Gown,
  In heat of all the day,
  Never would she say me no.
  Yet me thought she had though
Never enough of her, hy, &c.

8.

But gone she is [,] the blithest Lasse
  That ever trod on Plain.
What ever hath betided her,
  Blame not the Shepheard Swain.
  For why, she was her own foe,
  And gave her selfe the overthrowe,
By being too franke of her hy nonny nonny
  no.

A

A Ballad on Queen Elizabeth ;
to the tune of Sallengers round.

I Tell you all both great and small,
    And I tell you it truely,
That we have a very great cause,
    Both to lament and crie,
Oh fie, oh fie, oh fie, oh fie,
    Oh fie on cruell death ;
For he hath taken away from us
    Our Queen *Elizabeth*.

He might have taken other folk,
    That better might have been mist,
And let our gratious Queen alone,
    That lov'd not a Popish Priest.
She rul'd this Land alone of her self,
    And was beholding to no man.
She bare the waight of all affaires,
    And yet she was but a woman.

A woman said I ? nay that is more
    Nor any man can tell,
So chaste she was, so pure she was,
    That no man knew it well.

For whilst that she liv'd till cruel death
   Exposed her to all.
Wherefore I say lament, lament,
   Lament both great and small.

She never did any wicked thing,
   Might make her conscience prick her,
And scorn'd for to submit her self to him
   That calls himself Christ's Vicker:
But rather chose couragiously
   To fight under Christ's Banner,
Gainst Turk and Pope, I and King of *Spain*,
   And all that durst withstand her.

She was as Chaste and Beautifull,
   And Faire as ere was any;
And had from forain Countreys sent
   Her Suters very many.
Though *Mounsieur* came himself from *France*,
   A purpose for to woe her,
Yet still she liv'd and dy'd a Maid,
   Doe what they could unto her.

And if that I had *Argus* eyes,
   They were too few to weep,
For our sweet Queen *Elizabeth*,
   Who now doth lye asleep:
Asleep I say she now doth lye,
   Untill the day of Doome:
But then shall awake unto the disgrace
   Of the proud Pope of *Rome*.

A Ballad on King James ; *to the tune of*
   When Arthur *first in Court began.*

WHen *James* in *Scotland* first began,
   And there was crowned King,
He was not much more than a span,
   All in his clouts swadling.

But when he waxed into yeares,
   And grew to be somewhat tall,
And told his Lords, a Parliament
   He purposed to call.

That's over-much [,] quoth *Douglas* though,
   For thee to doe [,] I feare,
For I am Lord Protector yet,
   And will be one halfe yeare.

It pleaseth me well, quoth the King,
   What thou hast said to me,
But since thou standest on such tearmes,
   Ile prove as strict to thee.

And well he rul'd and well he curb'd
   Both *Douglas* and the rest ;
Till Heaven with better Fortune and Power,
   Had him to *England* blest.

        Then

Then into *England* straight he came
    As fast as he was able,
Where he made many a Carpet Knight,
    Though none of the Round Table.

And when he entered *Barwicke* Town,
    Where all in peace he found :
But when that roaring Megge went off,
    His Grace was like to swound.

Then up to *London* straight he came,
    Where he made no long stay,
But soon returned back again,
    To meet his Queen by th' way.

And when they met, such tilting was,
    The like was never seen ;
The Lords at each others did run,
    And neer a tilt between.

Their Horses backs were under them,
    And that was no great wonder,
The wonder was to see them run,
    And break no Staves in sunder.

They ran full swift and coucht their Speares,
    O ho quoth the Ladies then,

                                    They

They run for shew, quoth the people though,
   And not to hurt the men.

They smote full hard at Barriers too,
   You might have heard the sound,
As far as any man can goe,
   When both his legges are bound.

Upon the death of a Chandler.

The Chandler grew neer his end,
   Pale Death would not stand his friend;
But tooke it in foul snuff,
As having tarryed long enough :
Yet left this not to be forgotten,
Death and the Chandler could not Cotton.
Farre

1.

FArre in the Forrest of *Arden*,
There dwelt a Knight hight *Cassimen*,
    As bold as *Isenbras:*
Fell he was and eager bent
In battaile and in Turnament,
    As was the good Sr. *Topas.*

2.

He had (as Antique stories tell)
A daughter cleped *Dowsabell*,
    A Maiden faire and free,
Who, cause she was her fathers heire,
Full well she was y-tought the leire
    Of mickle courtesie.

3.

The Silke well could she twist and twine,
And make the fine Marchpine,
    And with the needle work.
And she could help the Priest to say
His Mattins on a Holy-day,
    And sing a Psalme in Kirk.

                              Her

4.

Her Frocke was of the frolique Green,
(Mought well become a Mayden Queen)
    Which seemely was to see:
Her Hood to it was neat and fine,
In colour like the Columbine,
    y-wrought full featuously.

5.

This Maiden in a morne betime,
Went forth when *May* was in her prime,
    To get sweet Scettuall,
The Honysuckle, the Horelock,
The Lilly, and the Ladies-Smock,
    To dight her summer Hall.

6.

And as she romed here, and there,
Y-picking of the bloomed brier,
    She chanced to espie
A Shepheard sitting on a bank,
Like Chanticleere—he crowed crank,
    And piped with merry glee.

7.

He leerd his Sheep as he him list,
When he would whistle in his fist,
    To feed about him round,

Whilst he full many a Caroll sung,
That all the fields, and meadowes rung,
   And made the woods resound.

8.

In favour this same Shepheard Swaine
Was like the Bedlam Tamerlaine,
   That kept proud Kings in awe.
But meek he was as meek mought be,
Yea like the gentle *Abell*, he
   Whom his lewd brother slew.

9.

This Shepheard ware a freeze-gray Cloake,
The which was of the finest locke,
   That could be cut with Sheere:
His Aule and Lingell in a Thong,
His Tar-box by a broad belt hung,
   His Cap of Minivere.

10.

His Mittens were of Bausons skin,
His Cockers were of Cordowin,
   His Breech of country blew:
All curle, and crisped were his Locks,
His brow more white then *Albion* Rocks:
   So like a Lover true.

                        And

11.

And piping he did spend the day,
As merry as a Popinjay,
   Which lik'd faire *Dowsabell*,
That wod she ought, or wod she nought,
The Shepheard would not from her thought,
   In love she longing fell:

12.

With that she tucked up her Frock,
(White as the Lilly was her Smock,)
   And drew the Shepheard nigh,
But then the Shepheard pip'd a good,
That all his Sheep forsook their food,
   To heare his melody.

13.

Thy Sheep (quoth she) cannot be lean,
That have so faire a Shepheard Swain,
   That can his Pipe so well:
I but (quoth he) the Shepheard may,
If Piping thus he pine away,
   For love of *Dowsabell*.

14.

Of love (fond boy) take thou no keep,
Look well (quoth she) unto thy Sheep;
   Lest they should chance to stray.

So

So had I done (quoth he) full well,
Had I not seen faire *Dowsabell*,
   Come forth to gather May.

15.

I cannot stay (quoth she) till night,
And leave my Summer Hall undight,
   And all for love of men.
Yet are you, quoth he, too unkind,
If in your heart you cannot find,
   To love us now and then.

16.

And I will be to thee as kind,
As *Collin* was to *Rosalinde*,
   Of courtesie the flower.
And I will be as true (quoth she)
As ever Lover yet mought be,
   Unto her Paramour.

17.

With that the Maiden bent her knee,
Down by the Shepheard kneeled she,
   And sweetly she him kist.
But then the Shepheard whoop'd for joy,
(Quoth he) was never Shepheards boy,
   That ever was so blist.

Upon the Scots *being beaten at* Muscleborough *field.*

ON the twelfth day of *December*,
　In the fourth year of King *Edwards* reign[,]
Two mighty Hosts (as I remember)
　At *Muscleborough* did pitch on a Plain.
For a down, down, derry derry down, Hey down a,
Down, down, down a down derry.

All night our English men they lodged there,
　So did the Scots both stout and stubborn,
But well-away was all their cheere,
　For we have served them in their own turn.
　　　For a downe, &c.j

All night they carded for our *English* mens Coats,
　(They fished before their Nets were spun)

A white for Six-pence, a red for two Groats;
   Wisdome would have stayd till they had been won.
         For a down, &c.

On the tewelfth day all in the morn,
   They made a fere as if they would fight;
But many a proud *Scot* that day was down born,
   And many a rank Coward was put to his flight.
         For a down, &c.

And the Lord *Huntley*, we hadden him there,
   With him he brought ten thousand men :
But God be thanked, we gave him such a Banquet,
   He carryed but few of them home agen.
         For a down, &c.

For when he heard our great Guns crack,
   Then did his heart fall untill his hose,
He threw down his Weapons, he turned his back,
   He ran so fast that he fell on his nose.
         For a down, &c.

We beat them back till *Edenbrough*,
   (There's men alive can witnesse this)

                                                But

But when we lookt our English men through,
   Two hundred good fellowes we did not misse.
      For a down, &c.

Now God preserve *Edward* our King,
  With his two Nuncles and Nobles all,
And send us Heaven at our ending:
  For we have given *Scots* a lusty fall.
For a down, down, derry derry down, Hey,
Down a down down, down a down derry.

Lipps and Eyes.

IN *Celia* a question did arise,
  Which were more beautifull her Lippes or Eyes.
We, said the Eyes, send forth those pointed darts,
Which pierce the hardest Adamantine hearts.
From us, (reply'd the Lipps) proceed the blisses
Which Lovers reape by kind words and sweet kisses.
Then wept the Eyes, and from their Springs did powre
Of liquid Orientall Pearle a showre:
Whereat the Lippes mov'd with delight and pleasure,
Through a sweet smile unlockt their pearly Treasure:
And bad Love judge, whether did adde more grace,
Weeping or smiling Pearles in *Celia's* face.

                                      On

On black Eyes.

Black Eyes; in your dark Orbs do lye,
My ill or happy destiny,
If with cleer looks you me behold,
You give me Mines and Mounts of Gold;
If you dart forth disdainfull rayes,
To your own dy, you turn my dayes.
    Black Eyes, in your dark Orbes by changes dwell,
    My bane or blisse, my Paradise or Hell.

That Lamp which all the Starres doth blind,
Yeelds to your lustre in some kind,
Though you do weare, to make you bright,
No other dresse but that of night:
He glitters only in the day.
You in the dark your Beames display.
    Black Eyes, &c.

The cunning Theif that lurkes for prize,
At some dark corner watching lyes;
So that heart-robbing God doth stand
In the dark Lobbies, shaft in hand,

To rifle me of what I hold
More pretious farre then *Indian* Gold.
      Black Eyes, &c.

Oh powerful Negromantick Eyes,
Who in your circles strictly pries,
Will find that *Cupid* with his dart,
In you doth practice the blacke Art:
And by th' Inchantment I'me possest,
Tryes his conclusion in my brest.
      Black Eyes, &c.

Look on me though in frowning wise,
Some kind of frowns become black eyes,
As pointed Diamonds being set,
Cast greater lustre out of Jet.
Those pieces we esteem most rare,
Which in night shadowes postur'd are.
Darknesse in Churches congregates the sight,
Devotion strayes in glaring light.
    Black Eyes, in your dark Orbs by changes dwell,
    My bane, or blisse, my Paradise or Hell.

CR V.

CRVELTY.

WE read of Kings, and Gods that kindly took
    A Pitcher fill'd with Water from the Brook.
But I have dayly tendred without thanks,
Rivers of tears that overflow their banks.
A slaughtred Bull will appease angry Jove,
A Horse the Sun, a Lamb the God of Love.
But she disdains the spotlesse sacrifice
Of a pure heart that at her Altar lyes:
Vesta [i]'s not displeas'd if her chaste Urn
Doe with repaired fuell ever burn;
But my Saint frowns, though to her honoured name
I consecrate a never dying flame:
Th' *Assyrian* King did none i th' furnace throw,
But those that to his Image did not bow:
With bended knees I dayly worship her,
Yet she consumes her own Idolater.
Of such a Goddesse no times leave record,
That burnt the Temple where she was ador'd.

A Sonnet.

What ill luck had I, silly Maid that I am,
    To be ty'd to a lasting vow;
Or ere to be laid by the side of a man,
    That woo'd, and cannot tell how;
Down didle down, down didle me.
Oh that I had a Clown that he might down diddle me,
With a courage to take mine down.

What punishment is that man worthy to have,
    That thus will presume to wedde,
He deserves to be layd alive in his grave,
    That woo'd and cannot in bed;
Down didle down [,] down didle me.
Oh that I had a Lad that he might down didle (me,
For I feare I shall run mad.

The Doctors *Touchstone.*

I Never did hold, all that glisters is Gold,
  Unless by the Touch it be try'd;
Nor ever could find, that it was a true signe,
  To judge a man by the outside.
A poor flash of wit, for a time may be fit
  To wrangle a question in Schools.
Good dressing, fine cloathes, with other fine shews,
  May serve to make painted fools.

That man will beguile, in your face that will smile,
  And court you with Cap and with knee:
And while you're in health, or swimming in wealth,
  Will vow that your Servant hee'l be.
That man Ile commend, and would have to my friend
  If I could tell where to choose him,
That wil help me at need, and stand me in stead,
  When I have occasion to use him.

I doe not him fear, that wil swagger & sweare,
  And draw upon every cross word,
And forthwith again if you be rough & plain,
  Be contented to put up his sword.

Him valiant I deem, that patient can seem,
   And fights not in every place,
But on good occasion, without seeking evasion [,]
   Durst look his proud Foe in the face.

That Physician shal pass that is all for his glass
   And no other sign can scan,
Who to practice did hop, from 'Apothecaries' shop,
   Or some old Physitians man.
He Physick shal give to me whilst I live,
   That hath more strings to his Bow,
Experience and learning, with due deserving,
   And will talk on no more then he know.

That Lawyer I hate, that wil wrangle & prate,
   In a matter not worth the hearing:
And if fees do not come, can be silent & dumb,
   Though the cause deserves but the clearing.
That Lawyers for me, that's not all for his fee,
   But will do his utmost endeavour
To stand for the right, and tug against might,
   And lift the truth as with a Leaver.

The Shark I do scorn, that's only well born,
   And brags of his antient house,
Yet his birth cannot fit, with money nor wit,
   But feeds on his friends like a Louse,
That man I more prize, that by vertue doth rise
   Unto some worthy degree,

                                           That

That by breeding hath got, what by birth he had not,
    A carriage that's noble and free.

I care not for him, that in riches doth swimme,
    And flants it in every fashion,
That brags of his Grounds and prates of his Hounds,
    And his businesse is all recreation.
For him I will stand, that hath wit with his Land,
    And will sweat for his Countreys good,
That will stick to the Lawes, and in a good cause
    Will adventure to spend his heart-blood.

That man I despise, that thinks himself wise,
    Because he can talk at Table,
And at a rich feast break forth a poor jest,
    To the laughter of others more able.
No, he hath more wit, that silent can sit,
    Yet knowes well enough how to do it,
That speaks with reason, & laughs in due seaso[n,]
    And when he is mov'd unto it.

I care not a fly, for a house that's built high,
    And yeelds not a cup of good beer,
Where scraps you may find, while Venison's in kind
    For a week or two in a yeare.
He a better house keeps, that every night sleeps
    Under a Covert of thatch,
Where's good Beef from the Stall, and a fire in the Hall,
    Where you need not to scramble nor snatch.

Then lend me your Touch, for dissembling there's
   Ile try them before I do trust.   (much,
For a base needy Slave, in shew may be brave,
   And a sliding Companion seem just.
The man that's down right, in heart & in sight,
   Whose life and whose looks doth agree,
That speaks what he thinks, and sleeps when he winks,
   O that's the companion for me.

A copy of Verses of a mon[e]y Marriage.

1.

NO Gypsie nor no Blackamore,
   No Bloomesbery, nor Turnbald whore,
Can halfe so black, so foule appeare,
As she I chose to be my Deare.
She's wrinkled, old, she's dry, she's tough,
Yet money makes her faire enough.

2.

Nature's hand shaking did dispose,
Her cheeks faire red unto her nose,
Which shined like that wanton light,
Misguideth wanderers in the night.
Yet for all this I do not care,
Though she be foul, her money's faire.

                                                  Her

3.

Her tangled Locks do show to sight,
Like Horses manes, whom haggs affright.
Her Bosome through her vaile of Lawne,
Shews more like Pork, her Neck like Brawn.
    Yet for all this I do not care,
      Though she be foul, her money's faire.

4.

Her teeth, to boast the Barbers fame,
Hang all up in his wooden frame.
Her lips are hairy, like the skin
Upon her browes, as lank as thin.
    Yet for all this I do not care,
      Though she be foul, her money's faire.

5.

Those that her company do keep,
Are rough hoarse coughs, to break my sleep.
The Palsie, Gout, and Plurisie,
And Issue in her legge and thigh.
    Yet me it grieves not, who am sure
      That Gold can all diseases cure.

6.

Then young men do not jeere my lot,
That beauty left, and money got:
For I have all things having Gold,
And beauty too, since beautie's sold.
    For Gold by day shall please my sight,
      When all her faults lye hid at night.

The baseness of Whores.

Trust no more, a wanton Whore,
   If thou lov'st health and freedom,
They are so base in every place,
   It's pity that bread should feed 'um.
All their sence is impudence,
   Which some call good conditions.
Stink they do, above ground too,
   Of Chirurgions and Physitians.

If you are nice, they have their spice,
   On which they'le chew to flout you,
And if you not discern the plot,
   You have no Nose about you.
Furthermore, they have in store,
   For which I deadly hate 'um,
Perfum'd geare, to stuffe each eare,
   And for their cheeks Pomatum.

Liquorish Sluts, they feast their guts,
   At Chuffs cost, like Princes,
Amber Plumes, and Mackarumes,
   And costly candy'd Quinces.
Potato plump, supports the Rump,
   Eringo strengthens Nature.
Viper Wine, so heats the chine,
   They'le gender with a Satyr.

Names they own were never known
    Throughout their generation,
Noblemen are kind to them,
    At least by approbation :
Many dote on one gay Coat,
    But mark what there is stampt on 't,
A stone Horse wild, with toole defil'd,
    Two Goats, a Lyon rampant.

Truth to say, Paint and Array,
    Makes them so highly prized.
Yet not one well, of ten can tell,
    If ever they were baptized.
And if not, then tis a blot
    Past cure of Spunge or Laver :
And we may sans question say
    The Divel was their God-father.

Now to leave them, he receive them,
    Whom they most confide in,
Whom that is, aske *Tib* or *Sis*,
    Or any whom next you ride in.
If in sooth, she speaks the truth,
    She sayes excuse I pray you,
The beast you ride, where I confide,
    Will in due time convey you.

A Lover disclosing his love to his Mistris.

LEt not sweet *St.* let not these eyes offend you,
   Nor yet the message, that these lines impart,
The message my unfeined love doth send you,
Love that your self hath planted in my heart.

For being charm'd by the bewitching art
Of those inveigling graces that attend you:
Love's holy fire kindled hath in part
These never-dying flames, my breast doth send you.

Now if my lines offend, let love be blam'd,
And if my love displease, accuse my eyes,
And if mine eyes sin, their sins cause only lyes
On your bright eyes, that hath my heart inflam'd.

Since eyes [,] love, lines erre, then by your direction,
Excuse my eyes, my lines, and my affection.

The contented Prisoner his praise of Sack.

How happy's that Prisoner
    That conquers his fates,
With silence, and ne're
    On bad fortune complaines,
But carelessely playes
    With his Keyes on the Grates,
And makes a sweet consort
    With them and his chayns.
He drowns care with Sack,
    When his thoughts are opprest,
And makes his heart float,
    Like a Cork in his Breast.

The Chorus.

Then,
Since we are all slaves,
　That Islanders be,
And our Land's a large prison,
　Inclos'd with the Sea :
Wee'l drink up the Ocean,
To set our selves free,
　For man is the World's Epitome.

Let Pirates weare Purple,
　Deep dy'd in the blood
Of those they have slain,
　The scepter to sway.
If our conscience be cleere,
　And our title be good,
With the rags we have on us,
　We are richer then they.
We drink down at night,
　What we beg or can borrow,
And sleep without plotting
　For more the next morrow.
　　　　　　Since we, &c.

Let the Usurer watch
　Ore his bags and his house,

To keep that from Robbers,
  He hath rackt from his debtors,
Each midnight cries Theeves,
  At the noyse of a mouse,
Then see that his Trunks
  Be fast bound in their Fetters.
When once he's grown rich enough
  For a State plot,
Buff in an hower plunders
  What threescore years got.

    Since we, &c.

Come Drawer fill each man
  A peck of Canary
This Brimmer shall bid
  All our senses good-night.
When old *Aristotle*
  Was frolick and merry,
By the juice of the Grape,
  He turn'd Stagarite.
Copernicus once
  In a drunken fit found,
By the coruse [course] of his brains,
  That the world turn'd round.

    Since we, &c.

      'Tis

'Tis Sack makes our faces
   Like Comets to shine,
And gives beauty beyond
   The Complexion mask,
Diogenes fell so
   In love with this Wine,
That when 'twas all out,
   He dwelt in the Cask.
He liv'd by the s[c]ent
   Of his Wainscoated Room;
And dying desir'd
   The Tub for his Tombe.

                Since we, &c.

Of DESIRE.

Fire, Fire!
    O how I burn in my desire.
For all the teares that I can strain
Out of my empty love-sick brain,
Cannot asswage my scorching pain.
Come Humber, Trent, and silver Thames,
The dread Ocean haste with all thy streames,
And if thou can'st not quench my fire,
Then drown both me and my Desire.

    Fire, Fire!
Oh there's no hell to my desire.
See how the Rivers backward lye,
The Ocean doth his tide deny,
For fear my flames should drink them drye.
Come heav'nly showers, come pouring down,
You all that once the world did drown.
You then sav'd some, and now save all,
Which else would burn, and with me fall.

Upon kinde and true Love.

'Tis not how witty, nor how free,
    Nor yet how beautifull she be,
But how much kinde and true to me.
Freedome and Wit none can confine,
And Beauty like the Sun doth shine,
But kinde and true are onely mine.

Let others with attention sit,
To listen, and admire her wit,
That is a rock where Ile not split.
Let others dote upon her eyes,
And burn their hearts for sacrifice,
Beauty's a calm where danger lyes.

But Kinde and True have been long try'd,
And harbour where we may confide,   [? An]
And safely there at anchor ride.
From change of winds there we are free,
And need not fear Storme's tyrannie,
Nor Pirat, though a Prince he be.

Upon his Constant Mistresse.

SHe's not the fairest of her name,
   But yet she conquers more than all the race,
For she hath other motives to inflame,
   Besides a lovely face.
There's Wit and Constancy   (the Eye.
   And Charms, that strike the soule more than
'Tis no easie lover knowes how to discover
   Such Divinity.

And yet she is an easie book,
   Written in plain language for the meaner wit,
A stately garb, and [yet] a gracious look,
   With all things justly fit.
But age will undermine
This glorious outside, that appeares so fine,
   When the common Lover
Shrinks and gives her over,
Then she's onely mine.

To the Platonick that applies
   His clear addresses onely to the mind;
The body but a Temple signifies,
   Wherein the Saints inshrin'd,
To him it is all one,
   Whether the walls be marble, or rough stone;
Nay, in holy places, which old time defaces,
   More devotion's shown.

The

The Ghost-Song.

'Tis late and cold, stir up the fire,
    Sit close, and draw the table nigher,
Be merry, and drink wine that's old,
A hearty medicine 'gainst the cold ;
Your bed['s] of wanton down the best,
Where you may tumble to your rest :
I could well wish you wenches too,
But I am dead, and cannot do.
Call for the best, the house will ring,
Sack, White and Claret, let them bring,
And drink apace, whilst breath you have,
You'l find but cold drinking in the grave ;
Partridge, Plover for your dinner,
And a Capon for the sinner,
You shall finde ready when you are up,
And your horse shall have his sup.
Welcome, welcome, shall flie round,
And I shall smile, though under ground.

You that delight in Trulls and Minions,
Come buy my four ropes of St. Omers Onions.

FINIS.

Table

Table of First Lines
To the Songs and Poems in
CHOICE DROLLERY, 1656.
(NOW FIRST ADDED.)

	page.
A Maiden of the Pure Society	44
A story strange I will you tell	31
A Stranger coming to the town	16
And will this wicked world never prove good?	40
As I went to Totnam	45
Blacke eyes, in your dark orbs do lye	81
Cloris, *now thou art fled away*	63
Come, my White-head, let our Muses	10
Deare Love, let me this evening dye	1
Down lay the Shepheards Swain	65
Drink boyes, drink boyes, drink and doe not spare	42
Farre in the Forrest of Arden	73
Fire! Fire! O, how I burn	97
Fuller of wish, than hope, methinks it is	62
He that a Tinker, a Tinker, a Tinker will be	52
Hide, oh hide those lovely Browes	53
How happy's that Prisoner that conquers, &c	93
I keeep my horse, I keep my W	60
I love thee for thy curled hair	49
I never did hold, all that glisters is gold	85
I tell you all, both great and small	68

Idol

Idol of our sex! Envy of thine own!	55
If at this time I am derided	9
In Celia *a question did arise*	80
In Eighty-eight, ere I was born	38
Let not, sweet saint, let not these eyes offend you	92
List, you Nobles, and attend	20
My Mother hath sold away her Cock	43
Never was humane soule so overgrown	17
No Gysie nor no Blackamore	88
Nor Love, nor Fate dare I accuse	4
Oh fire, fire, fire, where?	33
On the twelfth day of December	78
One night the great Apollo, *pleas'd with* Ben	5
Shall I think, because some clouds	15
She's not the fairest of her name	99
The Chandler grew neer his end	72
There is not halfe so warme a fire	61
This day inlarges every narrow mind	48
'Tis late and cold, stir up the fire	100
'Tis not how witty, nor how free	98
Trust no more a wanton Wh......	90
Uds bodykins, Chill work no more	57
We read of Kings, and Gods that kindly took	83
What ill luck had I, silly maid that I am	84
When first the magick of thine eye	8
When James *in Scotland first began*	70

AN

AN

'ANTIDOTE

AGAINST

MELANCHOLY:

Made up in PILLS.

Compounded of *Witty Ballads, Jovial Songs*, and *Merry Catches*.

These witty Poems though some time [*they*]
may seem to halt on crutches,
Yet they'l all merrily please you for your
Charge, which not much is.

Printed by *Mer. Melancholicus*, to be sold in *London* and *Westminster*, 1661.
[Aprill, 18.]

EDITORIAL
INTRODUCTION
TO THE
ANTIDOTE AGAINST MELANCHOLY,
1661.

Adalmar.—" An Antidote !
    Restore him whom thy poisons have laid low." . . . .
Isbrand.—" A very good and thirsty melody;
    What say you to it, my Court Poet ?
Wolfram.—" Good melody ! When I am sick o' mornings,
    With a horn-spoon tinkling my porridge pot,
    'Tis a brave ballad."
        (T. L. Beddoes: Death's Jest Book, Acts iv. & v.*)*

§ 1. REPRINT OF AN ANTIDOTE.

HAVING found that sixty-five of our previous pages, in the second volume of the *Drolleries Reprint*, were filled with songs and poems that also appear in the *Antidote against Melancholy,* 1661; and that all the remaining songs and poems of the *Antidote* (several being only obtainable therein) exceed not the compass of three additional sheets, or forty-eight pages, the Editor determined to include this valuable
                          book

book. Thus in our three volumes are given four entire works, to exemplify this particular class of literature, the Cavalier Drolleries of the Restoration.*

To that portion of our present Appendix which is devoted to *Notes to the Antidote against Melancholy*, 1661, we refer the reader for the admirable brief Introduction written by John Payne Collier, Esq. ; to whose handsome Reprint of the work we owe our first acquaintance with its pages. His knowledge of our old literature extends over nearly a century ; his opportunities for inspecting private and public libraries have been peculiarly great; and he has always been most generous in communicating his knowledge to other students, showing throughout a freedom from jealousy and exclusiveness reminding us of the genial Sir Walter Scott. He states :—" We have never seen a copy of an '*Antidote against Melancholy*' that was not either imperfect, or in some places illegible from dirt and rough usage, excepting the one we have employed: our single exemplar is as fresh as on the day it was issued from the press. There is an excellent and highly finished engraving on the title-page, of gentlemen and boors carousing ; but as the repetition

---

* Prefixed to " The Ex-Ale-tation of Ale" is given a Table of Contents (on page 112), enlarged from the one in the original " Antidote against Melancholy, made up in Pills, 1661, by references to such pages of " *Merry Drollery, Compleat,* 1670, 1691, as bear songs or poems in common with the " *Antidote.*"

of it for our purpose would cost more than double every other expense attending our reprint, we have necessarily omitted it. The same plate was afterwards used for one of Brathwayte's pieces; and we have seen a much worn impression of it on a Drollery near the end of the seventeenth century. It does not at all add to our knowledge of the subject of our reprint. J. P. C."

Nevertheless, the copper-plate illustration is so good, and connects so well with the Bacchanalian and sportive character of the "*Antidote against Melancholy*," and other *Drolleries*, that the present Editor not unwillingly takes up the graver to reproduce this frontispiece for the adornment of the volume and the service of subscribers. Our own Reprint and our engraving are made from the *perfect* specimen contained in the Thomason Collection, and dated 1661 (with "Aprill 18" in MS.; see p. 161). We make a rule always to go to the fountain-head for our draughts, howsoever long and steep may be the ascent. Flowers and rare fossils reward us as we clamber up, and in good time other students learn to trust us, as being pains-taking and conscientiously exact. The first duty of one who aspires to be honoured as the Editor of early literature is to faithfully reproduce his text, unmutilated and undisguised. To amend it, and elucidate it, so far as lies in his power, can be done
befitingly

befitingly in his notes and comments, while he gives his readers a representation of the original, so nearly in *fac-simile* as is compatible with additional beauty of typography. Throughout our labours we have held this principle steadily in view; and, whatever nobler work we may hereafter attempt, the same determination must guide us. There may be debate as to our wisdom in reproducing some questionable *facetiæ*, but there shall be none regarding our fidelity to the original text.

§ II. INGREDIENTS OF AN "ANTIDOTE."

A pleasant book it appeared to Cavaliers and all who were not quite strait-laced. It is almost unobjectionable, except for a few ugly words, and bears comparison honourably with "*Merry Drollery*" or "*Wit and Drollery*," both of the same date, 1661. Unlike the former, it is almost uninfected with political rancour or impurity. It is a jovial book, that roysters and revellers loved to sing their Catches from ; nay, if some laughing nymphs did not drop their eyes over its pages we are no conjurors. A vulgar phrase or two did not frighten them. Lucy Hutchinson herself, the Colonel's Puritan wife, fires many a volley of coarse epithets without blushing ; and, indeed, the Saintly Crew occasionally indulged in foul language as freely as the Malignants, though it was condoned as being theologic zeal and controversial phraseology.

In

In "The Ex-Ale-tation of Ale" we forgive the verbosity, for the sake of one verse on the noted Ballad-writer (see note in Appendix) :—

" For *ballads* ELDERTON never had peer ;
How went his wit in them, with how merry a gale,
And with all the sails up, had he been at the Cup,
And washed his beard with a *pot of good ale.*"

We find the character of the songs to be eminently festive : almost every one could be chanted over a cup of burnt Sack, and there was not entire forgetfulness of eating : witness "The Cold Chyne," on page 55 (our p. 148). The Love-making is seldom visible. Such glimpses as we gain of Puritans (Bishop Corbet's Hot-headed Zealot, Cleveland's " Rotundos rot,") are only suggestive of playful ridicule. The Sectaries, being no longer dangerous, are here laughed at, not calumniated. The odd jumble of nations brought together in those disturbed times is seen in the crowd of lovers around the " blith Lass of Falkland town" (p. 133) who is constant in her love of a Scottish blue bonnet :—" *If ever I have a man, blew-Cap for me !*" But, sitting at ease once more, not hunted into byeways or exile, and with enough of ready cash to wipe off tavern scores, or pay for braver garments than were lately flapping in the wind, the Cavaliers recall the exploits of their patron-saint, " St. George for England," the gay wedding of Lord Broghill, as described

described by Sir John Suckling in 1641, the still noisier marriage of Arthur o' Bradley, or that imaginary banquet afforded to the Devil, by Ben Jonson's Cook Lorrell, in the Peak of Derbyshire. Early contrasts, drawn by their own grandsires, between the Old Courtier of Queen Elizabeth and the New Courtier of King James, are welcomed to remembrance. They forgive " Old Noll," while ridiculing his image as " The Brewer," and they repeat the earlier Ulysses song of the " Blacksmith," by Dr. James Smith, if only for its chorus, " Which no body can deny." The grave solemnity wherewith Dr. Wilde's " Combat of Cocks" was told; the light-hearted buffoonery of " Sir Eglamore's Fight with the Dragon;" the spluttering grimaces of Ben Jonson's " Welchman's praise of Wales;" and the sustained humour as well as enthusiasm of Dr. Henry Edwards's " On the Vertue of Sack" (" Fetch me Ben Jonson's scull," &c.), are all crowned by the musical outburst of " The Green Gown:"—

"Pan leave piping, the Gods have done feasting,
There's never a goddess a hunting to-day," &c.

(see Appendix to *Westminster Drollery*, p. liv.) Our readers may thus additionally enjoy a full-flavoured bumper of the "*Antidote against Melancholy.*"

August, 1875.   J. W. E.

To the Reader.

THere's no Purge 'gainst *Melancholly*,
    But with *Bacchus* to be jolly :
All else are but Dreggs of Folly.

Paracelsus wanted skill
When he sought to cure that Ill :
No *Pectorals* like the *Poets* quill.

Here are *Pills* of every sort,
For the *Country*, *City*, *Court*,
Compounded and made up of sport.

If 'gainst *Sleep* and *Fumes* impure,
Thou, thy *Senses* would'st secure ;
Take this, Coffee's not half so sure.

Want'st thou *Stomack* to thy Meat,
And would'st fain restore the heat,
This does it more than *Choccolet*.

Cures the *Spleene*[,] Revives the *blood* [,]
Puts thee in a *Merry* Mood :
Who can deny such *Physick* good ?

Nothing like to Harmeles *Mirth*,
'Tis a Cordiall On earth
That gives *Society* a Birth.

Then be wise, and buy, not borrow,
Keep an *Ounce* still for to Morrow,
Better than a *pound* of *Sorrow*.

                N. D.

Ballads, Songs, and Catches in this Book.

	Original: page.	Our vols, page
1. The Exaltation of a *Pot of Good Ale*,	1	iii. 113
2. The Song of *Cook-Lawrel*, by Ben Johnson	9	ii. 214
3. The Ballad of *The Black-smith*,	11	.. 225
4. The Ballad of the *Old Courtier and the New*	14	iii. 125
5. The Ballad of the Wedding of *Arthur of Bradley*,	16	ii. 312
6. The Ballad of the *Green Gown*,	20	i.Ap.54
7. The Ballad of the *Gelding of the Devil*,	21	ii. 200
8. The Ballad of *Sir Eglamore*,	25	.. 257
9. The Ballad of *St. George for England*,	26	iii. 129
10. The Ballad of *Blew Cap for me*,	29	.. 133
11. The Ballad of the *Several Caps*,	31	.. 135
12. The Ballad of the *Noses*,	33	ii. 143
13. The Song of the *Hot-headed Zealot*,	35	.. 234
14. The Song of the *Schismatick Rotundos*,	37	iii. 139
15. A Glee in praise of *Wine* [*Let souldiers*],	39	ii. 218
16. Sir John Sucklin's Ballad of the *Ld. L. Wedding*.	40	.. 101
17. The *Combat of Cocks*,	44	.. 242
18. The *Welchman's prayse of Wales*,	47	iii. 141
19. The *Cavaleer's Complaint* [and *Answer*],	49	ii. 52
20. Three several Songs in praise of *Sack*		
[: *Old Poets Hipocrin*, &c.	52	iii. 143
Hang the Presbyter's Gill,	53	.. 144
'Tis Wine that inspires,	54	.. 145
[A Glee to the Vicar,		W.D.Int.
[On a Cold Chyne of Beef,	55	iii. 146
[A Song of *Cupid* Scorned,	56	.. 147
21. On the *Vertue of Sack*, by Dr. Hen. Edwards	57	ii. 293
22. The *Medly of Nations*, to several tunes,	59	.. 127
23. The Ballad of the Brewer,	62	.. 221
24. A Collection of 40 [34] more Merry Catches and Songs.	65-76	iii. 149
[Of these 34, ten are given in Merry Drollery, Complete, on pages 296, 304, 308, 232, 337, 300, 280, 318, 348, and 341. The others are added in this volume		iii. 52

Pills to Purge Melancholly.

The Ex-Ale-tation of ALE. [p. 1.]

Not drunken, nor sober, but neighbour to both,
    I met with a friend in *Ales-bury* Vale ;
He saw by my Face, that I was in the Case
    To speak no great harm of a *Pot of good Ale.*

Then did he me greet, and said, since we meet
    (And he put me in mind of the name of the Dale)
For *Ales-burys* sake some pains I would take,
    And not *bury* the praise of a *Pot of good Ale.*

The more to procure me, then he did adjure me
    If the *Ale* I drank last were nappy and stale,
To do it its right, and stir up my sprite,
    And fall to commend a *pot [of good ale]*.   [*passim.*]

Quoth I, To commend it I dare not begin,
    Lest therein my Credit might happen to fail ;
For, many men now do count it a sin,
    But once to look toward a *pot of good alc.*

Yet I care not a pin, For I see no such sin,
    Nor any thing else my courage to quail :
For, this we do find, that take it in kind,
    Much vertue there is in a *pot of good ale.*

                                      And

And I mean not to taste, though thereby much grac't,
   Nor the *Merry-go-down* without pull or hale,
Perfuming the throat, when the stomack's afloat,
   With the Fragrant sweet scent of a *pot of good ale.*

Nor yet the delight that comes to the *Sight*
   To see how it flowers and mantles in graile,
As green as a *Leeke*, with a smile in the cheek,
   The true Orient colour of a *pot of good ale.*

But I mean the *Mind*, and the good it doth find,
   Not onely the *Body* so feeble and fraile;
For, *Body* and *Soul* may blesse the *black bowle*,
   Since both are beholden to a *Pot of good ale.*

For, when *heavinesse* the mind doth oppresse,
   And *sorrow* and *grief* the heart do assaile,
No remedy quicker than to take off your Liquor,
   And to wash away *cares* with a *pot of good ale.*

The *Widow* that buried her Husband of late,
   Will soon have forgotten to weep and to waile,
And think every day twain, till she marry again,
   If she read the contents of a *pot of good ale.*

It is like a *belly-blast* to a *cold heart*,
   And warms and engenders the *spirits vitale:*
To keep them from domage all sp'rits owe their homage
   To the *Sp'rite of the buttery*, a *pot of good ale.*

And down to the *legs* the vertue doth go,
   And to a bad *Foot-man* is as good as a *saile:*
When it fill the Veins, and makes light the Brains,
   No *Lackey* so nimble as a *pot of good ale.*

The naked complains not for want of a coat,
   Nor on the cold weather will once turn his taile;
All the way as he goes, he cuts the wind with his Nose,
   If he be but well wrapt in a *pot of good ale.*

The hungry man takes no thought for his meat,
   Though his stomack would brook a *ten-penny* naile;
He quite forgets hunger, thinks on it no longer,
   If he touch but the sparks of a *pot of good ale.*

The *Poor man* will praise it, so hath he good cause,
   That all the year eats neither *Partridge* nor *Quaile,*
But sets up his rest, and makes up his Feast,
   With a crust of *brown bread,* and a *pot of good ale.*

The *Shepherd,* the *Sower,* the *Thresher,* the *Mower,*
   The one with his *Scythe,* the other with his *Flaile,*
Take them out by the poll, on the peril of my soll,
   All will hold up their hands to a *pot of good ale.*

The *Black-Smith,* whose bellows all Summer do blow,
   With the fire in his Face still, without e're a vaile,
Though his throat be full dry, he will tell you no lye,
   But where you may be sure of a *pot of good ale.*

Who ever denies it, the Pris'ners will prayse it,
  That beg at [the] Grate, and lye in the *Goale*,
For, even in their *fetters* they thinke themselves better,
  May they get but a two-penny black *pot of Ale.*

The begger, whose portion is alwayes his prayers,
  Not having a tatter to hang on his taile,
Is rich in his rags, as the churle in his bags,
  If he once but shakes hands with a *pot of good ale.*

It drives his poverty clean out of mind,
  Forgetting his *brown bread*, his *wallet*, and *maile*;
He walks in the house like a *six-footed Louse*,
  If he once be inricht with a *pot of good ale.*

And he that doth *dig* in the *ditches* all day,
  And wearies himself quite at the *plough-taile*,
Will speak no less things than of *Queens* and of *Kings*,
  If he touch but the top of a *pot of good ale.*

'Tis like a Whetstone to a *blunt wit*,
  And makes a supply where Nature doth fail:
The dullest wit soon will look quite through the Moon,
  If his temples be wet with a *pot of good ale.*

Then DICK to his *Dearling*, full boldly dares speak,
  Though before (silly Fellow) his courage did quaile,
He gives her the *smouch*, with his hand on his pouch,
  If he meet by the way with a *pot of good ale.*

                                                    And

And it makes the *Carter* a *Courtier* straight-way;
  With Rhetorical termes he will tell his tale;
With *courtesies* great store, and his Cap up before,
  Being school'd but a little with a *pot of good ale.*

The *Old man*, whose tongue wags faster than his teeth,
  (For old age by Nature doth drivel and drale)
Will frig and will fling, like a Dog in a string,
  If he warm his cold blood with a *pot of good ale.*

And the good *Old Clarke*, whose sight waxeth dark,
  And ever he thinks the Print is to[o] small,
He will see every Letter, and say Service better,
  If he glaze but his eyes with a *pot of good ale.*

The *cheekes* and the *jawes* to commend it have cause;
  For where they were late but even wan and pale,
They will get them a colour, no *crimson* is fuller,
  By the true die and tincture of a *pot of good ale.*

Mark her Enemies, though they think themselves wise,
  How *meager* they look, with how low a waile,
How their cheeks do fall, without sp'rits at all,
  That alien their minds from a *pot of good ale.*

And now that the grains do work in my brains,
  Me thinks I were able to give by retaile
Commodities store, a dozen and more,
  That flow to Mankind from a *pot of good ale.*

             The

The MUSES would muse any should it misuse:
   For it makes them to sing like a *Nightingale*,
With a lofty trim note, having washed their throat
   With the *Caballine* Spring of a *pot of good ale*.
                                    [? Castalian]

And the *Musician* of any condition,
   It will make him reach to the top of his *Scale:*
It will clear his pipes, and moisten his lights,
   If he drink *alternatim* a *pot of good ale*.

The *Poet* Divine, that cannot reach Wine,
   Because that his money doth many times faile,
Will hit on the vein to make a good strain,
   If he be but *inspir'd* with a *pot of good ale*.

For *ballads* ELDERTON never had Peer;
   How went his wit in them, with how merry a Gale,
And with all the Sails up, had he been at the Cup,
   And washed his beard with a *pot of good ale*.

And the power of it showes, no whit less in *Prose*,
   It will file one's Phrase, and set forth his Tale:
Fill him but a Bowle, it will make his Tongue troul,
   For *flowing speech* flows from a *pot of good ale*.

And *Master Philosopher*, if he drink his part,
   Will not trifle his time in the *huske* or the *shale*,
But go to the *kernell* by the depth of his Art,
   To be found in the bottom of a *pot of good ale*.
                                          Give

Give a *Scholar* of OXFORD a pot of *Sixteen*,
   And put him to prove that an *Ape* hath no *taile*,
And sixteen times better his wit will be seen,
   If you fetch him from *Botley* a *pot of good ale*.

Thus it helps *Speech* and *Wit:* and it hurts not a whit,
   But rather doth further the *Virtues Morale;*
Then think it not much if a little I touch
   The good moral parts of a *pot of good ale*.

To the *Church* and *Religion* it is a good Friend,
   Or else our Fore-Fathers their wisedome did faile,
That at every mile, next to the *Church* stile,
   Set a *consecrate house* to a *pot of good ale*.

But now, as they say, *Beer* bears it away ;
   The more is the pity, if right might prevaile:
For, with this same *Beer*, came up *Heresie* here,
   The old *Catholicke drink* is a *pot of good ale*.

The *Churches* much ow[e], as we all do know,
   For when they be drooping and ready to fall,
By a *Whitson* or *Church-ale*, up again they shall go,
   And owe their *repairing* to a *pot of good ale*.

Truth will do it right, it brings *Truth* to light,
   And many bad matters it helps to reveal :
For, they that will drink, will speak what they think :
   TOM *tell-troth* lies hid in a *pot of good ale*.

It

It is *Justices* Friend, she will it commend,
   For all is here served by *measure* and *tale;*
Now, *true-tale* and *good measure* are *Justices* treasure,
   And much to the praise of a *pot of good ale.*

And next I alledge, it is *Fortitudes* edge[,]
   For a very Cow-heard, that shrinks like a Snaile,
Will swear and will swagger, and out goes his Dagger,
   If he be but arm'd with a *pot of good ale.*

Yea, ALE hath her *Knights* and *Squires* of Degree,
   That never wore Corslet, nor yet shirts of Maile,
But have fought their fights all, twixt the pot and the wall,
   When once they were dub'd with a *pot of good ale.*

And sure it will make a man suddenly *wise,*
   Er'e-while was scarce able to tell a right tale:
It will open his jaw, he will tell you the *Law,*
   As make a right *Bencher* of a *pot of good ale.*

Or he that will make a *bargain* to gain,
   In *buying* or *setting* his goods forth to *sale,*
Must not plod in the mire, but sit by the fire,
   And seale up his Match with a *pot of good ale.*

But for *Soberness,* needs must I confess,
   The matter goes hard; and few do prevaile
Not to go too deep, but *temper* to keep,
   Such is the *Attractive* of a *pot of good ale.*

                                                But

But here's an amends, which will make all Friends,
　And ever doth tend to the best availe:
If you take it too deep, it will make you but sleep;
　So comes no great harm of a *pot of good ale*.

If (reeling) they happen to fall to the ground,
　The fall is not great, they may hold by the Raile:
If into the water, they cannot be drown'd,
　For that gift is given to a *pot of good ale*.

If drinking about they chance to fall out,
　Fear not that *Alarm*, though flesh be but fraile;
It will prove but some blowes, or at most a bloody nose,
　And Friends again straight with a *pot of good ale*.

And *Physic* will favour ALE, as it is bound,
　And be against *Beere* both tooth and naile;
They send up and down, all over the town
　To get for their Patients a *pot of good ale*.

Their *Ale-berries*, *cawdles*, and *Possets* each one,
　And *Syllabubs* made at the Milking-pale,
Although they be many, *Beere* comes not in any,
　But all are composed with a *pot of good ale*.

And in very deed the *Hop's* but a Weed,
　Brought o're against Law, and here set to sale:
Would the Law were renew'd, and no more *Beer* brew'd,
　But all men betake them to a *Pot of good ale*.

　　　　　　　　　　　　　　　　　　The

The *Law* that will take it under his wing,
  For, at every *Law-day*, or *Moot of the hale*,
One is sworn to serve our *Soveraigne* the KING,
  In the ancient *Office* of a CONNER of ALE.

There's never a Lord of *Mannor* or of a Town,
  By strand or by land, by hill or by dale,
But thinks it a *Franchise*, and a *Flow'r* of the CROWN,
  To hold the *Assize* of a *pot of good ale*.

And though there lie *Writs* from the *Courts Paramount*,
  To stay the proceedings of *Courts Paravaile;*
Law favours it so, you may come, you may go,
  There lies no *Prohibition* to a *pot of good ale*.

They talk much of *State*, both early and late,
  But if *Gascoign* and *Spain* their *Wine* should but faile,
No remedy then, with us *Englishmen*,
  But the *State* it must stand by a *pot of good ale*.

And they that sit by it are good men and quiet,
  No dangerous *Plotters* in the Common-weale
Of *Treason* and *Murder :* For they never go further
  Than to call for, and pay for a *pot of good ale*.

To the praise of GAMBRIVIUS that good *Brittish King*
  That devis'd for his Nation (by the *Welshmen's* tale)
Seventeen hundred years before CHRIST did spring,
  The happy invention of a *pot of good ale*.

The

The *North* they will praise it, and praise with passion,
    Where every *River* gives name to a *Dale:*
There men are yet living that are of th' old fashion,
    No *Nectar* they know but a *pot of good ale.*

The PICTS and the SCOTS for ALE were at lots,
    So high was the skill, and so kept under seale;
The PICTS were undone, slain each mothers son,
    For not teaching the SCOTS to make *Hether Eale.*

But hither or thither, it skils not much whether:
    For Drink must be had, men live not by *Keale*,
Not by *Havor-bannocks* nor by *Havor-jannocks*,
    The thing the SCOTS live on is a *pot of good ale.*

Now, if ye will say it, I will not denay it,
    That many a man it brings to his bale:
Yet what fairer end can one wish to his Friend,
    Than to dye by the part of a *pot of good ale.*

Yet let not the innocent bear any blame,
    It is their own doings to break o're the pale:
And neither the *Malt*, nor the good wife in fault,
    If any be potted with a *pot of good ale.*

They tell whom it kills, but say not a word,
    How many a man liveth both sound and hale,
Though he drink no *Beer* any day in the year,
    By the *Radical humour* of a *pot of good ale.*

                                             But

But to speak of *Killing*, that am I not willing,
  For that in a manner were but to raile:
But *Beer* hath its name, 'cause it brings to the *Biere*,
  Therefore well-fare, say I, to a *pot of good ale.*

Too many (I wis) with their deaths proved this,
  And, therefore (if ancient Records do not faile),
He that first brew'd the *Hop* was rewarded with a *rope*,
  And found his *Beer* far more *bitter* than ALE.

O ALE [!] *ab alendo*, the *Liquor* of LIFE,
  That I had but a mouth as big as a *Whale!*
For mine is too little to touch the least tittle
  That belongs to the praise of a *pot of good ale.*

Thus (I trow) some *Vertues* I have mark'd you out,
  And never a *Vice* in all this long traile,
But that after the *Pot* there cometh the *Shot*,
  And that's th' onely *blot* of a *pot of good ale.*—

With that my Friend said, that *blot* will I bear,
  ' You have done very well, it is time to strike saile,
Wee'l have six pots more, though I dye on the score,
  To make all this good of a *Pot of good ALE.*

[Followed by Ben Jonson's Cook Lorrel, and by The Blacksmith: for which see *Merry Drollery, Complete*, pp. 214-17, 225-30.]

An Old Song of an Old Courtier [p. 14.]
and a New.

With an Old Song made by an Old Ancient pate,
    Of an Old worshipful Gentleman who had a
        great Estate;
Who kept an old house at a bountiful rate,
    And an old Porter to relieve the Poore at his Gate,
        Like an old Courtier of the Queens.

With and old Lady whose anger and [? one] good word
        asswages,
Who every quarter payes her old Servants their wages,
Who never knew what belongs to Coachmen, Footmen,
        & Pages,
    But kept twenty thrifty old Fellows, with blew-coats
        and badges,
        Like an old Courtier of the Queens.

With an old Study fill'd full of Learned books,
    With an old Reverent Parson, you may judge him
        by his looks,
With an old Buttery hatch worn quite off the old hooks,
    And an old Kitching, which maintains half a dozen
        old cooks;
        Like an old Courtier of the Queens.

With an old Hall hung round about with Guns, Pikes,
    and Bowes,

With old swords & bucklers, which hath born[e]
    many shrew'd blows,   (hose,
And an old Frysadoe coat to cover his Worships trunk
And a cup of old Sherry to comfort his Copper Nose;
    Like an old Courtier of the Queens.

With an old Fashion, when *Christmas* is come,
    To call in his Neighbours with Bag-pipe and Drum,
And good chear enough to furnish every old Room,
    And old liquor able to make a cat speak, and a wise man dumb;
        like an Old [*Courtier of the Queens.*]

With an old Hunts-man, a Falkoner, and a Kennel of Hounds;
    Which never Hunted, nor Hawked but in his own Grounds;
Who like an old wise man kept himself within his own bounds,
    And when he died gave every child a thousand old pounds;
        like an Old [*Courtier of the Queens.*]

But to his eldest Son his house and land he assign'd,
    Charging him in his Will to keep the same bountiful mind,
To be good to his Servants, and to his Neighbours kind,
    But in th' ensuing Ditty you shall hear how he was enclin'd;
        like a young Courtier of the Kings.
                              [Part

[Part Second.]

Like a young Gallant newly come to his Land,
   That keeps a brace of Creatures at's own command,
And takes up a thousand pounds upon's own Band,
   And lieth drunk in a new Tavern, till he can neither
     go nor stand ;
        like a young [*Courtier of the Kings*].

With a neat Lady that is fresh and fair,
   Who never knew what belong'd to good house-
     keeping or care,
But buyes several Fans to play with the wanton ayre,
   And seventeen or eighteen dressings of other
     womens haire ;
        like a young [*Courtier of the Kings*].

With a new Hall built where the old one stood,
   Wherein is burned neither coale nor wood,
And a new Shuffel-board-table where never meat stood,
   Hung Round with Pictures, which doth the poor little
     good.
        like a young [*Courtier of the Kings*].

With a new study stuff't full of Pamphlets and playes,
   With a new Chaplin, that swears faster then he prayes,
With a new Buttery hatch that opens once in four or
     five dayes,

With a new *French-Cook* to make Kickshawes and Tayes;
    like a young Courtier of the Kings.

With a new Fashion, when *Christmasse* is come,
  With a journey up to *London* we must be gone,
And leave no body at home but our new Porter *John*,
  Who relieves the poor with a thump on the back with a stone;
    Like a young [Courtier of the Kings].

With a Gentleman-Vsher whose carriage is compleat,
  With a Footman, a Coachman, a Page to carry meat,
With a waiting Gentlewoman, whose dressing is very neat,
  Who when the master hath dyn'd gives the servants litle meat;
    Like a young [Courtier of the Kings].

With a new honour bought with his Fathers Old Gold,
  That many of his Fathers Old Manors hath sold,
And this is the occasion that most men do hold,
  That good Hous[e]-keeping is now-a-dayes grown so cold;
    Like a young Courtier of the Kings.

[Here

[Here follow, Arthur of Bradley (see *Merry Drollery, Compleat,* p. 312); The Green Gown: "Pan leave piping," (see *Westm. Droll.,* Appendix, p. 54); Gelding of the Devil: "Now listen a while, and I will you tell" (see *Merry D., C.,* p. 200); Sir Egle More (*ibid,* p. 257); and St. George for England (*ibid,* p. 309). But, as the variations are great, in the last of these, it is here given from the *Antidote ag. Mel.,* p. 26.]

The Ballad of St. George for England. [p. 26.]

WHy should we boast of *Arthur* and his Knights?
  Know[ing] how many men have perform'd fights;
Or why should we speak of Sir *Lancelot du Lake,*
Or Sir *Trestram du Leon,* that fought for the Lady's sake;
Read old storyes, and there you'l see
How St. *George,* St. *George,* did make the Dragon flee:
  St. *George* he was for *England,* St. *Denis* was for
    Sing *Hony soitt qui Mal y pense.* (*France,*

To speak of the Monarchy, it were two Long to tell;
And likewise of the *Romans,* how far they did excel,
Hannibal and *Scipio,* they many a field did fight;
Orlando Furioso he was a valiant Knight;
Romulus and *Rhemus* were those that ROME did build,
But St. *George,* St. *George,* the Dragon he hath kill'd;
  St. *George* he was, &c.

Jephtha and *Gidion* they led their men to fight
The *Gibeonites* and *Amonites,* they put them all to flight;   *Hercul'es*

Hercul'es Labour was in the Vale of Brass,
And *Sampson* slew a thousand with the Jaw-bone of
　　an Asse,
And when he was blind pull'd the Temple to the ground:
But St. *George*, St. *George*, the Dragon did confound.
　St. *George* he was, &c.

Valentine and *Orson* they came of *Pipins* blood,
Alphred and *Aldrecus* they were brave Knights and good,
The four sons of *Amnon* that fought with *Charlemaine*,
Sir *Hugh de Burdeaux* and *Godfray* of *Bolaigne*,
These were all *French* Knights the *Pagans* did Convert,
But St. *George*, St. *George*, pull'd forth the Dragon's
　St. *George* he was, &c.　　　　　　　　(heart:

Henry the fifth he Conquered all *France*,
He quartered their Armes, his Honour to advance,
He razed their Walls, and pull'd their Cities down,
And garnished his Head with a double treble Crown;
He thumbed the *French*, and after home he came!
But St. *George*, St. *George*, he made the Dragon *tame:*
　St. *George* he was, &c.

St. *David* you know, loves *Leeks* and tosted *Cheese*,
And *Jason* was the Man, brought home the *Golden*
St. *Patrick* you know he was St. *Georges* Boy, (Fleece;
Seven years he kept his Horse, and then stole him away,
For which Knavish act, a slave he doth remain;
　　　　　　　　　　　　　　　　　　But

But St. *George*, St. *George*, he hath the Dragon slain:
St. *George* he was, &c.

Tamberline, the Emperour, in Iron Cage did Crown,
With his bloody Flag's display'd before the Town;
Scanderbag magnanimous *Mahomets Bashaw* did dread,
Whose Victorious Bones were worn when he was dead;
His *Bedlerbegs*, his Corn like drags, *George Castriot*
  was he call'd,
But St. *George*, St. *George*, the Dragon he hath maul'd:
St. *George* he was for *England*, St. *Denis* was for
  Sing *Hony soit qui mal y pense*.   (*France*,

Ottoman, the *Tartar*, *Cham* of *Persia's* race,
The great *Mogul*, with his Chests so full of all his Cloves
  and Mace,
The *Grecian* youth *Bucephalus* he manly did bestride,
But those with all their Worthies Nine, St. *George* did
  them deride,
Gustavus Adolphus was *Swedelands* Warlike King,
But St. *George*, St. *George*, pull'd forth the Dragon's
  sting.
St. George he was for *England*, St. *Dennis* was for
  Sing *Hony soit qui mal y pense*.   (*France*,

Pendragon and *Cadwallader* of *British* blood doe boast,
Though *John* of *Gant* his foes did daunt, St. *George*
  shal rule the roast;

Agamemnon and *Cleomedon* and *Macedon* did feats,
But, compared to our Champion, they were but merely cheats;
Brave *Malta* Knights in *Turkish* fights, their brandisht swords out-drew,
But St. *George* met the Dragon, and ran him through and through:
St. *George* he was, &c.

Bidea, the Amazon, *Photius* overthrew,
As fierce as either *Vandal*, *Goth*, *Saracen*, or *Jew*;
The potent *Holophernes*, as he lay in his bed,
In came wise *Judith* and subtly stool[e] his head;
Brave *Cyclops* stout, with *Jove* he fought, Although he showr'd down Thunder;
But St. *George* kill'd the Dragon, and was not that a wonder:
St. *George* he was, &c.

Mark Anthony, Ile warrant you Plaid feats with *Egypts* Queen,
Sir *Egla More* that valiant Knight, the like was never seen,
Grim *Gorgons* might, was known in fight, old *Bevis* most men frighted,
The *Myrmidons* & *Presbyter John*, why were not those men knighted?

Brave

Brave *Spinola* took in *Breda, Nasaw* did it recover,
But St. *George*, St. *George*, he turn'd the Dragon over
 and over :
 St. *George* he was for *England*, St. *Denis* was for
Sing, *Hony soit qui mal y pense.* (*France,*

A Ballad call'd *Blew Cap for me.*

COme hither thou merriest of all the Nine, [p. 29]
 Come, sit you down by me, and let us be jolly ;
And with a full Cup of *Apollo's* wine,
 Wee'l dare our Enemy mad Melancholly ;
And when we have done, wee'l between us devise
A pleasant new Dity by Art to comprise :
 And of this new Dity the matter shall be,
If ever I have a man, blew cap for me.

There dwells a blith Lass in *Falkland* Town
And she hath Suitors I know not how many,
 And her resolution she had set down
That she'l have a *Blew Cap*, if ever she have any.
An *Englishman* when our geod Knight was there,
Came often unto her, and loved her dear,
 Yet still she replyed, Geod Sir, La be,
If ever I have a man, blew cap for me.

          A

A *Welchman* that had a long Sword by his side,
   Red Doublet, red Breech, and red Coat, and red
Was made a great shew of a great deal of pride, (Peard,
   Was tell her strange tales te like never heard ;
Was recon her pedegree long pefore *Prute*[,]
No body was near that could her Confute ;
   But still she reply'd, Geod Sir la be,
If ever I have a man, blew Cap for me.

A *Frenchman* that largely was booted and spurr'd,
   Long Lock with a ribbon, long points and long preeshes,
Was ready to kisse her at every word,
   And for the other exercises his fingers itches ;
You be prety wench *a Metrel, par ma Foy,*
Dear me do love you, be not so coy ;
   Yet still replyed, Geod Sir, la be ;
If ever I have a man, blew Cap for me.

An *Irishman*, with a long skeen in his Hose,
   Did think to obtain her, it was no great matter,
Up stairs to the chamber so lightly he goes,
   That she never heard him until he came at her,
Quoth he, I do love thee, by Fait and by Trot,
And if thou wilt know it, experience shall sho't,
   Yet still she reply'd, Geod sir, la be,
If ever I have a man, blew Cap for me.

A *Netherland* Mariner came there by chance,
    Whose cheekes did resemble two rosting pome-
        watters,
And to this Blith lasse this sute did advance;
    Experience had taught him to cog, lie, and flatter;
Quoth he, I will make thee sole Lady of the sea,
Both *Spanyard* and *English* man shall thee obey:
    Yet still she replyed, [Geod sir, La be,
If ever I have a man, blew cap for me].

At last came a *Scotchman* with a *blew Cap*,
    And that was the man for whom she had tarryed,
To get this Blyth lass it was his Giud hap,
    They gan to *Kirk* and were presently married;
She car'd not whether he were Lord or Leard,
She call'd him sick a like name as I ne'r heard,
    To get him from aw she did well agree,
And still she cryed, *blew Cap* thou art welcome to mee.

The Ballad of the Caps. [p. 30.]

THe Wit hath long beholding been
    Unto the Cap to keep it in;
But now the wits fly out amain,
    In prayse to quit the Cap again;

The

The Cap that keeps the highest part
   Obtains the place by due desert:
     For any Cap, &c. [*what ere it bee,*
     Is still the signe of some degree.]

The *Monmouth* Cap, the Saylors thrumbe,
   And that wherein the Tradesmen come,
The Physick Cap, the Cap Divine,
   And that which Crownes the Muses nine,
The Cap that fooles do Countenance,
   The goodly Cap of Maintenance.
     For any Cap, &c.

The sickly Cap both plain and wrought,
   The Fudling cap, how ever bought,
The worsted, Furr'd, the Velvet, Sattin,
   For which so many pates learn Latin;
The Cruel cap, the Fustian Pate,
   The Perewig, a Cap of late:
     For any Cap, &c.

The Souldiers that the *Monmoth* wear,
   On Castles tops their Ensigns rear;
The Sea-man with his Thrumb doth stand
   On higher parts then all the Land;
The Tradesmans Cap aloft is born,
   By vantage of a stately horn.
     For any Cap, &c.

The Physick Cap to dust can bring
   Without controul the greatest King:
The Lawyers Cap hath Heavenly might
   To make a crooked action straight;
And if you'l line him in the fist,
   The Cause hee'l warrant as he list.
     For any Cap, &c.

Both East and West, and North and South,
   Where ere the Gospel hath a mouth
The Cap Divine doth thither look:
   Tis Square like Scholars and their Books:
The rest are Round, but this is Square
   To shew their Wits more stable are:
     For any Cap, &c.

The Jester he a Cap doth wear,
   Which makes him Fellow for a Peer,
And 'tis no slender piece of Wit
   To act the Fool, where great Men sit,
But O, the Cap of *London* Town!
   I wis, 'tis like a goodly Crown.
     For any Cap, &c.

The sickly Cap [,] though wrought with silk,
   Is like repentance, white as milk;
When Caps drop off at health apace,
   The Cap doth then your head uncase,

                        The

The sick mans Cap (if wrought can tell)
   Though he be sick, his cap is well.
     For any Cap, &c.

The fudling Cap by *Bacchus* Might,
   Turns night to day, and day to night;
We know it makes proud heads to bend,
   The Lowly feet for to Ascend:
It makes men richer then before,
   By seeing doubly all their score.
     For any Cap, &c.

The furr'd and quilted Cap of age
   Can make a mouldy proverb sage,
The Satin and the Velvet hive
   Into a Bishoprick may thrive,
The Triple Cap may raise some hope,
   If fortune serve, to be a Pope;
     For any Cap, &c.

The Perewig, O, this declares
   The rise of flesh, though fall of haires,
And none but Grandsiers can proceed
   So far in sin, till they this need,
Before the King who covered are,
   And only to themselves stand bare.
     For any Cap, what ere it bee,
     Is still the signe of some degree.

                  [Next

[Next follow A Ballad of the Nose (see *Merry Drollery, Compleat*, p. 143), and A Song of the Hot-headed Zealot: *to the tune of* "Tom a Bedlam" (Dr. Richard Corbet's, *Ibid*, p. 234).]

A Song On the Schismatick Rotundos. [p. 37.]

ONce I a curious Eye did fix,
    To observe the tricks
Of the *schismaticks* of the Times,
To find out which of them
    Was the merriest Theme,
And best would befit my Rimes.
Arminius I found solid,
    Socinians were not stolid,
Much Learning for Papists did stickle.
    But ah, ah, ha, ha, ha, ha, Rotundos *rot,*
  Ah, ha, ha, ha, ha, Rotundos *rot,*
    'Tis you that my spleen doth tickle.

And first to tell must not be forgot,
    How I once did trot
With a great Zealot to a Lecture,
Where I a Tub did view,
    Hung with apron blew:
'Twas the Preachers, as I conjecture.
His life and his Doctrine too
Were of no other hue,
Though he spake in a tone most mickle;
    But ah, ha, ha, ha, &c.

He taught amongst other prety things
  That the Book of *Kings*
Small benefit brings to the godly,
  Beside he had some grudges
  At the Book of *Judges*,
And talkt of *Leviticus* odly.
Wisedome most of all
  He declares *Apocryphal*,
Beat *Bell* and the *Dragon* like *Michel* :
 But, ah, ah, ha, ha, ha, ha, &c.

Gainst Humaine Learning next he enveyes
  and most boldly say's,
'Tis that which destroyes Inspiration :
  Let superstitious sence
  And wit be banished hence,
With Popish Predomination :
Cut *Bishops* down in hast,
  And *Cathedrals* as fast
As corn that's fit for the sickle :
 But ah, ah, ha, ha, ha, ha, Rotundos, *rot,*
ah, ha, ha, ha, ha, ha Rotundos *rot,*
 T'is you that my spleen doth tickle.

[The three next in the *Antidote*, respectively by Aurelian Townshend (?), Sir John Suckling, and "by T. R." (or Dr. Thomas Wild?), are to be found also in our *Merry Drollery, Compleat*, pp. 218, 101, and 242. See Appendix Notes.]

The

The Welshmans Song, in praise of Wales. [p. 47.]

I 'S not come here to tauke of *Prut*,
From whence the *Welse* dos take hur root;
Nor tell long Pedegree of Prince *Camber*,
Whose linage would fill full a Chamber,
Nor sing the deeds of ould Saint *Davie*,
The Ursip of which would fill a Navie,
But hark me now for a liddell tales
Sall make a great deal to the creddit of *Wales*:
    For her will tudge your eares,
    With the praise of hur thirteen Seers,
    And make you as clad and merry,
    As fourteen pot of Perry.

'Tis true, was wear him Sherkin freize,
But what is that? we have store of seize, [*i.e.* cheese,]
And Got is plenty of Goats milk
That[,] sell him well[,] will buy him silk
Inough, to make him fine to quarrell
At *Herford* Sizes in new apparrell;
And get him as much green Melmet perhap,
Sall give it a face to his Monmouth Cap.
    But then the ore of *Lemster;*
    Py Cot is uver a Sempster;
    That when he is spun, or did[,]
    Yet match him with hir thrid.

Aull

Aull this the backs now, let us tell yee,
Of some provision for the belly :
As Kid and Goat, and great Goats Mother,
And Runt and Cow, and good Cows uther.
And once but tast on the Welse Mutton,
Your *Englis* Seeps not worth a button.
And then for your Fisse, shall choose it your disse,
Look but about, and there is a Trout,
    A Salmon, Cot, or Chevin,
    Will feed you six or seven,
    As taull man as ever swagger
    With *Welse* Club, and long dagger.

But all this while, was never think
A word in praise of our *Welse* drink:
And yet for aull that, is a Cup of *Bragat*,
Aull *England* Seer may cast his Cap at.
And what say you to Ale of *Webly* [?],
Toudge him as well, you'll praise him trebly,
As well as *Metheglin*, or *Syder*, or *Meath*,
Sall sake it your dagger quite out o' th seath.
    And Oat-Cake of *Guarthenion*,
    With a goodly Leek or Onion,
    To give as sweet a rellis
    As e'r did Harper *Ellis*.

And yet is nothing now all this,
If our Musicks we do misse ;   Both

Both Harps, and Pipes too; and the Crowd
Must aull come in, and tauk aloud,
As lowd as *Bangu, Davies* Bell,
Of which is no doubt you have hear tell :
As well as our lowder *Wrexam* Organ,
And rumbling Rocks in the Seer of *Glamorgan;*
  Where look but in the ground there,
  And you sall see a sound there :
  That put her all to gedder,
  Is sweet as measure pedder.

[Followed, in *An Antidote*, by the excellent poems, The Cavalier's Complaint; to the tune of (Suckling's) *I'le tell thee, Dick, &c.,* with The Answer. For these, see *Merry Drollery, Compleat,* pp. 52-56, and 367.]

On a Pint of SACK.   [p. 52.]

OLd poets Hipocrin admire,
   And pray to water to inspire
Their wit and Muse with heavenly fire ;
Had they this Heav'nly Fountain seen,
Sack both their Well and Muse had been,
And this Pint-pot their Hipocrin.

Had they truly discovered it
They had like me thought it unfit
To pray to water for their wit.
                                    And

And had adored Sack as divine,
And made a Poet God of Wine,
And this pint-pot had been a shrine.

Sack unto them had been in stead
Of Nectar, and their heav'nly bread,
And ev'ry boy a Ganimed;
Or had they made a God of it,
Or stil'd it patron of their wit,
This pot had been a temple fit.

Well then Companions is't not fit,
Since to this Jemme we ow[e] our wit,
That we should praise the Cabonet,
And drink a health to this divine,
And bounteous pallace of our wine [?] :
Die he with thirst that doth repine!

A Song in Praise of SACK. [p. 53.]

Hang the *Presbyters* Gill, bring a pint of Sack,
 More *Orthodox* of the two,   (*Will*,
Though a slender dispute, will strike the Elf mute,
 Here's one of the honester Crew.

           In

In a pint there's small heart, Sirrah, bring a Quart;
    There is substance and vigour met,
'Twill hold us in play, some part of the day,
    But wee'l sink him before Sun-set:

The daring old Pottle, does now bid us battle,
    Let us try what our strength can do;
Keep your ranks and your files, and for all his wiles,
    Wee'l tumble him down stayrs too.

Then summon a Gallon, a stout Foe and a tall one,
    And likely to hold us to't;
Keep but Coyn in your purse, the word is Disburse,
    Ile warrant he'le sleep at your foot.

Let's drain the whole Celler, Pipes, Buts, and the
    If the Wine floats not the faster;   (Dweller,
Will, when thou dost slack us, by warrant from *Bacchus*,
    We will cane thy tun-belli'd Master.

In the praise of WINE.   [p. 54.]

'TIs Wine that inspires,
    And quencheth Loves fires,
Teaches fools how to rule a S[t]ate:
    Mayds ne're did approve it
Because those that doe love it,
    Despise and laugh at their hate.

                    The

The drinkers of beer
  Did ne're yet appear
In matters of any waight;
  'Tis he whose designe
  Is quickn'd by wine
That raises things to their height.

We then should it prize
  For never black eyes
Made wounds which this could not heale,
  Who then doth refuse,
  To drink of this Juice
Is a foe to the Comon weale.

[Followed by A Glee to the Vicar, beginning, " Let the bells ring, and the boys sing:" for which see the Introduction to our edition of *Westminster Drollery*, pp. xxxvii-viii.]

On a Cold Chyne of BEEF. [p. 55.]

BRing out the Old Chyne, the Cold Chyne to me,
  And how Ile charge him come and see,
Brawn tusked, Brawn well sowst and fine,
With a precious cup of Muscadine :

CHORUS.
*How shall I sing, how shall I look,
In honour of the Master-Cook?*

The

The Pig shall turn round and answer me,
Canst thou spare me a shoulder [?], a wy, a wy.
The Duck, Goose and Capon, good fellows all three
Shall dance thee an antick[,] so shall the turkey;
    But O! the cold Chyne, the cold Chyne for me:

CHORUS.
How shall I sing, how shall I look,
In honour of the Master-Cook?

With brewis Ile noynt thee from head to th' heel,
Shal make thee run nimbler then the new oyld wheel [;]
With Pye-crust wee'l make thee
The eighth wise man to be;
    But O! the cold Chyne, the cold Chyne for me:

CHORUS.
How shall I sing, how shall I look,
In honour of the Master-Cook?

A Song of Cupid Scorn'd. [p. 56]

IN love [?] away, you do me wrong,
  I hope I ha' not liv'd so long
Free from the Treachery of your eyes,
Now to be caught and made a prize,

                  No,

No, Lady, 'tis not all your art,
Can make me and my freedome part.

Chorus.

Come, fill's a cup of sherry, and let us be merry.
  There shall nought but pure wine
  Make us love-sick or pine,
Wee'l hug the cup and kisse it, we'l sigh when ere
    we misse it;
  For tis that, that makes us jolly,
  And sing hy trololey lolly.

In love, 'tis true, with *Spanish* wine,
Or the *French* juice *Incarnadine;*
But truly not with your sweet Face,
This dimple, or that hidden grace,
  Ther's far more sweetnesse in pure Wine,
  Then in those Lips or Eyes of thine.

    Chorus *(Come, fill's a cup of sherry, &c.*

Your god[,] you say, can shoot so right,
Hee'l wound a heart ith darkest night :
Pray let him throw away a dart,
And try if he can hit my heart.
  No *Cupid*, if I shall be thine,
  Turn *Ganimed* and fill us Wine.

    Chorus *(Come, fill's a cup of sherry, &c.*
              [The

[The three next are common to the *Antidote* and *Merry Drollery, Compleat*, with a few verbal differences: On the Vertue of Sack, by Dr. Henry Edwards; The Medley of the Nations; and The Brewer, A Ballad made in the Year 1657, To the Tune of *The Blacksmith*. For them, see *M. D., C.*, pp. 293, 127, 221. These three poems are followed by "A Collection of Merry Catches," thirty-four in number, of which only ten are found in *Merry Drollery, Compleat*, (viz., 3. "Now that the Spring;" 5. "Call *George* again;" 9. "She that will eat;" 13. "The Wisemen were but Seven;" 14. "Shew a room!" 15. "O! the wily wily Fox;" 17. "Now I am married;" 19. "There was three Cooks in Colebrook;" 22. "If any so wise is;" and 29. "What fortune had I,") on pp. 296, 304, 308, 232, 337, 300, 280, 318, 348, and 341, respectively. See notes on them, also, in Appendix to *M. D., C.* One other, first in the *Antidote*, had appeared earlier in *Choice Drollery*, p. 52: "He that a Tinker," &c., *q. v.*]

A CATCH. [p. 65.]

2. YOu merry Poets[,] old Boyes
    Of *Aganippes* Well,
Full many tales have told boyes
    Whose liquor doth excell,
And how that place was haunted
    By those that love good wine;
Who tipled there, and chaunted
    Among the *Muses* nine:
Where still they cry'd [,] drink clear, boyes,
    And you shall quickly know it,
That 'tis not lowzy Beer, boyes,
    But wine, that makes a Poet.

A CATCH. [p. 66.]

4. Mong'st all the precious Juices
  Afforded for our uses,
Ther's none to be compar'd with Sack:
 For the body or the mind,
 No such Physick you shall find,
Therefore boy see we do not lack.

Would'st thou hit a lofty strain,
 With this Liquor warm thy brain,
And thou Swain shalt sing as sweet as *Sidney;*
 Or would'st thou laugh and be fat,
 Ther's not any like to that
To make *Jack Sprat* a man of kidney.

[It] Is the soul of mirth
 To poor Mortals upon Earth;
It would make a coward bold as *Hector*,
 Nay I wager durst a Peece,
 That those merry Gods of *Greece*
Drank old Sack and *Nector*.

A CATCH. [p. 67.]

6. COme, come away to the Tavern I say,
  For now at home 'tis washing day:
Leave your prittle prattle, and fill us a pottle [;]
You are not so wise as *Aristotle:*
Drawer come away, let's make it Holy day.
Anon, Anon, Anon, Sir: what is't you say [?]

          A

A CATCH.

7. THere was an old man at *Walton* cross, [Waltham]
Who merrily sung when he liv'd by the loss;
  Hey tro-ly loly lo.
He never was heard to sigh a hey ho,
But he sent it out with *Hey troly loly lo.*
  He chear'd up his heart,
  When his goods went to wrack[,]
  With a hem, boy, Hem !
  And a cup of old Sack ;
  Sing, *hey troly loly lo.*

A CATCH.

8. COme, let us cast *Dice* who shall drink,
Mine is *twelve*, and his *sice sink*,
Six and *Fowr* is thine, and he threw *nine.*
Come away, *Sink tray; Size ace*, fair play ;
Quater-duce is your throw Sir ; [p. 68.]
Quater-ace, they run low, sir :
Two Dewces, I see ; *Dewce ace* is but three :
Oh ! where is the Wine ? Come, fill up his glasse,
For here is the man has thrown *Ams-ace.*

A CATCH.
           (wife,
10. NEver let a man take heavily the clamor of his
But be rul'd by me, and lead a merry life ;
Let her have her will in every thing,
If she scolds, then laugh and sing,
  Hey derry, derry, ding.   A

A CATCH.

11. Let's cast away care, and merrily sing,
There is a time for every thing;
He that playes at work, and works at his play,
Neither keeps working, nor yet Holy day:
Set business aside, and let us be merry,
And drown our dull thoughts in Canary and Sherry.

A CATCH.

12. Hang sorrow, and cast away care,
And let us drink up our Sack:
They say 'tis good to cherish the blood,
And for to strengthen the back:
Tis Wine that makes the thoughts aspire,
And fills the body with heat;
Besides 'tis good, if well understood   [p. 69.]
To fit a man for the feat;
Then call, and drink up all,
The drawer is ready to fill:
Pox take care, what need we to spare,
My Father has made his will.

A CATCH.   [p. 70.]

16. My lady and her Maid, upon a merry pin,
They made a match at F . . ting, who
should the wager win.   (upright;
Jone lights three candles then, and sets them bolt
   With

With the first f . . . she blew them out,
With the next she gave them light :
In comes my Lady then, with all her might and main,
And blew them out, and in and out, and out and
  in again.

A CATCH.

18. AN old house end, an old house end,
And many a good fellow wants mon[e]y to
  If thou wilt borrow   (spend.
  Come hither to morrow
I dare not part so soon with my friend[.]
But let us be merry, and drink of our sherry,
But to part with my mon[e]y I do not intend[.]
Then a t . . d in thy teeth, and an old house end.

A CATCH.   [p. 71.]

20. WIlt thou lend me thy Mare to ride a mile
No; she's lame going over a stile,
But if thou wilt her to me spare
Thou shalt have mony for thy mare :
Oh say you so, say you so,
Mon[e]y will make my mare to go.

THE ANSWER.

21. YOur mare is lame ; she halts downe right,
Then shall we not get to *London* to night :
                                             You

You cry'd ho, ho, mon[e]y made her go,
But now I well perceive it is not so[.]
You must spur her up, and put her to't
Though mon[e]y will not make her goe, your spurs
    will do't.

A CATCH   [p. 72.]

23. GOod *Symon*, how comes it your Nose looks
    so red,
  And your cheeks and lips look so pale?
Sure the heat of the tost your Nose did so rost,
    When they were both sous't in Ale.
It showes like the Spire of *Pauls* steeple on fire,
Each Ruby darts forth (such lightning) Flashes,
While your face looks as dead, as if it were Lead,
    And cover'd all over with ashes.
Now to heighten his colour, yet fill his pot fuller
    And nick it not so with froth,
Gra-mercy, mine Host! it shall save the[e] a Toast:
    Sup *Simon*, for here is good broth.

A CATCH.

24. WIlt thou be Fatt, Ile tell thee how,
    Thou shalt quickly do the Feat;
And that so plump a thing as thou
Was never yet made up of meat:
Drink off thy Sack, twas onely that
Made *Bacchus* and *Jack Falstafe*, Fatt.
                       Now,

Now, every Fat man I advise,
That scarce can peep out of his eyes,
Which being set, can hardly rise ;   [p. 73.]
Drink off his Sack, and freely quaff:
'Twil make him lean, but me [to] laugh
To tell him how —— 'tis on a staff.

A CATCH.

25. OF all the *Birds* that ever I see,
    The *Owle* is the fairest in her degree;
For all the day long she sits in a tree,
And when the night comes, away flies she ;
    To whit, to whow, to whom drink['st] thou,
        Sir Knave to thou ;

This song is well sung, I make you a vow, [p. 73]
And he is a knave that drinketh now; (red Nose?
Nose, Nose, Nose, and who gave thee that jolly
[Cinnamon and gin-ger,]   (red Nose.
Nutmegs and Cloves, and that gave thee thy jolly

A CATCH.

26. THis Ale, my bonny Lads, is as brown as a berry,
    Then let us be merry here an houre,
      And drink it ere its sowre
      Here's to the[e], lad,
      Come to me, lad;
      Let it come ·Boy, To my Thumb boy.
    Drink it off Sir ; 'tis enough Sir ;
Fill mine Host, *Tom's* Pot and Toast.   A

A CATCH.

27. WHat! are we met? come, let's see
    If here's enough to sing this Glee.
Look about, count your number,
Singing will keep us from crazy slumber;
1, 2, and 3, so many there be that can sing,
The rest for wine may ring:
Here is *Tom Jack* and *Harry;*
Sing away and doe not tarry,
Merrily now let's sing, carouse, and tiple,
Here's *Bristow* milk, come suck this niple,
There's a fault sir, never halt Sir, before a criple.

A CATCH.

28. JOg on, jog on the Foot path-way,
    And merrily hen't the stile-a;
    Your merry heart go'es all the day,
    Your sad tires in a mile-a.
    Your paltry mony bags of Gold,
    What need have we to stare-for,
    When little or nothing soon is told,
    And we have the less to care-for?
    Cast care away, let sorrow cease,   [p. 74.]
    A Figg for Melancholly;
    Let's laugh and sing, or if you please,
    We'l frolick with sweet *Dolly*.

A SONG.
Translated out of Greek.

30. THe parcht *Earth* drinks the *Rain*,
    Trees drink it up again ;
The *Sea* the *Ayre* doth quaff,
Sol drinks the *Ocean* off ;
And when that Health is done,
Pale *Cinthia* drinks the sun :
Why, then, d'ye stem my drinking Tyde,
Striving to make me sad, I will, I will be mad.

A CATCH. [p. 75.]

31. FLy, Boy, Fly, Boy, to the Cellars bottom :
    View well your Quills and Bung, Sır.
Draw Wine to preserve the Lungs Sir ;
Not rascally Wine to Rot u'm.
If the Quill runs foul,
Be a trusty soul, and cane it ;
For the Health is such
An ill drop will much profane it.

UPON A WELCHMAN.

32. A Man of *Wales*, a litle before *Easter*
    Ran on his Hostes score for Cheese a teaster :
His Hostes chalkt it up behind the doore, (score :
And said, For Cheese (good Sir) Come pay the
Cod's *Pluternails* (quoth he) what meaneth these?
What dost thou think her knows not Chalk from
(Cheese?

A SONG.

33. Drink, drink, all you that think
To cure your souls of sadnesse;
Take up your Sack, 'tis all you lack,
All worldly care is madness.
Let Lawyers plead, and Schollars read,
And Sectaries still conjecture,
    Yet we can be as merry as they,
With a Cup of *Apollo's* nectar.

Let gluttons feed, and souldiers bleed,
And fight for reputation,
Physicians be fools to fill up close stools,
And cure men by purgation:
Yet we have a way far better than they,
Which *Galen* could never conjecture,
    To cure the head, nay quicken the dead,
With a cup of *Apollo's* Nectar.

We do forget we are in debt
When we with liquor are warmed;
We dare out-face the Sergeant's Mace,   [p. 76.]
And Martiall Troops though armed.
The *Swedish* King much honour did win,
And valiant was as *Hector;*
    Yet we can be as valiant as he,
With a cup of *Apollo's* Nectar.

Let

Let the worlds slave his comfort have,
And hug his hoards of treasure,
Till he and his wish meet both in a dish,
So dies a miser in pleasure.
'Tis not a fat farm our wishes can charm,
We scorn this greedy conjecture ;   (commend
    Tis a health to our friend, to whom we
This cup of *Apollo's* Nectar.

The Pipe and the Pot, are our common shot,
Wherewith we keep a quarter ;
Enough for to choak with fire and smoak
The Great *Turk* and the *Tartar.*
Our faces red, our ensignes spread,
Apollo is our Protector :
    To rear up the Scout, to run in and out,
And drink up this cup of Nectar.

A CATCH.

34. WElcome, welcome again to thy wits,
    This is a Holy day :
I'le have no plots nor melancholly fits,
But merrily passe the time away :
    They are mad that are sad ;
    Be rul'd, by me,
And none shall be so merry as we ;

The Kitchin shall catch cold no more,
And we'l have no key to the Buttery dore,
   The fidlers shall sing,
   And the house shall ring,
   And the world shall see
    What a merry couple,
     Merry couple,
      We will be.

FINIS.

EDITORIAL POSTSCRIPT:

I.—ON THE "AUTHOR" OF
AN ANTIDOTE AGAINST MELANCHOLY,
1661.

THANKS be to the worthy bookseller, George Thomason,* for prudence in laying aside the "tall copy" of this amusing book, from which we make our transcript of text and engraving. Probably it did not exceed two shillings, in price; (at least, we have seen

---

* *George Thomason.* It was in 1640 that this bookseller commenced systematically to preserve a copy of every pamphlet, broadside, and printed book connected with the political disturbances. Until after the Restoration in 1660, he continued his valuable collection, so far as possible without omission, but not without danger and interruption. In his will he speaks of it as "not to be paralleled," and it was intact at Oxford when he died in 1666. Charles II. had too many feminine claimants on his money and time to allow him to purchase the invaluable series of printed documents, as it had been desired that he should do. The sum of £4,000 was refused for this collection of 30,000 pamphlets, bound in 2,000 volumes; but, after several changes of ownership, they were ultimately purchased by King George the Third, for only three or four hundred pounds, and were presented by him to the nation. They are in the British Museum, known as the King's Pamphlets, and the *Antidote against Melancholy* is among the small quartos. See Isaac D'Israeli's *Amenities of Literature,* for an interesting account of the difficulties and perils attending their collection: article *Pamphlets,* pp. 685-691. edition 1868.

that Anthony à Wood's uncropt copy of "*Merry Drollery*," 1661, is marked in contemporary manuscript at " 1s. 3d.," each part). The title says :—

>These *witty Poems, though sometime* [*they*]
>   *may seem to halt on crutches,*
>*Yet they'l all merrily please you*
>   *for your charge, which not much is.*

Who was the "N. D." to whose light labours we are indebted for the compounding of these " Witty Ballads, jovial Songs, and merry Catches " in Pills warranted to cure the ills of Melancholy, had not hitherto been ascertained*; or whether he wrote anything beside the above couplet, and the humorous address To the Reader, beginning,

>*There's no Purge 'gainst* Melancholy,
>*But with* Bacchus *to be jolly :*
>*All else are but dreggs of Folly, &c.* (p. 111.)

---

* J. P. Collier, in his invaluable " *Bibliographical and Critical Account of the Rarest Books in the English Language*," 1865, acknowledges, in reference to "*An Antidote against Melancholy*," that "We are without information by whom this collection of Poems, Ballads, Songs, and Catches was made; but Thomas Durfey, about sixty years afterwards, imitated the title, when he called his six volumes '*Wit and Mirth, or Pills to Purge Melancholy*,' 8vo., 1719—20.' (*Bibliog. & Crit. Account*, vol. i. p. 26.) Again, " If N. D., whose initials are at the end of the rhyming address ' to the Reader,' were the person who made the selection, we are without any other clue to his name. There is no ground for imputing it to Thomas Jordan, excepting that he was accustomed to deal in productions of this class; but the songs and ballads he printed were usually of his own composition, and not the works of anterior versifyers." (*Ibid*, i. 27.)

As we suspected (flowing though his verse might be), he was more of bookseller than ballad-maker. His injunctions for us to "be wise and *buy*, not *borrow*," had a terribly tradesman-like sound. Yet he was right. Book-borrowing is an evil practice ; and book-lending is not much better. Woeful chasms, in what should be the serried ranks of our Library companions, remind us pathetically, in too many cases (book-cases, especially,) of some Coleridge-like "lifter" of Lambs, who made a raid upon our borders, and carried off plunder, sometimes an unique quarto, on other days an irrecoverable duodecimo : With Schiller, we bewail the departed,—

"*The beautiful is vanished, and returns not.*"

The title of "*Pills to Purge Melancholy*" was by Playford and Tom D'Urfey afterwards employed, and kept alive before the public, in many a volume from before 1684 until 1720, if not later. Whether " N. D." himself were the " Mer[cury] Melancholicus " whose name appears as printer, for the book to be " sold in London and Westminster," is to us not doubtful. By April 18, 1661,* Thomason had secured his

* It was a week of supreme rejoicing and frollic, being five days before the Coronation of Charles II. in Westminster Abbey, April 23rd. On the 19th were the ceremonies of the Knights of the Bath, at the Painted Chamber, and in the Chapel at Whitehall. On the 22nd, Charles went from the Tower to Whitehall, through well-built triumphal arches, and amid enthusiasm.

copy, and there need be no question that it was for sport, and not through any fear of rigid censorship or malicious pettifogging interference by the law, that, instead of printer's name, this pseudonym or nickname was adopted.

We believe that the mystery shrouding the personality of " N. D." can be dispelled. The discovery helps us in more ways than one, and connects the *Antidote against Melancholy*, of 1661, in an intelligible and legitimate manner, with much jocular literature of later date. To us it seems clear that N. D. was no other than [He]n[ry] [Playfor]d. The triplets addressed in 1661 To the Reader, beginning " There's no purge 'gainst Melancholy," are repeated at commencement of the 1684 edition of " *Wit and Mirth; or, an Antidote to Melancholy* " (the third edition of *Pills to Purge Melancholy*") where they are entitled " The Stationer to the Reader," and signed, not " N. D.," but " H. P.;" for Henry Playford, whose name appears in full as publisher "near the Temple Church." Thus, the repetition or alteration of the original title, " *An Antidote against Melancholy, made up in Pills*," or, as the head-line puts it, "*Pills to Purge Melancholy*," was, in all probability, a perfectly business-like reproduction of what Playford had himself originated. What relation Henry Playford was to John Playford, the publisher of " *Select Ayres*,"

"*Choice Ayres,*" 1652, &c., we are not yet certain. Thirteen of the longest and most important poems from the 1661 *Antidote** re-appear in that of 1684, beside four of the Catches. Indeed, the transmission of many of these Lyrics (by the editions of 1699, 1700, 1706, 1707) to the six volume edition, superintended by Tom D'Urfey in 1719-20, is unbroken; though we have still to find the edition published between 1661 and 1684.

But even the 1661 *Antidote* is not entitled to bear the credit of originating the phrase : *Pills to purge Melancholy.* So far as we know, by personal search, this belongs to Robert Hayman, thirty years earlier. Among his *Quodlibets*, 1628, on p. 74, we find the following epigram :—

"To one of the elders of the Sanctified Parlour of Amsterdam.

Though thou maist call my merriments, my folly,
They are my Pills to purge my melancholy ;
They would purge thine too, wert thou not foole-holy."

---

* These are the Blacksmith, the Brewer, Suckling's Parley between two West Countrymen concerning a Wedding, St. George and the Dragon, the Gelding of the Devil, the Old and Young Courtier, the Welchman's Praise of Wales, Ben Jonson's Cook Lorrel, "Fetch me Ben Jonson's scull," a Combat of Cocks, "Am I mad, O noble Festus?" "Old Poets Hypocrin admire," and "'Tis Wine that inspires." The Catches are "Drink, drink, all you that think;" "If any so wise is," "What are we met?" and "The thirsty earth drinks up the rain."

EDITORIAL POSTSCRIPT :

2.—ARTHUR O' BRADLEY.

(Merry Drollery, Compleat, p. 312, 395; *Antidote ag. Mel.,* p. 16.*)*

    "Before we came in we heard a great shouting,
      And all that were in it look'd madly ;
    But some were on Bull-back, some dancing a morris,
      And some singing Arthur-a-Bradley."
        —(Robin Hood's Birth, &c. Printed by Wm. Onlen, about 1650. In *Roxburghe Collection of Black-Letter Ballads,* i., 360.)

So long ago as the Editor can remember, the words and music of "Arthur o' Bradley's Wedding" rang pleasantly in his ears. The jovial rollicking strain prepared him to feel interest in the bridal attire of Shakespeare's Petruchio; who, not improbably, when about to be married unto "Kate the Curst," borrowed the details of costume and demeanour from this popular hero of song. Or *vice versa.* To this day, the *lilt* of the tune holds a fascination, and we sometimes behold, under favourable planetary aspects, the long procession of dancing couples who have, during three centuries, footed the grass, the rushes, or chalked floor, to that jig-melody, accompanied by the bagpipes or fiddle of some rustic Crowdero. Can it be possible? Yes, the line is headed by the venerable Queen Elizabeth, holding up her fardingale with tips of taper fingers, and looking preternaturally grim, to show that dancing is a serious undertaking for a virgin sovereign (especially when the Spanish Ambassador watches her, with comments of wonder that the Head of the Church can dance at all). Yet is there a sly under-glance that tells of fun, to those who are her Majesty's familiars. Her " Cousin James " is not the neatest figure as a partner (which accounts for her having chosen Leicester instead, let alone chronology); but we see him, close behind, with Anne of Denmark, twirling his crooked little legs about in obedience to the music, until his round hose swell like hemispheres on school-maps. " Baby Charles and Steenie," half mockingly, follow after with the Infanta. We did once catch a glimpse of handsome Carr and his wicked paramour, Frances Howard, trying to join the Terpsichorean revellers; but, beautiful as they both were, it was felt necessary to exclude them, "for the honour of Arthur o' Bradley," since they possessed none of their own. What a gallant assemblage of poets and dramatists covered the buckle and snapped their fingers gleefully to the merry notes! Foremost among them was rare Ben Jonson (unable to resist clothing Adam Overdo in Arthur's own mantle); and honest Thomas Dekker "followed after in a dream" (as had been memorably printed on our seventh page of *Choyce Drollery*), thinking of Bellafront's repentance, and her quotation of the well-known burden, "O brave Arthur o' Bradley, then!" A score of poets are junketting with merry milkmaids and Wives of Windsor. Richard Brathwaite (the creator of Drunken Barnaby) is not absent from among them; although he sees, outside the circle that for a moment has formed around a Maypole, an angry crowd of schismatic Puritans, who are scowling at them with malignant eyes, and denunciations misquoted from Scripture. Many a fair Precisian, nevertheless, yields to the honeyed pleading of a be-love-locked Cavalier, and the irresistible charms of "Arthur o' Bradley, ho!" showing the prettiest pair of ankles, and the most delightful mixture of bashfulness and enjoyment; until the Roundhead Buff-coats prove too numerous, and whisk her off to a conventicle, where, the sexes sitting widely apart, for aught we know, the crop-eared rout sing unpoetic versions of the Psalmist to the tune of Arthur o' Bradley, "godlified" and eke expurgated.

Cromwell, we know, loved music, withal, and it is not unlikely that those two ladies are his daughters, whom we behold dancing somewhat stifly in John Hingston's music-chamber; Mrs. Claypole and her sister, Mrs Rich : there are L'Estrange, who fiddles to them, and Old Noll, smiling pleasantly, though the tune be Arthur o' Bradley. Our Second Charles (not yet "Restored") is also dancing to it, at the Hague (as we see in Janssen's Windsor picture), with the Princess Palatine Elizabeth, and such a bevy of bright faces round them, that we lose our heart entirely. Can we not see him again—crowned now, and self-acknowledged as "Old Rowley"—at one of the many balls in Whitehall recorded by Samuel Pepys,* enter-

* *Ball at Court.*—"31st. [December, 1662.] Mr. Povy and I to White Hall; he taking me thither on purpose to carry me into the ball this night before the King. He brought me first to the Duke [of York]'s chamber, where I saw him and the Duchesse at supper; and thence into the room where the ball was to be; crammed with fine ladies, the greatest of the Court. By and by, comes the King and Queene, the Duke and Duchesse, and all the great ones; and after seating themselves, the King takes out the Duchesse of York; and the Duke, the Duchesse of Buckingham; the Duke of Monmouth, my Lady Castlemaine; and so other lords other ladies: and they danced the Brantle [? *Braule*]. After that the King led a lady a single Coranto; and then the rest of the lords, one after another, other ladies: very noble it was, and great pleasure to see. Then to country dances; the King leading the first, which he called for, which was, says he, 'Cuckolds all awry [a-row],' the old dance of England. Of the ladies that danced, the Duke of Monmouth's mistress, and my Lady Castlemaine, and a daughter of Sir Harry de Vicke's, were the best. The manner was, when the King dances, all the ladies in the room, and the Queene herself, stand up: and indeed he dances rarely, and much better than the Duke of York. Having staid here as long as I thought fit, to my infinite content, it being the greatest pleasure I could wish now to see at Court, I went home, leaving them dancing."—*(Diary of Samuel Pepys, Esq., F.R.S., Secretary to the Admiralty, &c.)*

ing gaily into all the mirth with that grave, swarthy face of his; not noticing the pouts of Catherine, who sits neglected while The Castlemaine laughs loudly, the fair Stewart simpers, and the little spaniels bark or caper through the palace, snapping at the dancers' heels? Be sure that pretty Nelly and saucy Knipp were also well acquainted with the music of "rare Arthur o' Bradley," as indeed were thousands of the play-goers to whom the former once sold oranges.

And lower ranks delighted in it. Pierce, the Bag-piper, is himself the central figure, when we look again, " with cheeks as big as a mitre," such time as that table-full of Restoration revellers (whom we catch sight of in our frontispiece to the *Antidote*, 1661) are beginning to shake a toe in honour of the music.

So it continues for two centuries more, with all varieties of costume and feature. Certain are we that plump Sir Richard Steele whistled the tune, and Dean Swift gave the Dublin ballad-singer a couple of thir-teens for singing it. Dr. Johnson grunted an accom-paniment whenever he heard the melody, and James Boswell insisted on dancing to it, though a little " overtaken," and got his sword entangled betwixt his legs, which cost him a fall and a plastered head-piece, by no means for the only time on record. It is re-ported that good old George the Third was seen en-deavouring to persuade Queen Charlotte to accompany him on the Spinnet, while he set their numerous olive-branches jigging it delightedly "*for the honour of* Arthur *o'* Bradley." But whenever Dr. John Wolcot was reported to be prowling near at hand, with Peter Pindaresque eyes, the motion ceased. Well was it loved by honest Joseph Ritson, *impiger, iracundus inexorabilis, acer*—better than vegetable diet and eccentric spelling, or the flagellation of inexact antiquarian Bishops. We ourselves may have beheld him in high glee perusing the black-letter ballad, and rectifying its corrupt text by the *Antidote against Melancholy's*. How lustily he skipped, shouting meanwhile the burden of "*brave* Arthur *o'* Bradley!" so that unconsciously he joined the ten-mile train of dancers. They are still winding around us, some in a Nineteenth-Century garb (a little tattered, but it adds to the picturesqueness), blithe Hop-pickers of West-Bridge Deanery. There are a few New Zealanders, we understand, waiting to join the throng, (including Macaulay's own particular circumnavigating meditator, yet unborn); so that as long as the world wags no welcome may be lacking to the mirth and melody, jigging and joustling,

"*For the honour of* Arthur *o'* Bradley,
O rare Arthur *o'* Bradley,
O brave Arthur *o'* Bradley,
Arthur *o'* Bradley. *O!*"

Having relieved our feelings, for once, we resume the sober duties of Annotation in a chastened spirit :—

In *Merry Drollery Compleat*, Reprint (Appendix, p. 401), we gave the full quotation from a Sixteenth Century Interlude, *The Contract of Marriage between Wit and Wisdom*, the point being this :—

" *For the honour of* Artrebradley,
This age would make me swear madly !"

Arthur o' Bradley is mentioned by Thomas Dekker, near the end of the first part of his *Honest Whore*, 1604; when Bellafront, assuming to be mad, hears that Mattheo is to marry her, she exclaims—

" *Shall he ? O brave* Arthur *of* Bradley, *then ?*"

In Ben Jonson's *Bartholomew Fair*, 1614, (which covers the Puritans with ridicule, for the delight of James Ist.), Act ii. Scene 1, when Adam Overdo, the Sectary, is disguised in a "garded coat" as Arthur o' Bradley, to gesticulate outside a booth, Mooncalf salutes him thus :—
"O Lord! do you not know him, Mistress? *'tis mad* Arthur *of* Bradley *that makes the orations.*— Brave master, old Arthur of Bradley, how do you do? Welcome to the Fair! When shall we hear you again, to handle your matters, *with your back against a booth*, ha?"

In Richard Brathwaite's *Strappado for the Diuell*, 1615, p. 225 (in a long poem, containing notices of Wakefield, Bradford, and Kendall, addressed " to all true-bred Northerne Sparks, of the generous Society of the Cottoneers," &c.) is the following reference to this tune, and to other two, viz. " Wilson's Delight," and Mal Dixon's Round :"

" *So each (through peace of conscience) rapt with pleasure*
Shall ioifully begin to dance his measure.
One footing aɕtiuely Wilson's *delight*, ...

The fourth is chanting of his Notes so gladly,
Keeping the tune for th' honour of Arthura Bradly ;
The 5th *so pranke he scarce can stand on ground,*
Asking who' le sing with him Mal Dixon's *round.*"

(By the way: The same author, Richard Brathwaite, in his amusing *Shepherds Tales*, 1621, p. 211, mentions as other Dance-tunes,

> *Roundelayes,* ‖ Irish-*hayes*,
> *Cogs and rongs and* Peggie Ramsie,
> *Spaniletto* ‖ *The Venetto,*
> John *come kisse me,* Wilson's *Fancie.*)

Again, Thomas Gayton writes concerning the hero :—
" 'Tis not alwaies sure that *'tis merry in hall when beards Wag all,* for these men's beards wagg'd as fast as they could tag 'em, but mov'd no mirth at all : They were verifying that song of—

> *Heigh, brave* Arthur *o'* Bradley,
> *A beard without hair looks madly.*"
> (*Festivous Notes on Don Quixot,* 1654, p. 141.)

On pp. 540, 604, of William Chappell's excellent work, *The Popular Music of the Olden Time,* are given two tunes, one for the *Antidote* version, and the other for the modern, as sung by Taylor, " Come neighbours, and listen a while." He quotes the two lines from Gayton, and also this from Wm. Wycherley's *Gentleman Dancing Master,* 1673, Act i, Sc. 2, where Gerrard says :—" Sing him '*Arthur of Bradley,*' or ' *I am the Duke of Norfolk.*' "

It is quite evident, from such passages, that during a long time a proverbial and popular character attached to this noisy personage: such has not yet passed away. The earliest complete imprint of "Arthur o' Bradley" as a Song, (from a printed original, of 1656, beginning "*All you that desire to merry be,"*) in our present APPENDIX, Part iv. Quite distinct from this hitherto unnoticed examplar, not already reprinted, is "*Saw you not* Pierce, *the piper,*" &c., the ballad reproduced by us, from *Merry Drollery,* 1661, Part 2nd., p. 124, (and ditto, *Compleat* 1670, 1691, p. 312); which agrees with the *Antidote against Melancholy,* same date, 1661, p. 16. More than a Century later, an inferior rendering was common, printed on broadsheets. It was mentioned, in 1797, by Joseph Ritson, as being a "much more modern ballad [than the *Antidote* version] upon this popular subject, in the same measure intitled *Arthur o' Bradley,* and beginning 'All in the merry month of May.'" *(Robin Hood,* 1797, ii. 211.) Of this we already gave two verses, (in Appendix to *M. Drollery C.,* p. 400), but as we believe the ballad has not been reprinted in this century, we may give all that is extant, from the only copy within reach, of ARTHUR O' BRADLEY :—

> "*All in the merry month of May,*
> *The maids* [*they will be gay,*
> *For*] *a May-pole they will have, &c.*
>   (See the present Appendix, Part iv.)

In this, doubtless, we detect two versions, garbed together. What is now the final verse is merely a variation of the sixth: probably the broadsheet-printer could not meet with a genuine eighth verse. Robert Bell denounced the whole as "a miserable composition" (even as he had declared against the amatory Lyrics of Charles the Second's time): but then, he might have added, with Goldsmith, "My Bear dances to none but the werry genteelest of tunes."

Far superior to this was the "Arthur o' Bradley's Wedding:

> "*Come, neighbours, and listen awhile,*
> *If ever you wished to smile,*" &c.,

which was sung by ... Taylor, a comic actor, about the beginning of this century. It is not improbable that he wrote or adapted it, availing himself of such traditional scraps as he could meet with. Two copies of it, duplicate, on broadsheets, are in the Douce Collection at Oxford, vol. iv. pp. 18, 19. A copy, also, in J. H. Dixon's *Bds. and Sgs. of the Peasantry*, Percy Soc., 1845, vol. xvii. (and in R. B.'s *Annotated Ed. B. P.*, p. 138.)

There is still another "Arthur o' Bradley," but not much can, or need, be said in its favour; except that it contains only three verses. Yet even these are more than two which can be spared. Its only tolerable lines are borrowed from the Roxburghe Ballad. It is the *nadir* of Bradleyism, and has not even a title, beyond the burden "*O rare* Arthur o' Bradley, *O!*" Let us, briefly, be in at the death: although Arthur makes not a Swan-like end, with the help of his Catnach poet. It begins thus:

*'Twas in the sweet month of May, I walked out to take
    the air,
My Father he died one day, and he left me his son and heir;
He left me a good warm house, that wanted only a
    thatch,
A strong oak door to my chamber, that only wanted a
    latch;
He left me a rare old cow, I wish he'd have left me a sow,
A cock that in fighting was shy, and a horse with a sharp
    wall eye, &c.*
                    (*Universal Songster*, 1826, i. 368.)

Even Ophelia could not ask, after Arthur sinking so low, "And will he not come again?"

September, 1875.   J. W. E.

176

[So far as possible, to give completeness to our Reprint of *Westminster Drollery* of 1671-2, and *Merry Drollery, Compleat*, 1670-1691, we now add the Extra Songs belonging to the former work, edition 1674; and to the latter, in its earlier edition, 1661: with their respective title-pages.]

Westminster

Westminster-Drollery.

Or, A Choice

COLLECTION

of the Newest

SONGS & POEMS

BOTH AT

Court and Theaters.

BY
A Person of Quality.

The third Edition, with many more Additions.

LONDON,
Printed for *H. Brome*, at the *Gun* in St. *Paul's*
Church Yard, near the West End.
MDCLXXIV.

ADDITIONAL SONGS

FROM THE

WESTMINSTER-DROLLERY:

Edition 1674.

A Song. [p. 111.]

1. SO wretched are the sick of Love,
    No Herb has vertue to remove
        The growing ill:
            But still,
    The more we Remedies oppose
    The Feaver more malignant grows.
        Doubts do but add unto desire,
        Like Oyl that's thrown upon the fire,
        Which serves to make the flame aspire;
            And not t' extinguish it:
    Love has its trembling, and its burning fit.

2. Fruition which the sick propose   [p. 112.]
To end, and recompence their woes,
          But turns them o're
              To more.
And curing one, does but prepare
A new, perhaps a greater care.
      Enjoyment even in the chaste,
      Pleases, not satisfies the taste,
      And licens'd Love the worst can fast.
          Such is the Lovers state,
Pining and pleas'd, alike unfortunate.

3. *Sabina* and *Camilla* share
An equal interest in care,
          Fear hath each brest
              Possest.
In different Fortunes, one pure flame
Makes their unhappiness the same.
      Love begets fear, fear grief creates,
      Passion still passion animates,
      Love will be love in all estates :
          His power still is one
Whether in hope or in possession.

                        A

A Song. [p. 113.]

1. TO Arms! to Arms! the Heroes cry,
    A glorious Death, or Victory.
Beauty and Love, although combin'd,
    And each so powerful alone,
Cannot prevail against a mind
    Bound up in resolution.
Tears their weak influence vainly prove,
Nothing the daring breast can move
Honour is blind, and deaf, ev'n deaf to Love.

2. The Field! the Field! where Valour bleeds,
Spurn'd into dust by barbed steeds,
        Instead of wanton Beds of Down
            Is now the Scene where they must try,
        To overthrow, or be o'rethrown;
            Bravely to overcome, or dye.
        Honour in her interest sits above
        What Beauty, Prayers, or tears can move:
Were there no Honour, there would be no Love.

[p. 114.]   *A Song.*

1. Beauty that it self can kill,
    Through the finest temper'd steel,
   Can those wounds she makes endure,
      And insult it o're the brave,
   Since she knows a certain cure,
      When she is dispos'd to save :
But when a Lover bleeding lies,
      Wounded by other Arms,
      And that she sees those harms,
   For which she knows no remedies ;
   Then Beauty Sorrows livery wears,
   And whilst she melts away in tears,
      Drooping in Sorrow shews
Like Roses overcharg'd with morning dews.

2. Nor do women, though they wear
The most tender character,
      Suffer in this case alone :
         Hearts enclos'd with Iron Walls,
      In humanity must groan
         When a noble Hero falls.

                              Pitiless

Pitiless courage would not be   [p. 115.]
    An honour, but a shame ;
    Nor bear the noble name
Of valour, but barbarity ;
The generous even in success
Lament their enemies distress :
    And scorn it should appear
Who are the Conquer'd, with the Conqueror.

A Song.

1. THe young, the fair, the chaste, the good,
    The sweet *Camilla*, in a flood
    Of her own Crimson lies
    A bloody, bloody sacrifice
To Death and man's inhumane cruelties.
    Weep Virgins till your sorrow swells
    In tears above the Ivory Cells
    That guard those Globes of light ;
Drown, drown those beauties of your eyes.
Beauty should mourn, when beauty dies ;
    And make a general night,
To pay her innocence its Funeral rite.

2. Death since his Empire first begun, [p. 116.]
So foul a conquest never won,
   Nor yet so fair a prize :
   And had he had a heart, or eyes,
Her beauties would have charm'd his cruelties.
   Even Savage Beasts will Beauty spare,
    Chaft Lions fawn upon the fair ; [Fierce Lions]
   Nor dare offend the chaste :
But vitious man, that sees and knows
The mischiefs his wild fury does,
   Humours his passions haste,
To prove ungovern'd man the greatest beast.

A Song.

1. HOw frailty makes us to our wrong
  Fear, and be loth to dye,
When Life is only dying long
   And Death the remedy !
   We shun eternity,
A nd still would gravel her beneath, [*Scil.*, grovel]
   Though still in woe and strife,
When Life's the path that leads to Death,
   And Death the door to Life.
          2. The

2. The Fear of Death is the disease   [p. 117.]
    Makes the poor patient smart;
Vain apprehensions often freeze
    The vitals in the heart,
    Without the dreaded Dart.
When fury rides on pointed steel
    Death's fear the heart doth seize,
Whilst in that very fear we feel
    A greater sting than his.

3. But chaste *Camilla's* vertuous fear
    Was of a noble kind,
Not of her end approaching near
    But to be left behind,
    From her dear Love disjoyn'd;
When Death in courtesie decreed,
    To make the fair his prize,
And by one cruelty her freed
    From humane cruelties.

CHORUS.

Thus heav'n does his will disguise,
To scourge our curiosities,
When too inquisitive we grow
Of what we are forbid to know.

                                           Fond

Fond humane nature that will try [p. 118.]
To sound th' Abiss of Destiny !
Alas ! what profit can arise
From those forbidden scrutinies,
When Oracles what they foretel
In such Ænigma's still conceal,
That self indulging man still makes
Of deepest truths most sad mistakes !
Or could our frailty comprehend
The reach those riddles do intend :
What boots it us when we have done,
To foresee ills we cannot shun ?
But 'tis in man a vain pretence,
To know or prophesie events,
Which only execute, and move,
By a dependence from above.
'Tis all imposture to deceive
The foolish and inquisitive,
Since none foresee what shall befal,
But providence that governs all.
Reason wherewith kind Heav'n has blest
His creature man above the rest,
Will teach humanity to know
All that it should aspire unto ;
And whatsoever fool relies
On false deceiving prophesies,
Striving by conduct to evade
The harms they threaten, or perswade, Too

Too frequently himself does run [p. 119.]
Into the danger he would shun,
And pulls upon himself the woe
Fate meant he should much later know.
By such delusions vertue strays
Out of those honourable ways
That lead unto that glorious end,
To which the noble ever bend.
Whereas if vertue were the guide,
Mens minds would then be fortified
With constancy, that would declare
Against supineness, and despair.
We should events with patience wait,
And not despise, nor fear our Fate.

[P. 120.]

WICKHAM WAKENED,

OR

The Quakers Madrigall In Rime Dogrell.

THe Quaker and his Brats,
   Are born with their Hats,
Which a point with two Taggs,
Ty's fast to their Craggs,
Nor King nor Kesar,
To such Knaves as these are,
Do signifie more than a Tinker.
   His rudeness and pride
   So puffs up his hide
That He's drunk though he be no drinker.

Chorus.

Now since Mayor and Justice
Are assured that thus 'tis
To abate their encrease and redundance
   Let us send them to WICKHAM
   For there's one will kick 'um
Into much better manners by abundance.

Once

Once the Clown at his entry
Kist his golls to the Gentry:
When the Lady took upon her,
'Twas God save your Honor:
But now Lord and Pesant,
Do make but one messe on't
Then farewel distinction 'twixt Plowman and Knight.
    If the world be thus tost
    The old Proverb is crost,
For Joan's as good as my Lady in th' Light.

Chorus.

Now since Mayor and Justice, &c.

'Tis the Gentry that Lulls 'um
While the Quaker begulls 'um:
They dandle 'um in their Lapps,
Who should strike of[f] their Capps;
And make 'um stand bare
Both to Justice and Mayor,
Till when 'twill nere be faire weather;
    For now the proud Devel
    Hath brought forth this Level
None Knows who and who is together.

Now since Mayor and Justice, &c.

Now

Now silence and listen [p. 122.]
Thou shalt hear how they Christen :
Mother Midnight comes out
With the Babe in a Clout,
Tis Rachell you must know tis,
Good friends all take notice,
Tis a name from the Scripture arising.
And thus the dry dipper
(Twere a good deed to whip her)
Makes a Christning without a Baptizing.

Now since Mayor and Justice, &c.

Their wedlocks are many,
But Marriages not any,
For they and their dull Sows,
Like the Bulls and the mull Cows,
Do couple in brutify'd fashion :
But still the Official,
Declares that it is all
Matrimoniall Fornication.

Now since Mayor and Justice, &c.

Their Lands and their Houses
W'ont fall to their Spouses :
They cannot appoint her
One Turff for a Joynter.

His

His son and his daughter, [p. 123.]
Will repent it hereafter ;
For when the Estate is divided ;
For the Parents demerit
Some Kinsman will inherit ;
Why then let them marry as I did.

But since Mayor and Justice, &c.

Now since these mad Nations
Do cheat their relations,
Pray what better hap then
Can we that are Chap men,
Expect from their Canting,
The sighing and panting ?
We are they use the house with a steeple,
And then they may Cozen
All us by the Dozen ;
For Israel may spoyle Pharaohs people.

Now since Mayor and Justice, &c.

The Quaker who before
Did rant and did roare ;
Great thrift will now tell yee on.
But it tends to Rebellion :
For his tipling being don,
He hath bought him a gun

Which

Which hee saves from his former vain spending.
    O be drunk agen *Quaker*,   [p. 124.]
    Take thy Canniken and shake her,
For thou art the worse for the mending.

    Now since Mayor and Justice, &c.

    Then looke we about,
    And give them a Rout,
    Before they Encumber
    The Land with their number:
    There can be no peace in
    These Vermins encreasing;
For tis plaine to all prudent beholders,
    That while we neglect,
    They do but expect
A new head to their old mans Shoulders.

    Now since Mayor and Justice
    Are assured that thus 'tis:
To abate their encrease and redundance
    Let us send them to WICKHAM
    For there's one will Kick 'um
Into much better manners by abundance.

[Here ends the 1674 edition; for account of which, and the 1661 *Merry Drollery*, see our present *Appendix*, Parts Third and Fourth.]

                                  MERRY

MERRY DROLLERY,

OR,

A COLLECTION

Of { Jovial Poems,
    Merry Songs,
    Witty Drolleries,

Intermixed with Pleasant CATCHES.

The First Part.

Collected by
W.N. *C.B.* *R.S.* *J.G.*
Lovers of Wit.

[1s. 3d.]

LONDON,
Printed by *J. W.* for *P. H.* and are to be Sold at the *New Exchange*, Westminster-Hall, Fleet Street, and *Pauls* Church-Yard. [May 1661.]

EXTRA SONGS & POEMS,
IN
Merry Drollery, 1661:

(Omitted from the Editions of 1670, 1691, when New Songs were substituted for them.)

I.—IN PART FIRST.

A Puritan. [fol. 2.]

A Puritan of late,
    And eke a holy Sister,
A Catechizing sate,
And fain he would have kist her
    For his Mate.

But she a Babe of grace,
A Child of reformation,
Thought kissing a disgrace,
A Limbe of prophanation
    In that place.

                                    He

He swore by yea and nay   [fol. 2b.]
He would have no denial,
The Spirit would it so,
She should endure a tryal
    Ere she go.

Why swear you so, quoth she?
Indeed, my holy Brother,
You might have forsworn be
Had it been to another [,]
    Not to me.

He laid her on the ground,
His Spirits fell a ferking,
Her Zeal was in a sound,   [i.e. swoon,]
He edified her Merkin
    Upside down.

And when their leave they took,
And parted were asunder,
My Muse did then awake,
And I turn'd Ballad-monger
    For their sake.

Loves

Loves Dream. [page 11.]

I Dreamt my Love lay in her bed,
   It was my chance to take her,
Her arms and leggs abroad were spread,
She slept, I durst not wake her;
O pitty it were, that one so rare
Should crown her head with willow:
The Tresses of her golden hair
Did crown her lovely Pillow.   [*al. lect.*, Did kisse]

Me thought her belly was a hill
Much like a mount of pleasure,
At foot thereof there springs a well,
The depth no man can measure;
About the pleasant Mountain head
There grows a lofty thicket,
Whither two beagles travelled
To rouze a lively Pricket.

They hunted him with chearful cry
About that pleasant Mountain,
Till he with heat was forc'd to fly
And slip into that Fountain;
The Dogs they follow'd to the brink,
And there at him they baited:
They plunged about and would not sink,   [p. 12.]
His coming out they waited.   Then

Then forth he came as one half lame,
All very faint and tired,
Betwixt her legs he hung his head,
As heavy heart desired;
My dogs then being refresht again,
And she of sleep bereaved,
She dreamt she had me in her arms,
And she was not deceived.

The good Old Cause.

Now *Lambert's* sunk, and valiant *M*—   [*Monk*]
   Does ape his General *Cromwel*,
And *Arthur's* Court, cause time is short,
   Does rage like devils from hell;
Let's mark the fate and course of State,
   Who rises when t'other is sinking,
And believe when this is past
   'Twill be our turn at last
To bring the Good Old Cause by drinking.

First, red nos'd *Nol* he swallowed all,
   His colour shew'd he lov'd it:
But *Dick* his Son, as he were none,
   Gav't off, and hath reprov'd it;

                                                              But

But that his foes made bridge of's nose,
    And cry'd him down for a Protector,
Proving him to be a fool that would undertake to rule
    And not drink and fight like *Hector*.

The Grecian lad he drank like mad,   [p. 13.]
    Minding no work above it;
And *Sans question* kill'd *Ephestion*
    Because he'd not approve it;
He got command where God had land,
    And like a *Maudlin* Yonker,
When he tippled all and wept, he laid him down to
    Having no more Worlds to conquer.   (sleep,

Rump-Parliament would needs invent
    An Oath of abjuration,   (fashion:
But Obedience and Allegiance are now come into
    Then here's a boul with heart and soul
To *Charles*, and let all say Amen to 't;
    Though they brought the Father down
From a triple Kingdom Crown,
    We'll drink the Son up again to 't.

A Song.

Riding to *London*, on *Dunstable* way
   I met with a Maid on *Midsummer* day,
Her Eyes they did sparkle like Stars in the sky,
Her face it was fair, and her forehead was high:
The more I came to her, the more I did view her,
The better I lik'd her pretty sweet face,
I could not forbear her, but still I drew near her,
And then I began to tell her my case:

Whither walk'st thou, my pretty sweet soul?
She modestly answer'd to *Hockley-i'th'-hole.*
I ask'd her her business; she had a red cheek,
She told me, she went a poor service to seek;
I said, it was pitty she should leave the City,
And settle her self in a Country Town;
She said it was certain it was her hard fortune
To go up a maiden, and so to come down.

With that I alighted, and to her I stept,
I took her by th' hand, and this pretty maid wept;
Sweet [,] weep not, quoth I: I kist her soft lip;
I wrung her by th' hand, and my finger she nipt;
So long there I woo'd her, such reasons I shew'd her,
That she my speeches could not controul,
But cursied finely, and got up behind me,
And back she rode with me to *Hockley-i'-th'-hole.*
                             When

When I came to *Hockley* at the sign of the Cock,
By [a]lighting I chanced to see her white smock,
It lay so alluring upon her round knee,
I call'd for a Chamber immediately;
I hugg'd her, I tugg'd her, I kist her, I smugg'd her,
And gently I laid her down on a bed,
With nodding and pinking, with sighing & winking,
She told me a tale of her Maidenhead.

While she to me this story did tell,
I could not forbear, but on her I fell;
I tasted the pleasure of sweetest delight, [p. 16.]
We took up our lodging, and lay there all night;
With soft arms she roul'd me, and oft times told me,
She loved me deerly, even as her own soul:
But on the next morrow we parted with sorrow,
And so I lay with her at *Hockley-i'th'-hole.*

Maidens delight. [p. 27.]

A Young man of late, that lackt a mate,
   And courting came unto her,
With Cap, and Kiss, and sweet Mistris,
But little could he do her;
                                    Quoth

Quoth she, my friend, let kissing end,
Where with you do me smother,
And run at Ring with t'other thing:
    A little o' th t'on with t'other.

Too much of ought is good for nought,
Then leave this idle kissing;
Your barren suit will yield no fruit
If the other thing be missing:
As much as this a man may kiss
His sister or his mother;
He that will speed must give with need
    A little o' th' t'on with t'other.

Who bids a Guest unto a feast,
To sit by divers dishes,
They please their mind untill they find
Change, please each Creatures wishes;
With beak and bill I have my fill,
With measure running over;
The Lovers dish now do I wish,
    A little o' th' t'on with t'other.

To gull me thus, like *Tantalus*,
To make me pine with plenty,
With shadows store, and nothing more,   [p. 28.]
Your substance is so dainty;

A fruitless tree is like to thee,
Being but a kissing lover,
With leaves joyn fruit, or else be mute ;
      A little o' th' t'on with t'other.

Sharp joyn'd with flat, no mirth to that ;
A low note and a higher,
Where Mean and Base keeps time and place,
Such musick maids desire :
All of one string doth loathing bring,
Change, is true Musicks Mother,
Then leave my face, and sound the base,
      A little o' th' t'on with t'other.

The golden mine lies just between   [? golden mean]
The high way and the lower ;
He that wants wit that way to hit
Alas [!] hath little power ;
You'l miss the clout if that you shoot
Much higher, or much lower :
Shoot just between, your arrows keen,
      A little o' th' t'on with t'other.

No smoake desire without a fire,
No wax without a Writing :
If right you deal give Deeds to Seal,
And straight fall to inditing ;
                                  Thus

Thus do I take these lines I make,
As to a faithful Lover,
In order he'll first write, then seal,
    A little o' th' t'on with t'other.

Thus while she staid the young man plaid   [p. 29.]
Not high, but low defending;   [? descending;]
Each stroak he strook so well she took,
She swore it was past mending;
Let swaggering boys that think by toyes
Their Lovers to fetch over,
Lip-labour save, for the maids must have
    A little o' th' t'on with t'other.

A Song.   [p. 32.]

A Young man walking all alone
    Abroad to take the air,
It was his chance to meet a maid
Of beauty passing fair:
Desiring her of curtesie
Down by him for to sit;
She answered him most modestly,
    O nay, O nay not yet.

                        Forty

Forty Crowns I will give thee,
Sweet heart, in good red Gold,
If that thy favour I may win
With thee for to be bold :
She answered him with modesty,
And with a fervent wit,
Think'st thou I'll stain my honesty?
      O nay, O nay not yet.

Gold and silver is but dross,   [p. 33.]
And worldly vanity;
There's nothing I esteem so much
As my Virginity;
What do you think I am so loose,   [al. lect., mad]
And of so little wit,
As for to lose my maidenhead?
      O nay, O nay not yet.

Although our Sex be counted base,
And easie to be won,
You see that I can find a check
Dame Natures Games to shun;
Except it be in modesty,
That may become me fit,
Think'st I am weary of my honesty?
      O nay, O nay not yet.

                              The

The young man stood in such a dump,
Not giving no more words,
He gave her that in quietness
Which love to maids affords:
The maid was ta'n as in a trance,
And such a sudden fit,
As she had almost quite forgot
   Her nay, O nay not yet.

The way to win a womans love
Is only to be brief,
And give her that in quietness
Will ease her of her grief:
For kindness they will not refuse
When young men proffer it,
Although their common speeches be
   O nay, O nay not yet.

     Admiral Deans *Funeral.* [p. 56.]

       1.

N*Ick Culpepper*, and *William Lilly*,
 Though you were pleas'd to say they were silly,
Yet something these prophesi'd true, I tell you, [? ye,]
 Which no body can deny.

         2.

2.

In the month of *May*, I tell you truly,
Which neither was in *June* nor *July*,
The Dutch began to be unruly,
    Which no body can deny.

3,

Betwixt our *England* and their *Holland*,
Which neither was in *France* nor *Poland*,
But on the Sea, where there was no Land,
    Which no body can deny.

4.

They joyn'd the Dutch, and the English Fleet,
[In] Our Authors opinion then they did meet,
Some saw't that never more shall see't,
    Which no body can deny.

5.

There were many mens hearts as heavy as lead, [p.57.]
Yet would not believe *Dick Dean* to be dead,
Till they saw his Body take leave of his head,
    Which no body can deny.

6.

Then after the sad departure of him,
There was many a man lost a Leg or a Lim,
And many were drown'd 'cause they could not swim,
    Which no body can deny.   One

7.

One cries, lend me thy hand [,] good friend,
Although he knew it was to no end,
I think, quoth he, I am going to the Fiend,
    Which no body can deny.

8.

Some, 'twas reported, were kill'd with a Gun,
And some stood that knew not whether to run,
There was old taking leave of Father and Son,
    Which no body can deny,

9.

There's a rumour also, if we may believe,
We have many gay Widdows now given to grieve,
'Cause unmannerly Husbands ne'er came to take
    Which no body can deny.   (leave,

10.

The Ditty is sad of our *Deane* to sing;
To say truth, it was a pittiful thing
To take off his head and not leave him a ring.
    Which no body can deny.

11.

From *Greenwich* toward the Bear at Bridge foot
He was wafted with wind that had water to't,
But I think they brought the devil to boot,
    Which no body can deny.   The

12.

The heads on *London* Bridge upon Poles,   [p. 58.]
That once had bodies, and honester soules
Than hath the Master of the Roules,
    Which no body can deny,

13.

They grieved for this great man of command,
Yet would not his head amongst theirs should stand;
He dy'd on the Water, and they on the Land,
    Which no body can deny.

14.

I cannot say, they look'd wisely upon him,
Because people cursed that parcel was on him;
He has fed fish and worms, if they do not wrong him,
    Which no body can deny.

15.

The Old Swan, as he passed by,
Said, she would sing him a dirge, and lye down & die:
Wilt thou sing to a bit of a body, quoth I?
    Which no body can deny.

16.

The Globe on the bank, I mean, on the Ferry,
Where Gentle and simple might come & be merry,
Admired at the change from a Ship to a Wherry,
    Which no body can deny.

17.
Tom Godfreys Bears began for to roare,
Hearing such moans one side of the shore,
They knew they should never see *Dean* any more,
    Which no body can deny.

18.
Queenhithe, *Pauls*-Wharf, and the Fryers also,
Where now the Players have little to do,
Let him pass without any tokens of woe,
    Which no body can deny.

[p. 59.]
19.   (names,
Quoth th' Students o'th' Temple, I know not their
Looking out of their Chambers into the Thames,
The Barge fits him better than did the great *James*,
    Which no body can deny.

20.
Essex House, late called Cuckold's Hall,
The Folk in the Garden staring over the wall,
Said, they knew that once *Pride* would have a fall,
    Which no body can deny.

21.
At Strand Gate, a little farther then,
Were mighty Guns numbred to sixty and ten,
Which neither hurt Children, Women, nor Men,
    Which no body can deny.   22.

22.

They were shot over times one, two, three, or four,
'Tis thought one might 'heard th' bounce to th' Tower,
Folk report, the din made the Buttermilk sower,
    Which no body can deny.

23.

Had old Goodman *Lenthal* or *Allen* but heard 'um,
The noise worse than *Olivers* voice would 'fear'd 'um,
And out of their small wits would have scar'd 'um.
    Which no body can deny.

24.

Sommerset House, where once did the Queen lye,
And afterwards *Ireton* in black, and not green, by,
The Canon clattered the Windows really,
    Which no body can deny.

25.

The *Savoys* mortified spittled Crew,
If I lye, as *Falstaffe* saies, I am a Jew,   (spew,
Gave the Hearse such a look it would make a man
    Which no body can deny.

26.

The House of S—— that Fool and Knave, [p. 60.]
Had so much wit left lamentation to save
From accompanying a traytorly Rogue to his grave,
    Which no body can deny.   27.

27.

The Exchange, and the ruines of *Durham* House eke,
Wish'd such sights might be seen each day i' th' week,
A Generals Carkass without a Cheek,
    Which no body can deny.

28.

The House that lately Great *Buckinghams* was,
Which now Sir *Thomas Fairfax* has,
Wish'd it might be Sir *Thomas's* fate so to pass,
    Which no body can deny.

29.

Howards House, *Suffolks* great Duke of Yore,
Sent him one single sad wish, and no more,
He might flote by *Whitehall* in purple gore,
    Which no body can deny.

30.

Something I should of *Whitehall* say,
But the Story is so sad, and so bad, by my fay,
That it turns my wits another way,
    Which no body can deny.

31.

To *Westminster*, to the Bridge of the Kings,
The water the Barge, and the Barge-men[,] brings
The small remain of the worst of things,
    Which no body can deny.

32.

They interr'd him in triumph, like *Lewis* the eleven,
In the famous Chappel of *Henry* the seven,
But his soul is scarce gone the right way to heaven,
    Which no body can deny.

A merrie Journey to France.   [p. 64.]

I Went from *England* into *France*,
  Not for to learn to sing nor dance,
    To ride, nor yet to fence,
But for to see strange sights, as those
That have return'd without a nose
    They carried away from hence.

As I to *Paris* rode along,
Like to *John Dory* in the Song,
    Upon a holy Tyde,
Where I an ambling Nag did get,
I hope he is not paid for yet,
    I spurr'd him on each side.

First, to Saint *Dennis* then I came,
To see the sights at *Nostredame*,
    The man that shews them snaffles:
That who so list, may there believe
To see the Virgin *Maries* Sleeve,
    And eke her odd Pantafles.   [? old]

The breast-milk, and the very Gown
That she did wear in *Bethlehem* Town,
      When in the Barn she lay:
But men may think that is a Fable,   [p. 65]
For such good cloaths ne'er came in Stable
      Upon a lock of hay.

No Carpenter can by his trade
Have so much Coin as to have made
      A gown of such rich Stuff:
But the poor fools must, for their credit,
Believe, and swear old *Joseph* did it,
      'Cause he received enough.   [*al. lect.*, deserv'd]

There is the Lanthorn which the Jews,
When *Judas* led them forth, did use,
      It weighs my weight down-right;
And then you must suppose and think
The Jews therein did put a Link,
      And then 't was wondrous bright.   [? light]

There is one Saint has lost his nose,
Another his head, but not his toes,
      An elbow, and a thumb;
When we had seen those holy rags,
We went to the Inne and took our Nags,
      And so away we come.

                                            We

We came to *Paris*, on the *Seine*,
'Tis wondrous fair, but little clean,
  'Tis *Europes* greatest Town:
How strong it is I need not tell it,
For every one may easily smell it
  As they ride up and down.

There's many rare sights for to see,
The Palace, the great Gallery,
  Place-Royal doth excell;
The Newbridge, and the Statute stairs,   [p. 66.]
At *Rotterdam*, Saint *Christophers*,   [? *Nostre Dame*]
  The Steeple bears the Bell.

For Arts, the University,
And for old Cloaths, the Frippery,
  The Queen the same did build;
Saint *Innocent*[*s'*], whose earth devours
Dead Corps in four and twenty hours,
  And there the King was kill'd.

The *Bastile*, and Saint *Dennis* street,
The *Chastelet*, like *London* Fleet;
  The Arsenal is no toy;
But if you will see the pretty thing,
Oh go to Court and see the King,
  Oh he is a hopeful boy.

       He

He is of all [his] Dukes and Peers
Reverenc'd for wit as well as years;
    Nor must you think it much
That he with little switches play,
And can make fine dirt-pies of Clay,
    O never King made such.

Birds round about his Chamber stands,
The which he feeds with his own hands,
    'Tis his humility:
And if they want [for] any thing,
They may but whistle to their King
    And he comes presently.

A bird that can but catch a Fly,
Or prate to please his Majesty,   [*al. lect.*, doth please]
    It's known to every one;
The Duke *De Guise* gave him a Parrot,   [p. 67]
And he had twenty Cannons for it
    For his great Gallion.

O that it e'er might be my hap
To catch the bird that in the Map
    They call the Indian Chuck,
I'd give it him, and hope to be
As great and wise a man as he,
    Or else I had ill luck.

                        Besides

Besides, he hath a pretty firk,
Taught him by Nature, for to work
   In Iron with much ease :
And then uuto the Forge he goes,
There he knocks, and there he blows,
   And makes both locks and Keys.

Which puts a doubt in every one
Whether he be *Mars* or *Vulcans* Son,
   For few believe his Mother :
For his Incestuous House could not
Have any Children, unless got
   By Uncle, or by Brother.

Now for these virtues needs he must
Intituled be *Lewis* the Just,
   Heneries Great Heir ;
Where to his Stile we add more words,
Better to call him King of Birds
   Than of the Great *Navar*.

His Queen, she is a little Wench,
Was born in *Spain*, speaks little French,
   Ne'er like to be a Mother :
But let them all say what they will,   [p. 68.]
I do beleeve, and shall do still,
   As soon the one as t'other.

          Then

Then why should *Lewis* be so just,
Contented be to take his lust   [? he]
    With his lascivious Mate,
Or suffer this his little Queen,
From all her Sex that e'er had been,
    Thus to degenerate?

'Twere charity to have it known,
Love other Children as his own
    To him it were no shame:
For why should he near greater be
Than was his Father *Henery*,
    Who, some say, did the same?

Englands Woe.   [p. 85.]

I Mean to speak of *Englands* sad fate,
   To help in mean time the King, and his Mate,
That's ruled by an Antipodian State,
    Which no body can deny.

But had these seditious times been when
We had the life of wise Poet *Ben*,
Parsons had never been Parliament men,
    Which no body can deny.

                                      Had

Had Statesmen read the Bible throughout,
And not gone by the Bible so round about,
They would have ruled themselves without doubt,
    Which no body can deny.

But Puritans now bear all the sway,
They'll have no Bishops as most men say,
But God send them better another day,
    Which no body can deny.

Zealous *Pryn* has threatned a great downfall,
To cut off long locks that is bushy and small,
But I hope he will not take ears and all,
    Which no body can deny.

Prin, [and] *Burton*, saies women that's leud and loose,
Shall wear no stallion locks for a bush, [*Italian* ... abuse]
They'll only have private boyes for their use, [*al lect.*, Keyes]
    Which no body can deny.

They'll not allow what pride it brings,   [p. 86.]
Nor favours in hats, nor no such things,
They'l convert all ribbands to Bible strings,
    Which no body can deny.

God bless our King and Parliament,
And send he may make such K—— repent   [Knaves]
That breed our Land such discontent,
    Which no body can deny.   And

And bless our Queen and Prince also,
And all true Subjects both high and low,
The brownings can pray for themselves you know,
    Which no body can deny.

Ladies Delight.   [p. 88.]

Hang Chastity [!] it is for the milking pail,
    Ladies ought to be more valiant :
Not to be confin'd in body and mind
    Is the temper of a right she Gallant ;
Hither all you Amazons that are true
    To this famous Dildoe profession,
She is no bonny Lass that fears to transgress
    The Act against Fornication.

The Country Dame, that loves the old sport,
    Or delights in a new invention,
May be fitted here, if they please to repair
    To this high ranting Convention ;
If you are weary of your Coyn,
    Or of your Chastity,
Here is costly toyes, or hot-metled boyes,
    That will ease you presently.
                                    Both

Both curious heads and wanton tailes
    May here have satisfaction ;
Here is all kind of ware, that useful are
    For pride or provocation ;
Here's Drugs to paint, or Powder to perfume,
    Or Ribbon of the best fashion ;
Here's dainty meat will fit you for the feat
    Beyond all expectation.

Here's curious patches to set out your faces, [p. 89.]
    And make you resemble the sky ;
Or here's looking-glasses to shew the poor Asses,
    Your Husbands, their destiny ;
Here's bawbles too to play withall,
    And some to stand in stead ;
This place doth afford both for your brow,
    And stallions for your head.

Old Ladies here may be reliev'd,
    If Ushers they do lack,
Or if they'll not discharge their husbands at large,
    But grow foundred in the back ;
Green visag'd Damsels, that are sick
    Of a troubled Maidenhead,
May here, if they please, be cur'd of the disease
    And their green colours turn'd to red.

The

The Tyrannical Wife. [p. 95.]

IT was a man, and a jolly old man,
    Come love me whereas I lay,
And he would marry a fair young wife
    The clean contrary way.

He woo'd her for to wed, to wed,
    Come love me whereas I lay,
And even she kickt him out of the bed
    The clean contrary way.

Then for her dinner she looked due,
    Come love me whereas I lay,
Or else would make her husband rue
    The clean contrary way.

She made him wash both dish and spoon,
    Come love me whereas I lay,
He had better a gone on his head to *Rome*
    The clean contrary way.

She proved a gallant huswife soon,
    Come love me whereas I lay,
She was every morning up by noon
    The clean contrary way,

She made him go to wash and wring, [p. 96.]
    Come love me whereas I lay,
And every day to dance and sing
    The clean contrary way.

She made him do a worse thing than this,
    Come love me whereas I lay,
To father a child was none of his,
    The clean contrary way.

Hard by a bush, and under a brier,
    Come love me whereas I lay,
I saw a holy Nun lye under a Frier
    The clean contrary way.

To end my Song I think it long,
    Come love me whereas I lay,
Come give me some drink and I'll be gone
    The clean contrary way.

The Tinker. [p. 134.]

[Some of these verses are evidently misplaced: We keep them unchanged, but add side-notes to rectify.]

THere was a Lady in this Land
    That lov'd a Gentleman,
And could not have him secretly,
    As she would now and then,   Till

Till she devis'd to dress him like
    A Tinker in Vocation:
And thus, disguis'd, she bid him say,
    He came to clout her Cauldron.

His face full fair she smother's black   [2.]
    That he might not be known,
A leather Jerkin on his back,   [p. 135.]
    His breeches rent and torn;
With speed he passed to the place,
    To knock he did not spare:
Who's that, quoth the lady ['s Porter] then,
    That raps so rashly there.

I am a Tinker, then quoth he,   [3.]
    That worketh for my Fee,
If you have Vessels for to mend,
    Then bring them unto me:
For I have brass within my bag,
    And target in my Apron,
And with my skill I can well clout,
    And mend a broken Cauldron.

Quoth she, our Cauldron hath most need,   [? verse 7.]
    At it we will begin,
For it will hold you half an hour
    To trim it out and in:

                                                But

But first give me a glass of drink,
    The best that we do use,
For why [,] it is a Tinkers guise
    No good drink to refuse.

Then to the Brew-house hyed they fast,   [? verse 8.]
    This broken piece to mend,
He said he would no company,
    His Craft should not be kend,
But only to your self, he said,
    That must pay me my Fee :
I am no common Tinker,
    But work most curiously.

And I also have made a Vow,   [? verse 9. p. 136.]
    I'll keep it if I may,
There shall no mankind see my work,
    That I may stop or stay :
Then barred he the Brew-house door,
    The place was very dark,
He cast his Budget from his back,
    And frankly fell to work.

And whilst he play'd and made her sport,   [? verse 10.]
    Their craft the more to hide,
She with his hammer stroke full hard
    Against the Cauldron side :

                            Which

Which made them all to think, and say,
    The Tinker wrought apace,
And so be sure he did indeed,
    But in another place.

The Porter went into the house,   [? verse 4.]
    Where Servants us'd to dine,
Telling his Lady, at the Gate
    There staid a Tinker fine:
Quoth he, much Brass he wears about,
    And Target in his Apron,
Saying, that he hath perfect skill
    To mend your broken Cauldron.

Quoth she, of him we have great need,   [? verse 5.]
    Go Porter, let him in,
If he be cunning in his Craft
    He shall much money win:
But wisely wist she who he was,
    Though nothing she did say,
For in that sort she pointed him
    To come that very day.

When he before the Lady came,   [? verse 6. p. 137.]
    Disguised stood he there,
He blinked blithly, and did say,
    God save you Mistris fair;

                            Thou'rt

Thou'rt welcome, Tinker, unto me,
    Thou seem'st a man of skill,
All broken Vessels for to mend,
    Though they be ne'er so ill;
I am the best man of my Trade,
    Quoth he, in all this Town,
For any Kettle, Pot, or Pan,
    Or clouting of a Cauldron.

Quoth he, fair Lady, unto her,   [verse 11.]
    My business I have ended,
Go quickly now, and tell your Lord
    The Cauldron I have mended:
As for the Price, that I refer
    Whatsoever he do say,
Then come again with diligence,
    I would I were away.

The Lady went unto her Lord,   [12.]
    Where he walkt up and down,
Sir, I have with the Tinker been,
    The best in all the Town:
His work he doth exceeding well,
    Though he be wondrous dear,
He asks no less than half a Mark
    For that he hath done here.

                                Quoth

Quoth he, that Target is full dear, [13]
    I swear by Gods good Mother :
Quoth she, my Lord, I dare protest,
    'Tis worth five hundred other ;
He strook it in the special place, [p. 138.]
    Where greatest need was found,
Spending his brass and target both,
    To make it safe and sound.

Before all Tinkers in the Land,
    That travels up and down,
Ere they should earn a Groat of mine,
    This man should earn a Crown :
Or were you of his Craft so good,
    And none but I it kend,
Then would it save me many a Mark,
    Which I am fain to spend.

The Lady to her Coffer went,
    And took a hundred Mark,
And gave the Tinker for his pains,
    That did so well his work ;
Tinker, said she, take here thy fee,
    Sith here you'll not remain,
But I must have my Cauldron now
    Once scoured o'er again.

                                      Then

Then to the former work they went,
    No man could them deny;
The Lady said, good Tinker call
    The next time thou com'st by:
For why [,] thou dost thy work so well,
    And with so good invention,
If still thou hold thy hand alike,
    Take here a yearly Pension.

And ev'ry quarter of the year
    Our Cauldron thou shalt view;
Nay, by my faith, her Lord gan say,   [p. 139.]
    I'd rather buy a new;
Then did the Tinker take his leave
    Both of the Lord and Lady,
And said, such work as I can do,
    To you I will be ready.
From all such Tinkers of the trade
    God keep my Wife, I pray,
That comes to clout her Cauldron so,
    I'll swinge him if I may.

[A song follows, beginning "There were three birds that built very low." With other four, commencing respectively on pp. 146, 153, 161, and 168, it is degraded from position here; for substantial reasons; and (with a few others, afterwards to be specified,) given separately. Nothing but the absolute necessity of making this a genuine Antiquarian Reprint, worthy of the confidence of all mature students of our Early Literature, compels the Editor to
admit

admit such prurient and imbecile pieces at all. They are tokens of a debased taste that would be inconceivable, did we not remember that, not more than twenty years ago, crowds of MP.s, Lawyers, and Baronets listened with applause, and encored tumultuously, songs far more objectionable than these (if possible) in London Music Halls, and Supper Rooms. Those who recollect what R .. s sang (such as " The Lock of Hair," " My name it is Sam Hall, Chimbley Sweep," &c.), and what " Judge N——" said at his Jury Court, need not be astonished at anything which was sung or written in the days of the Commonwealth and at the Restoration. A few words we suppress into dots in *Supplement*, &c.]

The Maid a bathing. [p. 148.]

UPon a Summers day,
  'Bout middle of the morn,
I spy'd a Lass that lay
  Stark nak'd as she was born;
'Twas by a running Pool,
  Within a meddow green,
And there she lay to cool,
  Not thinking to be seen.

Then did she by degrees
  Wash every part in rank,
Her Arms, her breasts, her thighs,
  Her Belly, and her Flank;
Her legs she opened wide,
  My eyes I let down steal,
Untill that I espy'd
  Dame natures privy Seal.   I

I stript me to the skin,
    And boldly stept unto her,
Thinking her love to win,
    I thus began to wooe her:
Sweet heart be not so coy,
    Time's sweet in pleasure spent,
She frown'd, and cry'd, away,
    Yet, smiling, gave consent.

Then blushing, down she slid,   [p. 149]
    Seeming to be amazed,
But heaving up her head,
    Again she on me gazed;
I seeing that, lay down,
    And boldly 'gan to kiss,
And she did smile, and frown,
    And so fell to our bliss.

Then lay she on the ground
    As though she had been sped,
As women in a swoon,
    Yield up, and yet not dead:
So did this lively maid,
    When hot bloud fill'd her vein,
And coming to her self she said,
    I thank you for your pain.

[Part

[Part First, 1661, ends on pages 171-175, with *The new Medley of the Country man, Citizen, and Souldier* (which in the 1670 and 1691 editions are on pp. 182-187). The 1661 edition of SECOND PART has a complete title-page of its own, in black and red, exactly agreeing with its own First Part, except that the words are prefixed "THE || Second Part || OF." A contemporary MS. note in Ant. à Wood's copy, says, of each part, " 1s. 3d." as the original price. There is also, in the 1661 edition (and in that only), another address, here, which runs as follows :—

"To the Reader :

"Courteous Reader,

"*W*E *do here present thee with the Second part of* Merry Drollery, *not doubting but it will find good Reception with the more Ingenious; The deficiency of this shall be supplied in a third, when time shall serve: In the mean time*
         Farewel."

The *Third Part*, mentioned above, never appeared.

The woodcut Initial W represents Salome, the daughter of Herodias, receiving from the Roman-like *Stratiotes* the head of John the Baptist (whose body lies at their feet), she holding her charger. The Editor hopes to engrave it for the Introduction to this present volume.

The pagination commences afresh in the 1661 Second Part; but continues in the 1670, and the 1691 editions.]

Merry

Merry Drollery, 1661 :

EXTRA SONGS IN PART SECOND.

(Omitted in 1670 and 1691 Editions.)

The Force of Opportunity. [Part 2nd., p. 21.]

YOu gods that rule upon the Plains,
    Where nothing but delight remains ;
You Nymphs that haunt the Fairy Bowers,
Exceeding *Flora* with her flowers ;
The fairest woman that earth can have
Sometimes forbidden fruit will crave,
        For any woman, whatsoe'r she be,
        Will yield to Opportunity.

Your Courtly Ladies that attends,
May sometimes dally with their friends ;
And she that marries with a Knight
May let his Lodging for a night ;
And she that's only Worshipful
Perhaps another friend may gull :
        For any woman, &c.

The

The Chamber-maid that's newly married
Perhaps another man hath carried;
Your City Wives will not be alone,
Although their husbands be from home;
The fairest maid in all the town
For green will change a russet Gown;
    For any woman, &c.

And she that loves a Zealous brother,
May change her Pulpit for another;
Physitians study for their skill,   [p. 22.]
Whiles wives their Urinals do fill;
The Lawyers wife may take her pride
Whilst he their Causes doth decide;
    For every woman, &c.

The Country maid, that milks the Cow,
And takes great pains to work and do,
I'th' fields may meet her friend or brother,
And save her soul to get another;
And she that to the Market[']s gone
May horn her man ere she come home;
    For any woman, &c.

You Goddesses and Nymphs so bright,
The greater Star, the lesser light;
To Lords, as well as mean estates,
  Belongeth husbands horned baites,   [? pates.] Then

Then give your Ladies leave to prove
The things the which your selves do love;
    For any woman, what ere she be,
    Will yield to Opportunity.

Lusty Tobacco.   [p. 22.]

YOu that in love do mean to sport,
    Tobacco, Tobacco,
First take a wench of a meaner sort,
    Tobacco, Tobacco,
But let her have a comely grace,
Like one that came from *Venus* race,
Then take occasion, time, and place,
  To give her some Tobacco.

You —— gamesters must be bound,   [p. 23.]
    Tobacco, Tobacco,
Their bullets must be plump and round,
    Tobacco, Tobacco,
Your Stopper must be stiff and strong,
Your Pipe it must be large and long,
Or else she'll say you do her wrong,
    She'll scorn your weak Tobacco.

And if that you do please her well,
    Tobacco, Tobacco,   All

All others then she will expell,
    Tobacco, Tobacco.
She will be ready at your call
To take Tobacco, Pipe, and all,
So willing she will be to fall
    To take your strong Tobacco.

And when you have her favour won,
    Tobacco, Tobacco,
You must hold out as you begun,
    Tobacco, Tobacco,
Or else she'll quickly change her mind,
And seek some other Friend to find,
That better may content her mind
    In giving her Tobacco.

And if you do not do her right,
    Tobacco, Tobacco,
She'll take a course to burn your Pipe,
    Tobacco, Tobacco,
And if you ask what she doth mean,
She'll say she doth't to make it clean,
Then take you heed of such a Quean
    For spoyling your Tobacco,

As I my self dare boldly speak,   [p. 24.]
    Tobacco, Tobacco,

                                            Which

Which makes my very heart to break,
    Tobacco, Tobacco,
For she that I take for my friend,
Hath my Tobacco quite consum'd,
She hath spoil'd my Pipe, and there's an end
    Of all my good Tobacco.

On the Goldsmiths-Committee.   [p 29.]

Come Drawer, some wine,
    Or we'll pull down the Sign,
        For we are all jovial Compounders:
We'll make the house ring,
With healths to the KING,
        And confusion light on his Confounders.

Since Goldsmiths Committee
Affords us no pitty,
        Our sorrows in wine we will steep 'um,
They force us to take
Two Oaths, but we'll make
        A third, that we ne'r mean to keep 'um.

And next, who e'r sees,
We drink on our knees,
        To the King, may he thirst that repines.

A

A fig for those traitors
That look to our waters,
  They have nothing to do with our wines.

And next here's a Cup
To the Queen, fill it up,
  Were it poyson, we would make an end o'nt:
May *Charles* and She meet,
And tread under feet
  Both Presbyter and Independent.

To the Prince, and all others,
His Sisters and Brothers,
  As low in condition as high born,
We'll drink this, and pray,   [p .30.]
That shortly they may,
  See all them that wrongs them at *Tyburn*.

And next here's three bowls
To all gallant souls,
  That for the King did, and will venter,
May they flourish when those
That are his, and their foes
  Are hang'd and ram'd down to the Center.

And next let a Glass
To our undoers pass,
  Attended with two or three curses: May

May plagues sent from hell
Stuff their bodies as well,
    As the Cavaliers Coyn doth their purses.

May the *Cannibals* of *Pym*
Eat them up limb by limb,
    Or a hot Fever scorch 'um to embers,
Pox keep 'um in bed
Untill they are dead,
    And repent for the loss of their Members.

And may they be found
In all to abound,
    Both with heaven and the countries anger,
May they never want Fractions,
Doubts, Fears, and Distractions,
    Till the Gallow-tree choaks them from danger.

Insatiate Desire. [p. 31.]

O That I could by any Chymick Art
   To sperme, convert my spirit and my heart,
That at one thrust I might my soul translate,
And in her w . . . my self degenerate,
There steep'd in lust nine months I would remain,
Then boldly —— my passage back again.

The

The Horn exalted.

Listen Lordings to my Story,
 I will sing of Cuckolds glory,
And thereat let none be vext,
None doth know whose turn is next;
And seeing it is in most mens scorn,
'Tis Charity to advance the *Horn*.

Diana was a Virgin pure,
Amongst the rest chaste and demure;
Yet you know well, I am sure,
What *Acteon* did endure,
If men have *Horns* for [such] as she,
I pray thee tell me what are we?

Let thy friend enjoy his rest,
What though he wear *Acteons* creast?
Malice nor Venome at him spit,
He wears but what the gods thinks fit;
Confess he is by times Recorder
Knight of great *Diana's* Order.

Luna was no venial sinner,
Yet she hath a man within her,
And to cut off Cuckolds scorns,
She decks her head with Silver horns
And if the moon in heaven [']s thus drest,
The men on earth like it are blest.

[*A Droll of a Louse* (p. 33), seven verses of seven lines each, beginning " Discoveries of late have been made by adventures," is reserved. *Vide ante* p. 213.]

A Letany. [p. 38.]

From *Essex* Anabaptist Laws,
And from *Norfolk* Plough-tail Laws, [? taws]
From *Abigails* pure tender Zeal,
Whiter than a *Brownists* veal,
From a Serjeants Temple pickle,
And the Brethrens *Conventicle*,
From roguish meetings, or Cutpurse hall,
And *New-England*, worst of all,
    Libera nos Domine.

From the cry of *Ludgate* debters, [p. 39.]
And the noise of Prisoners Fetters,
From groans of them that have the Pox,
And coyl of Beggars in the Stocks,
From roar o' th' *Bridge*, and *Bedlam* prate,
And with Wives met at *Billingsgate*,
From scritch-owles, and dogs night-howling,
From Sailers cry at their main bowling,
    Libera nos domine.

From *Frank Wilsons* trick of *mopping*,
And her ulcered h . . . with *popping*,   From

From Knights o' th' post, and from decoys,
From *Whores*, *Bawds*, and roaring *Boys*,
From a *Bulker* in the dark,
And *Hannah* with St. *Tantlins* Clark,
From Biskets Bawds have rubb'd their gums,
And from purging-Comfit plums,
    Libera nos Domine.

From *Sue Prats* Son, the fair and witty,
The Lord of *Portsmouth*, sweet and pretty,
From her that creeps up *Holbourne* hill,
And *Moll* that cries, *God-dam-me* still,
From backwards-ringing of the Bells,
From both the Counters and Bridewells,
From blind *Robbin* and his *Bess*,
And from a Purse that's penniless;
    Libera nos Domine.

From gold-finders, and night-weddings,
From *Womens* eyes false liquid sheddings,
From *Rocks*, *Sands*, and *Cannon-shot*,
And from a stinking Chamber-pot,
From a hundred years old sinner,   [p. 40.]
And Duke *Humphreys* hungry dinner,
From stinking breath of an old Aunt [,]
From Parritors and Pursevants [,]
    Libera nos Domine.

                          From

From a Dutchmans snick and sneeing,
From a nasty Irish being [,]
From a *Welchmans* lofty bragging,
And a Monsieur loves not drabbing,

From begging Scotchmen and their pride,
From striving 'gainst both wind and tide,
From too much strong Wine and Beer,
Enforcing us to domineer,
    Libera nos Domine.

[Following the above comes a group of more than usually objectionable Songs, viz., *John* and *Joan*, beginning "If you will give ear (p. 46); "Full forty times over I have strived to win," same title (p. 61); The Answer to it, " He is a fond Lover that doateth on scorn" (p. 62); Love's Tenement, " If any one do want a house" (p. 64) ; and A New Year's Gift, " Fair Lady, for your New Year's Gift" (p. 81). These are all reserved for the Chamber of Horrors. *Vide ante*, p. 213].

      New England *described.*   [p. 103.]

A Mong the purifidian Sect,
    I mean the counterfeit Elect :
Zealous bankrupts, Punks devout,
Preachers suspended, rabble rout,
Let them sell all, and out of hand
Prepare to go to *New England*,
    To build new *Babel* strong and sure,
    Now call'd a Church unspotted pure.
                      There

There Milk from Springs, like Rivers, flows,
And Honey upon hawthorn grows ;
Hemp, Wool, and Flax, there grows on trees,
The mould is fat, it cuts like cheese ;
All fruits and herbs spring in the fields,
Tobacco it good plenty yields ;
  And there shall be a Church most pure,
  Where you may find salvation sure.

There's Venison of all sorts great store,
Both Stag, and buck, wild Goat, and Boar,
And all so tame, that you with ease
May take your fill, eat what you please ;
There's Beavers plenty, yea, so many,
That you may buy two skins a penny,
  Above all this, a Church most pure,
  Where to be saved you may be sure.

There's flight of Fowl do cloud the skie,
Great Turkies of threescore pound weight,
As big as as Estriges, there Geese,   [p. 104.]
With thanks, are sold for pence a piece ;
Of Duck and Mallard, Widgeon, Teale,
Twenty for two-pence make a meale ;
  Yea, and a Church unspotted pure,
  Within whose bosome all are sure.

Loe, there in shoals all sorts of fish,
Of the salt seas, and water fresh :
         Ling,

Ling, Cod, Poor-John, and Haberdine,
Are taken with the Rod and Line;
A painful fisher on the shore
May take at least twenty an houre;
    Besides all this a Church most pure,
    Where you may live and dye secure.

There twice a year all sorts of Grain
Doth down from heaven, like hailstones, rain;
You ne'r shall need to sow nor plough,
There's plenty of all things enough:
Wine sweet and wholsome drops from trees,
As clear as chrystal, without lees;
    Yea, and a Church unspotted, pure,
    From dregs of Papistry secure.

No Feasts nor festival set daies
Are here observed, the Lord be prais'd,
Though not in Churches rich and strong,
Yet where no Mass was ever Sung,
The Bulls of *Bashan* ne'r met there [;]
Surplice and *Cope* durst not appear;
    Old Orders all they will abjure,
    This Church hath all things new and pure.

No discipline shall there be used,   [p. 105.]
The Law of Nature they have chused [;]
                                 All

All that the spirit seems to move
Each man may choose and so approve,
There's Government without command,
There's unity without a band;
  A Synagogue unspotted pure,
  Where lust and pleasure dwells secure.

Loe in this Church all shall be free
To Enjoy their Christian liberty;
All things made common, void of strife,
Each man may take anothers wife,
And keep a hundred maids, if need,
To multiply, increase, and breed,
  Then is not this Foundation sure,
  To build a Church unspotted, pure?

The native People, though yet wild,
Are altogether kind and mild,
And apt already, by report,
To live in this religious sort;
Soon to conversion they'l be brought
When *Warrens Mariery* have wrought,
  Who being sanctified and pure,
  May by the Spirit them alure.

Let *Amsterdam* send forth her Brats,
Her Fugitives and Runnagates:

Let Bedlam, Newgate, and the Clink
Disgorge themselves into this sink;
Let Bridewell and the stews be kept,
And all sent thither to be swept;
    So may our Church be cleans'd and pure,
    Keep both it self and state secure.

The insatiate Lover. [p. 106]

Come hither my own sweet duck,
  And sit upon my knee,
That thou and I may truck
  For thy Commodity,
If thou wilt be my honey,
  Then I will be thine own,
Thou shalt not want for money
  If thou wilt make it known;
With hey ho my honey,
  My heart shall never rue,
For I have been spending money
  And amongst the jovial Crew.

I prethee leave thy scorning,
  Which our true love beguiles,
Thy eyes are bright as morning,
  The Sun shines in thy smiles,
Thy gesture is so prudent,

Thy language is so free,
That he is the best Student
   Which can study thee;
With hey ho, &c.

The Merchant would refuse
   His Indies and his Gold
If he thy love might chuse,
   And have thy love in hold:
Thy beauty yields more pleasure
   Than rich men keep in store,
And he that hath such treasure   [p. 107.]
   Never can be poor;
With hey ho, &c.

The Lawyer would forsake
   His wit and pleading strong:
The Ruler and Judge would take
   Thy part wer't right or wrong;
Should men thy beauty see
   Amongst the learned throngs,
Thy very eyes would be
   Too hard for all their tongues;
With hey ho, &c.

Thy kisses to thy friend
   The Surgeons skill out-strips,

For

For nothing can transcend
   The balsome of thy Lips,
There is such vital power
   Contained in thy breath,
That at the latter hour
   'Twould raise a man from death ;
With hey, ho, &c.

Astronomers would not
   Lye gazing in the skies
Had they thy beauty got,
   No Stars shine like thine eyes :
For he that may importune
   Thy love to an embrace,
Can read no better fortune
   Then what is in thy face.
With hey ho, &c.

The Souldier would throw down   [p. 108.]
   His Pistols and Carbine,
And freely would be bound
   To wear no arms but thine :
If thou wert but engaged
   To meet him in the field,
Though never so much inraged
   Thou couldest make him yield,
With hey ho, &c.

The seamen would reject   [Seaman]
   To sayl upon the Sea,
And his good ship neglect
   To be aboard of thee:
When thou liest on thy pillows
   He surely could not fail
To make thy brest his billows,
   And to hoyst up sayl;
With hey ho, &c.

The greatest Kings alive
   Would wish thou wert their own,
And every one would strive
   To make thy Lap their Throne,
For thou hast all the merit
   That love and liking brings;
Besides a noble spirit,
   Which may conquer Kings;
With hey ho, &c.

Were *Rosamond* on earth
   I surely would abhor her,
Though ne'r so great by birth
   I should not change thee for her;
Though Kings and Queens are gallant,   [p. 109.]
   And bear a royal sway,

                                                The

The poor man hath his Talent,
   And loves as well as they,
With hey ho, &c.

Then prethee come and kiss me,
   And say thou art mine own,
I vow I would not miss thee
   Not for a Princes Throne;
Let love and I perswade thee
   My gentle suit to hear:
If thou wilt be my Lady,
   Then I will be thy dear;
With hey ho, &c.

I never will deceive thee,
   But ever will be true,
Till death I shall not leave thee,
   Or change thee for a new;
We'll live as mild as may be,
   If thou wilt but agree,
And get a pretty baby
   With a face like thee,
With hey ho, &c.

Let these perswasions move thee
   Kindly to comply,
There's no man that can love thee
   With so much zeal as I;

Do thou but yield me pleasure,
   And take from me this pain,
I'll give thee all the Treasure
   Horse and man can gain;
With hey ho, &c.

I'll fight in forty duels   [p. 110.]
   To obtain thy grace,
I'll give thee precious jewels
   Shall adorn thy face;
E'r thou for want of money
   Be to destruction hurl'd,
For to support my honey
   I'll plunder all the world;
With hey ho, &c.

That smile doth show consenting,
   Then prethee let's be gone,
There shall be no repenting
   When the deed is done;
My bloud and my affection,
   My spirits strongly move,
Then let us for this action
   Fly to yonder grove,
With hey ho, &c.

Let us lye down by those bushes
   That are grown so high,
                           Where

Where I will hide thy blushes;
  Here's no standers by
This seventh day of *July*,
  Upon this bank we'll lye,
Would all were, that love truly,
  As close as thou and I ;
With hey ho [,] my honey,
  My heart shall never rue,
For I have been spending money
  Amongst the jovial Crew.

[Followed, in 1661 edition by " Now that the Spring," &c., and the three other pieces which are to be found in succession, already printed in our *Merry Drollery, Compleat* of 1670, 1691, pp. 296—301 : The last of these being the Song, " She lay all naked in her bed." This begins on p. 115, of Part 2nd, 1661; p. 300, 1691. In the former edition it is followed by "The Answer," beginning "She lay up to," &c., which, like other extremely objectionable pieces, is kept apart. Next follow, in 1661 edition, The Louse, and the Concealment.]

The Louse. [p. 149.]

IF that you will hear of a Ditty
  That's framed by a six-footed Creature,
She lives both in Town and in City,
She is very loving by nature ;
She'l offer her service to any,
She'l stick close but she'l prevail,
She's entertained by too many
Till death, she no man will fail.

Fenner

Fenner once in a Play did describe her,
How she had her beginning first,
How she sprung from the loyns of great *Pharaoh*,
And how by a King she was nurs'd :
How she fell on the Carkass of *Herod*,
A companion for any brave fighter,
And there's no fault to be found with her,
But that she's a devillish backbiter.

With Souldiers she's often comraded
And often does them much good,
She'l save them the charge of a Surgeon
In sickness for letting them blood ;
Corruption she draws like a horse-leech, [p. 150]
Growing she'll prove a great breeder,
At night she will creep in her cottage,
By day she's a damnable feeder.

She'l venture as much in a battel
As any Commander may go,
But then she'l play Jack on both sides,
She cares not a fart for her Foe :
She knows that alwaies she's shot-free,
To kill her no sword will prevaile,
But if she's taken prisoner,
She's prest to death by the naile.

She

She doth not esteem of your rich men,
But alwaies sticks close to the poor ;
Nor she cares not for your clean shifters,
Nor for such as brave cloaths wear ;
She loves all such as are non-suited,
Or any brave fellow that lacks ;
She's as true a friend to poor Souldiers,
As the shirt that sticks close to their backs.

She cannot abide your clean Laundress,
Nor those that do set her on work,
Her delight is all in foul linnen,
Where in narraw seams she may lurk :
From her and her breed God defend me,
For I have had their company store,
Pray take her among you [,] Gentry,
Let her trouble poor souldiers no more.

[As already mentioned, this is followed, in the 1661 Part Second, page 151, by The Concealment, beginning " I loved a maid, she loved not me," which is the last of the songs or poems peculiar to that edition. See the end of our Supplement : so paged that it may be either omitted or included, leaving no *hiatus*. We add, after the Supplement, the title-page of the 1670 edition of *Merry Drollery, Compleat ;* when reissued in 1691, the *same sheets* held the fresh title-page prefixed, such as we gave in second Volume. Readers now possess the entire work, all three editions, comprehended in our Reprint : which is the Fourth Edition, but the first Annotated. J. W. E.]

Appendix.

APPENDIX.

Notes, Illustrations, Various Readings, and Emendations of Text.
(NOW FIRST ADDED.)

Arranged in Four Parts :—
  1.—*Choyce Drollery*, 1656.
  2.—*Antidote against Melancholy*, 1661.
  3.—*Westminster-Drollery*, 1674.
  4.—*Merry Drollery*, 1661 ; and Additional Notes to 1670-1691 editions : with Index.

READERS, who have accompanied the Editor both in text and comment throughout these three volumes of Reprints from the *Drolleries of the Restoration*, can scarcely have failed to see that he has desired to present the work for their study with such advantages as lay within his reach. Certainly, he never could have desired to assist in bringing these rare volumes into the hands of a fresh generation, if he believed not that their few faults were far outweighed by their merits ; and that much may be learnt from both of these. Every antiquary is well aware that during the troubled days of the Civil War, and for the remaining years of the seventeenth century, books were printed with such an abundance of typographical errors that a pure text of any author cannot easily be recovered. In the case of all unlicensed publications, such as anonymous pamphlets, *facetiæ*, broad-sheet Ballads, and the more portable *Drolleries*, these imperfections were innumerable. Dropt lines and omitted verses, corrupt readings and perversions of meaning, sometimes amounting to a total destruction of intelligibility, might drive an Editor to despair.

In regard to the *Drolleries*-literature, especially, if we remember, as we ought to do, the difficulties and dangers attendant on the printing of these political squibs and pasquinades, we shall be less inclined to rail at the original collector, or "author," and printers. If we ourselves, as Editor, do our best to examine such other printed books and manuscripts of the time, as may assist in restoring what for awhile was corrupted or lost from the text *(keeping these corrections and additions clearly distinguished, within square brackets, or in Appendix Notes* to each successive volume), we shall find ourselves more usefully employed than in flinging stones at the Cavaliers of the Restoration, because they left behind them many a doubtful reading or an empty flaggon.

We have given back, to all who desire to study these invaluable records of a memorable time, four complete unmutilated works (except twenty-seven necessarily dotted words): and we could gladly have furnished additional information regarding each and all of these, if further delay or increased bulk had not been equally inexpedient.

1.—In *Choyce Drollery*, 1656, are seen such fugitive pieces of poetry as belong chiefly to the reign of Charles 1st., and to the eight years after he had been judicially murdered.

2.—In *Merry Drollery*, 1661, and in the *Antidote against Melancholy* of the same date, we receive an abundant supply of such Cavalier songs, ballads, lampoons or pasquinades, social and political, as may serve to bring before us a clear knowledge of what was being thought, said, and done during the first year of the Restoration; and, indeed, a reflection of much that had gone recently before, as a preparation for it.

3.—In such *additional* matter as came to view in the *Merry Drollery, Compleat*, of 1670 (N.B., precisely the same work as what we have reprinted, from the 1691 edition, in our second volume); and still more in the delightful *Westminster-Drolleries* of 1671, 1672, and 1674, we enjoy the humours of the Cavaliers at a later date: Songs from theatres as well as those in favour at Court, and more than a few choice pastorals and ditties of much earlier date, lend variety to the collection.

.We could easily have added another volume; but enough has surely been done in this series to show how rich are the materials. Let us increase the value of all, before entering in detail on our third series of Appendix Notes, by giving entirely the deeply-interesting Address to the Reader, written and published in 1656 (exactly contemporary with our *Choyce Drollery*), by Abraham Wright, for his rare collection of University Poems, known as "*Parnassus Biceps.*"

It is "An Epistle in the behalfe of those now doubly-secluded and sequestered Members, by one who himselfe is none."

"To the Ingenuous   [Sheet sig. A 2.]

READER.

SIR,

Hese leaves present you with some few drops of that Ocean of Wit, which flowed from those two brests of this Nation, the *Universities;* and doth now (the sluces being puld up) overflow the whole Land: or rather like those Springs of Paradice, doth water and enrich the whole world; whilst the Fountains themselues are dryed up, and that Twin-Paradise become desart. For then were these Verses Composed, when *Oxford* and *Camebridge* were Universities, and a Colledge [A 2, *reverso*] more learned then a Town-Hall, when the Buttery and Kitchin could speak Latine, though not Preach; and the very irrational Turnspits had so much knowing modesty, as not to dare to come into a Chappel, or to mount any Pulpits but their own. Then were these Poems writ, when peace and plenty were the best Patriots and Mæcenasses to great Wits; when we could sit and make Verses under our own Figtrees, and be inspired from the juice of our own Vines: then,

when it was held no sin for the same man to be both a
Poet, and a Prophet; and to draw predictions no lesse
from his Verse then his Text. Thus you shall meet here
St. *Pauls* Rapture in a Poem, and the fancy as high and
as clear as the third Heaven, into which [A. 3] that
Apostle was caught up : and this not onely in the ravish-
ing expressions and extasies of amorous Composures and
Love Songs; but in the more grave Dorick strains of
sollid Divinity : Anthems that might have become *Davids*
Harpe, and *Asaphs* Quire, to be sung, as they were made,
with the Spirit of that chief Musitian. Againe, In this
small Glasse you may behold your owne face, fit your own
humors, however wound up and tuned; whether to the
sad note, and melancholy look of a disconsolate Elegy, or
those more sprightly jovial Aires of an Epithalamium, or
Epinichion. Further, would you see a Mistresse of any
age, or face, in her created, or uncreated complexion :
this mirrour presents you with more shapes then a Con-
jurers [*verso*] Glasse, or a Limner's Pencil. It will also
teach you how to court that Mistresse, when her very
washings and pargettings cannot flatter her; how to raise
a beauty out of wrinkles fourscore years old, and to fall
in love even with deformity and uglinesse. From your
Mistresse it brings you to your God; and (as it were
some new Master of the Ceremonies) instructs you how
to woe, and court him likewise; but with approaches and
distances, with gestures and expressions suitable to a
Diety [Deity]; addresses clothed with such a sacred
filial horror and reverence, as may invite and embolden
the most despairing condition of the saddest gloomy Sinner; and withall dash out of countenance the greatest
confidence of the most glorious Saint : and not with that
blasphemous familiarity [A 4] of our new enlightened and
inspired men, who are as bold with the Majesty and glory
of that Light that is unapproachable, as with their own
ignes fatui; and account of the third Person in the
blessed Trinity for no more then their Fellow-Ghost;
thinking him as much bound to them for their vertiginous
blasts and whi[r]le-winds, as they to him for his own
most holy Spirit. Your Authors then of these few sheets

are Priests, as well as Poets; who can teach you to pray in verse, and (if there were not already too much phantasticknes in that Trade) to Preach likewise : while they turn Scripture-chapters into Odes, and both the Testaments into one book of Psalmes : making *Parnassus* as sacred as Mount *Olivet*, and the nine Muses no lesse religious then a Cloyster of Nuns. [*verso.*] But yet for all this I would not have thee, *Courteous Reader*, pass thy censure upon those two Fountains of Religion and Learning, the *Universities*, from these few small drops of wit, as hardly as some have done upon the late *Assemblies* three-half-penny Catechisme : as if all their publick and private Libraries, all their morning and evening watchings, all those pangs and throwes of their Studies, were now at length delivered but of a Verse, and brought to bed onely of five feet, and a Conceit. For although the judicious modesty of these men dares not look the world in the face with any of *Theorau Johns* Revelations, or those glaring New-lights that have muffled the Times and Nation with a greater confusion and darknes, then ever benighted [A 5] the world since the first Chaos : yet would they please but to instruct this ignorant Age with those exact elaborate Pieces, which might reform Philosophy without a Civil War, and new modell even Divinity its selfe without the ruine of either Church, or State; probably that most prudent and learned Order of the Church of *Rome*, the *Jesuite*, should not boast more sollid, though more numerous Volum[e]s in this kind. And of this truth that Order was very sensible, when it felt the rational Divinity of one single *Chillingworth* to be an unanswerable twelve-years-task for all their English Colledges in Chrisendome. And therefore that *Society* did like its selfe, when it sent us over a War instead of an Answer, and proved us Hereticks by the Sword : which [*verso*] in the first place was to Rout the *Universities*, and to teach our two Fountains of Learning better manners, then for ever heareafter to bubble and swell against the *Apostolick Sea*. And yet I know not whether the depth of their Politicks might not have advised to have kept those Fountains within their own

banks, and there to have dammd them and choakd them
up with the mud of the Times, rather then to have let
those Protestant Streams run, which perchance may effect
that now by the spreading Riverets, which they could
never have done through the inclosed Spring : as it had
been a deeper State-piece and Reach in that Sanedrim,
the great Councell of the Jewish Nation, to have confined
the Apostles to *Jerusalem,* and there to have muzzeld
them [A 6] with Oaths, and Orders; rather then by a
fruitful Persecution to scatter a few Gospel Seeds, that
would spring up the Religion of the whole world : which
had it been Coopd within the walls of that City, might (for
all they knew) in few years have expired and given up
the ghost upon the same *Golgotha* with its Master. And
as then every Pair of Fishermen made a Church and
caught the sixt part of the world in their Nets; so now
every Pair of Ce[o]lledge-fellows make as many several
Universityes; which are truly so call'd, in that they are
Catholick, and spread over the face of the whole earth;
which stand amazed, to see not onely Religion, but
Learning also to come from beyond the *Alpes* ; and that
a poor despised Canton and nook of the world should
contain as much of each [*verso*] as all the other Parts besides. But then, as when our single Jesus was made an
universall Saviour, and his particular Gospel the Catholick Religion; though that Jesus and this Gospel did
both take their rise from the holy City ; yet now no City
is more unholy and infidel then that ; insomuch that there
is at this day scarce any thing to be heard of a Christ at
Jerusalem, more then that such a one was sometimes
there, nor any thing to be seen of his Gospel, more
then a Sepulcher : just so it is here with us; where
though both Religion and Learning do owe their
growth, as well as birth, to those Nurseryes of
both, the Universityes; yet, since the Siens of those
Nurseryes have been transplanted, there's little remaines
in them now (if they are not belyed) either of the old [A 7]
Religion and Divinity, more then its empty Chair & Pulpit, or of the antient Learning & Arts, except bare
Schools, and their gilded Superscriptions : so far have we

beggard our selves to enrich the whole world. And thus, *Ingenuous Sir*, have I given you the State and Condition of this *Poetick Miscellany*, as also of the *Authors;* it being no more then some few slips of the best Florists made up into a slender Garland, to crown them in their Pilgrimage, and refresh thee in thine : if yet their very Pilgrimage be not its selfe a Crown equall to that of Confessors, and their Academicall Dissolution a Resurrection to the greatest temporall glory : when they shall be approved of by men and Angels for a chosen Generation, a Royal Priesthood, a peculiar People. In the interim let this [*verso*] comfort be held out to you, *our secluded University members*, by him that is none; (and therefore what hath been here spoken must not be interpreted as out of passion to my self, but meer zeal to my Mother) that according to the generally received Principles and Axioms of Policy, and the soundest Judgment of the most prudential Statesmen upon those Principles, the date of your sad Ostracisme is expiring, and at an end; but yet such an end, as some of you will not embrace when it shall be offered; but will chuse rather to continue Peripateticks through the whole world, then to return, and be so in your own Colledges. For as that great Councell of *Trent* had a Form and Conclusion altogether contrary to the expectation and desires of them that procured it; so our great Councels of *England* [A 8] (our late Parliament) will have such a result, and Catastrophe, as shall no ways answer the Fasts and Prayers, the Humiliations, and Thanksgivings of their Plotters and Contrivers : such a result I say, that will strike a palsie through Mr. *Pims* ashes, make his cold Marble sweat; and put all those several Partyes, and Actors, that have as yet appeard upon our tragical bloudy Stage, to an amazed stand and gaze: when they shall confess themselves (but too late) to be those improvident axes and hammers in the hand of a subtle *Workman;* whereby he was enabled to beat down, and square out our Church and State into a Conformity with his own. And then it will appeare that the great Worke, and the holy Cause, and the naked Arme, so much talked of for [*verso*] these fifteen years, were but the work, and the cause, and the arme of that *Hand*, which hath all this while reached us over the *Alpes;* dividing, and composing, winding us up, and letting us down, untill our very discords have set and tuned us to such notes, both in our Ecclesiastical, and Civill Government; as may soonest conduce to that most necessary Catholick Unison and Harmony, which is an essential part of Christs Church here upon Earth, and the very Church its selfe in Heaven. And thus far, *Ingenuous Reader*, suffer him to be a Poet in his Prediction, though not in his Verse; who desires to be known so far to thee, as that he is a friend to persecuted Truth and Peace; and thy most affectionate Christian Servant,

Ab: Wright."

(From *Parnassus Biceps: or, Severall Choice Pieces of* POETRY, *composed by the best* WITS *that were in both the Universities before their* DISSOLUTION. London: Printed for *George Eversden* at the Signe of the *Maidenhead* in St. *Pauls* Church-yard, 1656.)

1.—CHOYCE DROLLERY, 1656.

Note, on *The Address to the Reader*, &c.

The subscribed initials, " R. P." are those of Robert Pollard; whose name appears on the title-page (which we reproduce), preceding his address. Excepting that he was a bookseller, dwelling and trading at the " Ben Jonson's Head, behind the Exchange," in business-connection with John Sweeting, of the Angel, in Pope's Head Alley, in 1656; and that he had previously issued a somewhat similar Collection of Poems to the *Choyce Drollery* (successful, but not yet identified), we know nothing more of Robert Pollard. The books of that date, and of that special class, are extremely rare, and the few existing copies are so difficult of access (for themost part in private possession, almost totally inaccessible except to those who know not how to use them), that information can only be acquired piecemeal and laboriously. Five years hence, if the Editor be still alive, he may be able to tell much more concerning the authors and the compilers of the *Restoration Drolleries*.

We are told that there is an extra leaf to *Choyce Drollery*, "only found in a few copies, containing ten lines of verse, beginning *Fame's windy trump*, &c. This leaf occurs in one or two extant copies of *England's Parnassus*, 1600. Many of the pieces found here are much older than the date of the book [viz., 1656]. It contains notices of many of our early poets, and, unlike some of its successors, is of intrinsic value. Only two or three copies have occurred." *(W. C. H.'s Handb. Pop. Lit. G. B.*, 1867, p. 168.*)* "Cromwell's Government ordered this book to be burned." *(Ibid.)* On this last item see our Introduction, section first. J. P. Collier, who prepared the Catalogue of Richard Heber's Collection, *Bibliotheca Heberiana*, Pt. iv., 1834 (a rich storehouse for bibliographical students, but not often gratefully acknowledged by them), thus writes of *Choyce Drollery :*—"This is one of the most intrinsically valuable of the *Drolleries*, if only for the sake of the very interesting poem in which characters are given of all the following Poets : Shakespeare, Jonson, Beaumont and Fletcher, Massinger, Chapman, Daborne, Sylvester, Quarles, May, Sands, Digges, Daniel, Drayton, Withers, Brown, Shirley, Ford, Middleton, Heywood, Churchyard, Dekker, Brome, Chaucer, Spencer, Basse, and finally John Shank, the Actor, who is said to have been famous for a jig. Other pieces are much older, and are here reprinted from previous collections" [mostly lost]. P. 90.

It is also known to J. O. Halliwell-Phillips; (but, truly, what is *not* known to him?) See *Shakespeare Society's Papers*, iii. 172, 1847.

In our copy of *England's Parnassus* (unindexed, save subjects), 1600, we sought to find "*Fame's windy trump*." [We hear that the leaf was in *E. P.* at Tite's sale, 1874.]

As we have never seen a copy of *Choyce Drollery* containing the passage of "ten lines," described as beginning "Fame's Windy Trump," we cannot be quite certain of the following, from *England's Parnassus*, 1600, being the one in question, but believe that it is so. Perhaps it ran, "*Fame's Windy Trump, whatever sound out-flies,*" &c. There are twenty-seven lines in all. We distinguish the probable portion of "ten lines" by enclosing the other two parts in brackets :—

FAME.

[A *Monster swifter none is under sunne;*
Encreasing, as in waters we descrie
The circles small, of nothing that begun,
Which, at the length, unto such breadth do come,
That of a drop, which from the skies doth fall,
The circles spread, and hide the waters all:
So Fame, in flight encreasing more and more;
For, at the first, she is not scarcely knowne,
But by and by she fleets from shore to shore,
To clouds from th' earth her stature straight is growne.
There whatsoever by her trumpe is blowne,]

The sound, that both by sea and land out-flies,
Rebounds againe, and verberates the skies.
They say, the earth that first the giants bred,
For anger that the gods did them dispatch,
Brought forth this sister of those monsters dead,
Full light of foote, swift wings the winds to catch:
Such monsters erst did nature never hatch.
As many plumes she hath from top to toe,
So many eyes them underwatch or moe;
And tongues do speake: so many eares do harke.

[*By night 'tweene heaven she flies and earthly shade,*
And, shreaking, takes no quiet sleepe by darke:
On houses roofes, on towers, as keeper made,
She sits by day, and cities threates t' invade;
And as she tells what things she sees by view,
She rather shewes that's fained false, then true.]

[Legend of Albanact.]   I. H., *Mirror of Magist.*

Page 1. *Deare Love, let me this evening dye.*

This beautiful little love-poem re-appears, as Song 77, in *Windsor Drollery*, 1672, p. 63. (There had been a previous edition of that work, in 1671, which we have examined : it is not noted by bibliographers, and is quite distinct.) A few variations occur. Verse 2. are *wrack'd;* 3. In *love* is not commended; *only* sweet, All praise, *no* pity; who *fondly;* 4. *Shall shortly* by dead Lovers lie; *hallow'd;* 5. *He* which *all others* els excels, That *are;* 6. *Will,* though thou; 7. *the* Bells *shall* ring; *While* all to *black is*; (last line but two in parenthesis;) Making, like Flowers, &c.

Page 4. *Nor Love nor Fate dare I accuse.*

By RICHARD BROME, in his "*Northerne Lasse,*" 1632, Act ii., sc. 6. It is also given in *Westminster-Drollery,* 1671, i. 83 (the only song in common). But compare with it the less musical and tender, "*Nor Love, nor Fate can I accuse of hate,*" in same vol. ii. 90, with Appendix Note thereunto, p. lxiii.

Page 5. *One night the great* Apollo, *pleased with* Ben.

This remarkable and little-known account of "THE TIME-POETS" is doubly interesting, as being a contemporary document, full of life-like portraiture of men whom no lapse of years can banish from us; welcome friends, whom we grow increasingly desirous of beholding intimately. Glad are we to give it back thus to the world; our chief gem, in its rough Drollery-setting: lifted once more into the light of day, from out the cobwebbed nooks where it so long-time had lain hidden. Our joy would have been greater, could we have restored authoritatively the lost sixteenth-line, by any genuine discovery among early manuscripts; or told something conclusive about the author of the poem, who has laid us under obligation for these vivid portraits of John Ford, Thomas Heywood, poor old Thomas Churchyard, and Ben's courageous foeman, worthy of his steel, that Thomas Dekker who "followed after in a dream."

In deep humility we must confess that nothing is yet learnt as to the authorship. Here, in the year 1656, almost at fore-front of *Choyce Drollery*, the very strength of its van-guard, appeared the memorable poem. Whether it were then and there for the first time in print, or borrowed from some still more rare and now-lost volume, none of us can prove. Even at this hour, a possibility remains that our resuscitation of *Choyce Drollery* may help to bring the unearthing of explanatory facts from zealous students. We scarcely dare to cherish hope of this. Certainly we may not trust to it. For Gerard Langbaine knew the poem well, and quoted oft and largely from it in his 1691 *Account of the English Dramatick Poets*. But he met with it nowhere save in *Choyce Drollery*, and writes of it continually in language that proves how ignorant he was of whom we are to deem the author. Yet he wrote within five-and-thirty years behind the date of its appearance; and might easily have learnt, from men still far from aged, who had read the *Drollery* on its first publication, whatever they could tell of "The Time-Poets:" if, indeed, they could tell anything. Five years earlier, William Winstanley had given forth his *Lives of the most famous English Poets*, in June, 1686; but he quotes not from it, and leaves us without an *Open Sesame*. Even Oldys could not tell; or Thomas Hearne, who often had remembered whatever Time forgot.

As to the date: we believe it was certainly written between 1620 (inclusive) and 1636; nearer the former year.

We reconcile ourselves for the failure, by turning to such other and similar poetic groupings as survive. We listen unto Richard Barnfield, when he sings sweetly his "Remembrance of some English Poets," in 1598. We cling delightedly to the words of our noble Michael Drayton—whose descriptive map of native England, *Polyolbion*, glitters with varie-coloured light, as though it were a mediæval missal: to whom, enditing his Epistle to friend Henry Reynolds—"A Censure of the Poets"— the Muses brought each bard by turn, so that the picture might be faithful: even as William Blake, idealist and spiritual Seer, believed of spirit-likenesses in his own experience. And, not without deep feeling (marvelling, meanwhile, that still the task of printing them with Editorial care is unattempted), we peruse the folio manuscripts of that fair-haired minstrel of the Cavaliers, George Daniel of Beswick, while he also, in his "Vindication of Poesie," sings in praise of those whose earlier lays are echoing now and always "through the corridors of Time :"—

> *Truth speaks of old, the power of Poesie;*
> Amphion, Orpheus, *stones and trees could move;*
> *Men, first by verse, were taught Civilitie;*
> *'Tis known and granted; yet would it behove*
>   *Mee, with the Ancient Singers, here to crowne*
>   *Some later Quills, some Makers of our owne.*

Nor should we fail to thank the younger Evelyn, for such graphic sketches as he gives of Restoration-Dramatists, of Cowley, Dryden, Wycherley, "Sedley and easy Etherege;" a new world of wits, all of whose works we prize, without neglecting for their sakes the older Masters who "so did take Eliza, and our James."

Something that we could gladly say, will come in befittingly on after-pages of this volume, in the "Additional Note on Sir John Suckling's 'Sessions of the Poets,'" as printed in our *Merry Drollery, Compleat,* page 72.

Are we stumbling at the threshold, *absit omen!* even amid our delight in perusing "the Time-Poets," when we wonder at the precise meaning of the statement in our opening couplet?

> *One night the great* Apollo, *pleas'd with* Ben,
> *Made the odd number of the Muses ten.*

By whom additional? Who is the lady, thus elevated? We see only one solution: namely, that furnished by the conclusion of the poem. It was the *Faerie Queene* herself whom the God lifted thus, in honour of her English Poets, to rank as the Tenth Muse, an equal with Urania, Clio, Euterpe, and their sisterhood. Yet something seems wanting, next to it; for we never reach a full-stop until the end of the 39th (or *query*, the 40th) line; and all the confluent nominatives lack a common verbal-action. Our mind, it is true, accepts intelligibly the onward rush of each and all (but later, "with equal pace each of them softly creeps"). It may be only grammatical pedantry which craves some such phrase, absent from the text, as—

> [*While throng'd around his comrades and his peers,*
> *To list the 'sounding Music of the Spheres:*]

But, since a momentary rashness prompts us here to dare so much, as to imagine the *hiatus* filled, let us suppose that the lost sixteenth-line ran someway thus (each reader being free to try experiments himself, with chance of more success):—

> *Divine-composing* Quarles, *whose lines aspire*
> [*And glow, as doth with like etherial fire*]   16th.
> *The April of all Poesy in* May,
> *Who makes our English speak* Pharsalia;

It is with some timidity we let this stand: but, as the text is left intact, our friends will pardon us; and foes we never quail to meet. As to BEN JONSON, see our "Sessions," in Part iv. Of BEAUMONT and FLETCHER, we write in the note on final page of *Choyce Drollery*, p. 100. Of "Ingenious SHAKESPEARE" we need say no more than give the lines of Richard Barnfield in his honour, from the *Poems in diuers humors*, 1598:—

A REMEMBRANCE OF SOME ENGLISH POETS.

Liue Spenser *euer, in thy* Fairy Queene:
Whose like (for deepe Conceit) was neuer seene.
Crownd mayst thou bee, vnto thy more renowne,
(As King of Poets) with a Lawrell Crowne.

And Daniell, *praised for thy sweet-chast Verse:*
Whose Fame is grav'd in Rosamonds *blacke Herse.*
Still mayst thou liue: and still be honored,
For that rare Worke, The White Rose and the Red.

> *And* Drayton, *whose wel-written Tragedies*
> *And sweet Epistles, soare thy fame to skies.*
> *Thy learned Name, is æquall with the rest ;*
> *Whose stately Numbers are so well addrest.*
>
> *And* Shakespeare *thou, whose hony-flowing Vaine,*
> *(Pleasing the World) thy Praises doth obtaine.*
> *Whose* Venus, *and whose* Lucrece *(sweete and chaste)*
> *Thy Name in fames immortall Booke hath plac't.*
> *Liue euer you, at least in Fame liue euer :*
> *Well may the Bodye dye, but Fame dies neuer.*

The praise of MASSINGER will not seem overstrained; although he never affects us with the sense of supreme genius, as does Marlowe. The recognition of GEORGE CHAPMAN'S grandeur, and the power with which this recognition is expressed, show how tame is the influence of Massinger in comparison. There need be little question that it was to Dekker's mind and pen we owe the nobler portion of the Virgin Martyr. Massinger, when alongside of Marlow, Webster, and Dekker, is like Euripides contrasted with Æschylus and Sophocles. We think of him as a Playwright, and successful; but these others were Poets of Apollo's own body-guard. Drayton sings :

> *Next* MARLOW, *bathed in the* Thespian *springs,*
> *Had in him those brave translunary things*
> *That the first poets had, his raptures were*
> *All air and fire, which made his verses clear ;*
> *For that fine madness still he did retain,*
> *Which rightly should possess a poet's brain.*

ROBERT DABORNE is chiefly interesting to us from his connection in misfortunes and dramatic labours with Massinger and Nat Field; and as joining them in the supplication for advance of money from Philip Henslow, while they lay in prison. The reference to Daborne's clerical, as well as to his dramatic vocation, and to his having died (in Ireland, we believe, leaving behind him sermons,) "Amphibion by the Ministry," confirms the general belief.

Jo: SYLVESTER's translation of Du Bartas, 1621; THOMAS MAY's of Lucan's Pharsalia, GEORGE SANDYS' of Ovid's Metamorphoses, need little comment here; some being referred to, near the end of our volume.

DUDLEY DIGGES (1612-43), born at Chilham Castle, near Canterbury (now the seat of Charles S. Hardy, Esq.); son of Sir Dudley Digges, Master of the Rolls, wrote a reverent Elegy for *Jonsonus Virbius*, 1638. L[eonard] Digges had, fifteen years earlier, written the memorial lines beginning "Shake-speare, at length thy pious fellows give || The World thy Workes:" which appear at beginning of the first folio *Shakespeare*, 1623.

To SAMUEL DANIEL's high merits we have only lately awakened: his "Complaint of Rosamond" has a sustained dignity and pathos that deserve all Barnfield's praise; the "Sonnets to Delia" are graceful and impressive in their purity; his "Civil Wars" may seem heavy, but the fault lies in ourselves, if unsteady readers, not the poet: thus we suspect, when we remember the true poetic fervour of his Pastoral,

O happy Golden Age!

and his Description of Beauty, from Marino.

Of "Heroick DRAYTON" we write more hereafter: He grows dearer to us with every year. His "Dowsabell" is on p. 73. Was his being coupled as a "Poet-Beadle," in allusion to his numerous verse-epistles, showing an acquaintance with all the worthies of his day, even as his *Polyolbion* gives a roll-call of the men, and a gazetteer of the England they made illustrious? For, as shown in the *Apophthegmmes of Erasmus*, 1564, Booke 2nd, (p. 296 of the Boston Reprint,) it is "the proper office and dutie of soche biddelles (who were called in latin *Nomenclators*) to have perfecte knowlege and remembrance of the names, of the surnames, and of the titles of dignitees of all persones, to the ende that thei maie helpe the remembraunce of their maisters in the same when neede is." To our day the office of an Esquire Beddell is esteemed in Cambridge University. But, we imagine, George Wither is styled a "Poets Beadle" with a very different significance. It was the

Bridewell-Beadles' whip which he wielded vigorously, in flagellation of offenders, that may have earned him the title. See his "*Abuses Stript and Whipt,*" 1613, and turn to the rough wood-cut of cart's-tail punishment shown in the frontispiece to *A Caueat or Warening for Common Cursetors, vulgarly called Vagabones,* set forth by Thomas Harman, Esquier for the utilitie and profit of his naturall country, &c., 1566, and later (Reprinted by E. E. Text Soc., and in *O. B. Coll. Misc.,* i. No. 4, 1871).

GEORGE WITHER was his own worst foe, when he descended to satiric invective and pious verbiage. True poet was he; as his description of the Muse in her visit to him while imprisoned in the Marshalsea, with almost the whole of his "Shepherd's Hunting" and "Mistress of Phil'arete," prove incontestibly. He is to be loved and pitied: although perversely he will argue as a schismatick, always wrong-headed and in trouble, whichever party reigns, To him, in his sectarian zeal or sermonizing platitudes—all for our good, alas!—we can but answer with the melancholy Jacques: "I do not desire you to please me. I do desire you to *sing!*"

"Pan's Pastoral *Brown*" is, of course, WM. BROWNE, author of "Britannia's Pastorals." Like JAMES SHIRLEY, last in the group of early Dramatists, his precocious genius is remembered in the text. Regretting that no painted or sculptured portrait of JOHN FORDE survives, we are thankful for this striking picture of him in his sombre meditation. We could part, willingly, with half of our dramatic possessions since the nineteenth century began, to recover one of the lost plays by Ford. No writer holds us more entirely captive to the tenderness of sorrow; no one's hand more lightly, yet more powerfully, stirs the affections, while admitting the sadness, than he who gave us "The Broken Heart," and "'Tis pity she's a whore."

Not unhappily chosen is the epithet "The Squibbing MIDDLETON," for he almost always fails to impress us fully by his great powers. He warms not, he enlightens not, with steady glow, but gives us fireworks instead of stars or altar-burnings. We except from this rebuke his

"Faire Quarrel," 1622, which shows a much firmer grasp and purpose, fascinating us the while we read. Perhaps, with added knowledge of him will come higher esteem.

Of THOMAS HEYWOOD the portrait is complete, every word developing a feature : his fertility, his choice of subjects, and rubicund appearance.

Nor is the humourous sadness, of the figure shewn by the aged THOMAS CHURCHYARD, less touching because it is dashed in with burlesque. " Poverty and Poetry his Tomb doth enclose" *(Camden's Remains)*. His writings extend from the time of Edward VI. to early in the reign of James I. (he died in 1604); some of the poems in *Tottel's Miscellany*, 1557, were claimed by him, but are not identified, and J. P. Collier thought him not unlikely to have partly edited the work, His " Tragedie of Shore's Wife," (best edit. 1698),in the *Mirror for Magistrates*, surpasses most of his other poems ; yet are there biographical details in *Churchyard's Chips*, 1575, that reward our perusal. Gascoigne and several other poets added *Tam Marti quàm Mercurio* after their names ; but Churchyard could boast thus with more truth as a Soldier. He says :—

Full thirty yeers, both Court and Warres I tryed,
And still I sought acquaintaunce with the best,
And served the Staet, and did such hap abyed
As might befall, and Fortune sent the rest :
When drom did sound, a souldier was I prest,
 To sea or lande, as Princes quarrell stoud,
 And for the saem, full oft I lost my blood.

But, throughout, misfortune dogged him :—

 . . . To serve my torn [i.e., turn] *in service of the Queen :*
But God he knoes, my gayn was small, I ween,
For though I did my credit still encreace,
I got no welth, by warres, ne yet by peace.
   (C.'s Chips : *A Tragicall Discourse of the*
    unhappy man's Life ; verses 9, 26.)

Of THOMAS DEKKER, or Decker (about 1575-1638), "*A priest in Apollo's Temple, many yeares,*" with his " Old

Fortunatus," both parts of his "Honest Whore," his "Satiromastix," and "Gull's Hornbook," &c.,—which take us back to all the mirth and squabbling of the day—we need add no word but praise. We believe that a valuable clue is afforded by the allusion in our text to the pamphlet "Dekker his Dreame," 1620, (reprinted by J. O. Halliwell, 1860.) We may be certain that "The Time-Poets" was not written earlier than 1620, or any later than 1636 (or probably than 1632), and before Jonson's death.

Page 7. "*Rounce, Robble, Hobble, he that writ so big.*"

In this 50th line the word "high" is evidently redundant (probably an error in printer's MS., not erased when the true word "big" was added): we retain it, of course, though in smaller type; as in similar cases of excess. But who was "*Rounce, Robble, Hobble?*" Most certainly it was no other than RICHARD STANYHURST (1547-1618), whose varied adventures, erudition, and eccentricities of verse combined to make him memorable. His Hexameter translation of the *Æneis* Books i-iv, appeared in 1583; not followed by any more during the thirty-five years succeeding. Gabriel Harvey praised him, in his "*Foure Letters*," &c., although Thomas Nashe, in 1592, declares that "Master Stanyhurst (though otherwise learned) trod a foule, lumbring, boystrous, wallowing measure in his translation of Virgil. He had never been praised by Gabriel [Harvey] for his labour, if therein he had not been so famously absurd." *(Strange Newes.)* This *Æneid* had a limited reprint in 1839. Warton in *Hist. Eng. Poetry* gives examples (misnaming him Robert, but Camden says "*Eruditissimus ille nobilis Richardus Stanihurstus.*" In his preface to Greene's *Arcadia*, Nash quotes Stanyhurst's description of a Tempest:—

> *Then did he make heauens vault to rebound*
>   *With rounce robble bobble,* [N.B.]
> *Of ruffe raffe roaring,*
>   *With thicke thwacke thurly bouncing:*

and indicates his opinion of the poet, "as of some thrasonical huffe-snuffe," indulging in "that quarrelling kind of verse." One more specimen, to justify our text, regarding "he that writ so big:" in the address to the winds, *Æn.*. Bk. i., Neptune thus rails :—

Dare ye, lo, curst baretours, in this my Seignorie regal,
Too raise such racks iacks on seas and danger unorder'd?

The recent death of Stanyhurst, 1618, strengthens our belief that *the Time-Poets* was not later than 1620-32.

To WILLIAM BASSE we owe the beautiful epitaph on Shakespeare, printed in 1633, "*Renowned* Spencer, *lye a thought more nigh To learned* Chaucer, *etc.*, and at least two songs (beside "Great Brittaine's Sunnes-set, 1613), viz., the Hunter in his Career, beginning "Long ere the Morn," and one of the best Tom o' Bedlam's; probably, "Forth from my sad and darksome cell."

The name of JOHN SHANKE, here suggestively famous "for a jigg," occurs in divers lists of players (see J. P. C.'s *Annals of the Stage, passim)*, he having been one of Prince Henry's Company in 1603. That he was also a singer, we have this verse in proof, written in the reign of James I. (*Bibliog. Acc.* i. 163) :—

That's the fat foole of the Curtin,
And the lean fool of the Bull :
Since Shanke *did leave to sing his rimes*
He is counted but a gull.
The Players on the Banckeside,
The round Globe *and the* Swan,
Will teach you idle tricks of love,
But the Bull *will play the man.*
(W. Turner's *Common Cries of London Town*, 1662.)

"Broom" is RICHARD BROME (died 1652), whose racy comedies have been, like Dekker's, lately reprinted. The insinuation that Ben Jonson had "sent him before to sweep the way," alludes, no doubt, to the fact of Brome having earlier been Jonson's servant, and learning from his personal discourse much of dramatic art. Neither was it meant nor accepted as an insult, when, (printed 1632,)Jonson wrote ("according to Ben's own nature and custom, magisterial enough," as their true friend Alexander Brome admits),

> *I had you for a Servant once,* Dick Brome;
> *And you perform'd a Servant's faithful parts* :
> *Now, you are got into a nearer room*
> *Of* Fellowship, *professing my old Arts.*
> *And you do doe them well, with good applause,*
> *Which you have justly gained from the Stage,* &c.

It is amusing to mark the survival of the old joke in our text, about sweeping (it came often enough, in *Figaro in London,* &c., at the time of the 1832 Reform Bill, as to Henry Brougham and Vaux); when we see it repeated, almost literally, in reference to Alexander Pope's fellow-labourer on the Odyssey translation, the Rev. William Broome, of our St. John's College, Cambridge :—

> Pope *came off clean with* Homer, *but they say,*
> Broome *went before, and kindly swept the way.*

Leaving a few words on the matchless BEN himself for the "Sessions of the Poets" Additional Note, we end this commentary on our book's chief poem with a few more stanzas from the Beswick Manuscript, by George Daniel, (written in great part before, part after, 1647,) in honour of Ben Jonson, but preceded by others relating to Sir Philip Sidney, Spenser, Daniel, Drayton, Shakespeare, Beaumont, and Donne :—

> *I am not bound to honour antique names,*   [8th verse]
> *Nor am I led by other men to chuse*
> *Any thing worthy, which my judgment blames;*
> *Heare better straines, though by a later Muse ;*
>   *The sweet* Arcadian *singer first did raise*
>   *Our Language current, and deserv'd his Baies.*

> *That Lord of* Penhurst, Penhurst *whose sad walls*
> *Yet mourne their master, in the* Belgicke *fray*
> *Untimely lost ; to whose dear funeralls*
> *The* Medwaie *doth its constant tribute paye ;*
>   *But glorious* Penhurst, Medwaies *waters once*
>   *With* Mincius *shall, and* Mergeline *advance ;*

The Shepherds Boy; *best knowen by that name*
Colin : *upon his homely Oaten Reed.*
With Roman Tityrus *may share in ffame ;*
But when a higher path hee strains to tread,
   This is my wonder: for who yet has seene
   Soe cleare a Poeme as his Faierie Queene ?

The sweetest Swan of Avon ; *to the faire*
And cruel Delia, *passionatelie sings* :
Other mens weaknesses and follies are
Honour and Wit in him ; each Accent brings
   A sprig to crowne him Poet; and contrive
   A Monument, in his owne worke to live.

Draiton *is sweet and smooth : though not exact,*
Perhaps to stricter Eyes ; yet he shall live
Beyond their Malice: to the Scene and Act,
Read Comicke Shakespeare ; *or if you would give*
   Praise to a just Desert, crowning the Stage,
   See Beaumont, *once the honour of his Age.*

The reverent Donne ; *whose quill God purely fil'd,*
Liveth to his Character : so though he claim'd
A greater glory, may not be exil'd
This Commonwealth, &c.

Here pause a little; for I would not cloy   [verse 15]
The curious Eare, with recitations ;
And meerily looke at names ; attend with joy,
Unto an English *Quill, who rivall'd once*
   Rome, *not to make her blush ; and knowne of late*
   Unenvied ('cause unequall'd) Laureate.

This, this was JONSON; *who in his own name*
Carries his praise ; and may he shine alone ;
I am not tyed to any generall ffame,
Nor fixed by the Approbation
   Of great ones : But I speake without pretence
   Hee was of English *Dramatiskes, the Prince.*

Page 10. *Come, my White-head, let our Muses.*

This was written by SIR SIMEON STEWARD, or Stewart. The numbers 1 and 2 of our text are twice incorrect in original, viz. the 10th and 14th verses, each assigned to 1 (Red-head), whereas they certainly belong to 2 (Whitehead). From third verse the figure "1" has unfortunately dropt in printing. By aid of Addit. MS. No. 11, 811, p. 36, we are enabled to correct a few other errors, some being gross corruptions of sense; although, as a general rule, regarding poems that had appeared in print, the private MS. versions abound with blunders of the transcriber, additional to those of the original printer. It is, in the MS., entitled "A Dialogue between *Pyrrotrichus* and *Leucothrix*," the latter taking verses 2, 4, 6, 8, 10, 12, and the final verse, 14 (marked *Leuc*). His earliest verse reads, in the MS., "*And higher, Rufus,* who would pass; were *some* ; 3rd. v. 'Tis *this* that; 6th. The Roman *King who ;* be *lopt ;* Ruddy *pates ;* 8th v. Red like *unto ; colour ;* 9th. *Nay* if; doth *beare* no; side *looks* as fair; other *doth* my; bear *my* [?]; 10th. *Therefore,* methinks ; Besides, *of* all the; 12th. N.B.—Yet *what thy head must buy with* yeares, Crosses ; That *hath* nature *giv'n ;* 13th, be *two* friendly peeres; let us *joyn ;* make *one* beauteous ; 14th, [*Leucothrix.*] We *joyn'd* our heads; beat them *to heart* [i.e. to boot]; Was *just* but; *of* our head. In the Reresby Memoirs, we believe, is mention of an ancestress, who, about 1619, married this (?) "Sir Simeon Steward."

Page 15. *A Stranger coming to the town.*

In Wm. Hickes his *Oxford Drollery,* 1671, in Part 3rd, ("Poems made at Oxford, long since"), p. 157, this Epigram appears, with variations. The second verse reads : *But being there a little while,* || *He met with one so right* || *That upon the* French *Disease* || *It was his chance to light.* The final couplet is :—*The* French-man's *Arms are the sign without,* || *But the* French-man's *harms are within.*

Throughout the first half of the Seventeenth century the abundance of Epigrams produced is enormous; whole volumes of them, divided into Books, like J. Heywood's, being issued by poets of whom nothing else is known,

Choyce Drollery, 1656. 283

except the name, unless Anthony à Wood has fortunately preserved some record. These have not been systematically examined, as they deserve to be. Amid much rubbish good things lie hid. Perhaps the Editor may have more to say on them hereafter. Meanwhile, take this, by Robert Hayman, as alike a specimen and a summary :—

To the Reader :

SErmons and Epigrams have a like end,
 To improve, to reprove, and to amend :
Some passe without this vse, 'cause they are witty ;
And so doe many Sermons, more's the pitty.
(*Quodlibets*, 1628, Book IV., p. 59.)

Page 20. *List, your Nobles, and attend.*

This was (perhaps, by JOHN ELIOT,) certainly written in anticipatory celebration of the event described, the Reception of Queen Henrietta Maria by the citizens of London, 1625. The full title is this :—" The Author intending to write upon the Duke of *Buckingham*, when he went to fetch the Queen, prepared a new Ballad for the Fidlers, as might hold them to sing between *Dover* and *Callice*." It is thus the poem reappears, with some variations (beginning " *Now list, you Lordlings, and attend,* || *Unto a Ballad newly penned,*" &c.,) among the *Choyce Poems, being Songs, Sonnets, Satyrs, and Elegies. By the Wits of both Universities*, London," &c., 1661, p. 83. This was merely the earlier edition (of June, 1658), reissued with an irregular extra sheet at beginning. The original title-page (two issued in 1658) was "*Poems or Epigrams, Satyrs, Elegies, Songs and Sonnets, upon several persons and occasions. By no body must know whom, to be had every body knows where, and for any body knows what.* [MS. The Author John Eliot.] London, Printed for Henry Brome, at the *Gun* in Ivie Lane, 1658." It is mentioned that "These poems were given me neer sixteen years since [therefore about 1642] by a Friend of the Authors, with a desire they might be printed, but I conceived the Age then too squeemish to endure the freedom which the Author useth, and therefore I have hitherto smothered them, but being desirous they should not perish, and the world be deprived of so much clean Wit and Fancy, I have adventured to expose them to thy view; . . . The Author writes not pedantically, but like a gentleman; and if thou art a gentleman of thy own making thou wilt not mislike it."

Verse 8th. *Gondomar* was the Spanish Ambassador at the Court of James I., to whom, with his "one word" of "Pyrates, Pyrates, Pyrates," we in great part owe the slaughter of Raleigh. Of course, the date '526, four lines lower, is a blunder. The rash visit to Madrid was in March, 1623.

Title, and verse 8th. A *Jack-a-Lent* was a stuffed puppet, set up to be thrown at, during Lent. Perhaps it was a substitute for a live Cock; or else the Cock-throwing may have been a later "improvement:" See Hone's *Every Day Book*, for an illustrated account, i. 249. Trace of the habit survives in our modern "Old Aunt Sally," by which yokels lose money at Races (although Dorset Rectors try to abolish Country Fairs, while encouragment is given to gambling at Chapel Bazaars with raffles for pious purposes). In the *Merry Wives of Windsor*, Act iii. sc. 3, Mrs. Page says to the boy, "You little *Jack-a-Lent*, have you been true to us?" Quarles alludes to the practice :—

> How like a Jack-a-Lent
> He stands, for boys to spend their Shrove-tide throws,
> Or like a puppet made to frighten crows.
>   (J. O. Halliwell's *M. W. of W.*, Tallis ed., p. 127.)

John Taylor (the Water-Poet) wrote a whim-wham entitled "*Jack a Lent: his Beginning and Entertainment*," about 1619, printed 1630; as "of the Jack of Jacks, great Jack a Lent." And Cleveland devoted thus a Cavalier's worn suit : "Thou shalt make *Jack-a-Lents* and Babies first." (*Poems*, 1662, p. 56.)

Martin Llewellyn's Song on Cock-throwing begins "Cock a doodle doe, 'tis the bravest game;" in his *Men-Miracles*, &c., 1646, p. 61.

Page 31. *A Story strange I will you tell.*

As to the burden (since some folks are inquisitive about the etymology of Down derry down, or Ran-dan, &c.), we may note that in a queer book, *The Loves of Hero and Leander*, 1651, p. 3, is a six-line verse ending thus :

> *Oh,* Hero, Hero, *pitty me,*
> *With a dildo, dildo, dildo dee.*"

By which we may guess that the Rope-dancer's Song, in our text, was probably written about, or even before, 1651. Some among us (the Editor for one) saw Madame Sacchi in 1855 mount the rope, although she was seventy years old, as nimbly as when the first Napoleon had been her chief spectator. During the Commonwealth, rope-dancing and tumbling were tolerated at the Red-Bull Theatre, while plays were prohibited. See (Note to p. 210) our Introduction to *Westminster Drollery*, pp. xv.-xx, and the Frontispiece reproduced from Kirkman's "*Wits*," 1673, representing sundry characters from different "Drolls," grouped together, viz.: Falstaff and Dame Quickly, from "the Bouncing Knight;" the French Dancing-Master, from the Duke of Newcastle's "Variety," Clause, from Beaumont and Fletcher's "Beggar's Bush," Tom Greene as Bubble the Clown uttering "Tu Quoque" from John Cooke's "City Gallant" (peeping through the chief-entrance, reserved for dignitaries); also Simpleton the Smith, and the Changeling, from two of Robert Cox's favourite Drolls. We add now, illustrative of practical suppression under the Commonwealth, a contemporary record :—

A Song.

1.

The fourteenth of September
I very well remember,
   When people had eaten and fed well,
Many men, they say,
Would needs go see a Play,
   But they saw a great rout at the red Bull.

2.

The Soldiers they came,
(The blind and the lame)
  To visit and undo the Players;
And women without Gowns,
They said they would have Crowns;
  But they were no good Sooth-sayers.

3.

Then Jo: Wright they met,
Yet nothing could get,
  And Tom Jay i' th' same condition:
The fire men they
Would ha' made 'em a prey,
  But they scorn'd to make a petition.

4. [p. 89.]

The Minstrills they
Had the hap that day,
  (Well fare a very good token)
To keep (from the chase)
The fiddle and the case,
  For the instruments scap'd unbroken.

5.

The poor and the rich,
The wh ... and the b ....,
  Were every one at a losse,
But the Players were all
Turn'd (as weakest) to the wall,
  And 'tis thought had the greatest losse. [? cross.]
(Wit's Merriment, or Lusty Drollery, 1656, p. 88.)

One such raid on the poor actors (and probably at this very theatre, the Red Bull, St. John's Street, Clerkenwell) is recorded, as of 20th December, 1649:—" Some Stage-players in St. John's-Street were apprehended by troopers, their clothes taken away, and themselves carried to prison" (Whitelocke's *Memorials,* 435, edit. 1733, cited by J. P. C., *Annals,* ii. 118). It was a serious business, as we see from the Ordinance of 11 Feb., 1647-8; the demolishing of seats and boxes, the actors " to be apprehended and openly and publicly whipt in some market town . . . to enter into recognizances with two sufficient sureties, never to act or play any Play or Interlude any more," &c.

As for the Light-skirts, so elegantly referred to in the Song now reprinted (as far as we are aware, for the first time), they were certainly not actresses, but courtezans frequenting the place to ensnare visitors. Although English women did not *publicly* perform until after the Restoration, except on one occasion (of course, at Court Masques and private mansions, the Queen herself and her ladies had impersonated characters), yet so early as 8th November, 1629, some French professional actresses vainly attempted to get a hearing at Blackfriars Theatre, and a fortnight later at the Red Bull itself, as three weeks afterwards at the Fortune. Evidently, they were unsuccessful throughout. We hear a good deal about the far-more objectionable " Ladies of Pleasure," who beset all places of amusement. Thomas Cranley, addressing one such, in his *Amanda*, 1635, describes her several alluring disguises and habits :—

> *The places thou dost usually frequent*
> *Is to some playhouse in an afternoon,*
> *And for no other meaning and intent*
> *But to get company to sup with soon ;*
> *More changeable and wavering than the moon.*
> > *And with thy wanton looks attracting to thee*
> > *The amorous spectators for to woo thee.*
>
> *Thither thou com'st in several forms and shapes*
> *To make thee still a stranger to the place,*
> *And train new lovers, like young birds, to scrapes,*
> *And by thy habit so to change thy face ;*
> *At this time plain, to-morrow all in lace :*
> > *Now in the richest colours to be had ;*
> > *The next day all in mourning, black and sad.* &c.

Page 33. *Oh fire, fire, fire, where?*

Despite our repugnance to mutilate a text (see Introduction to *Westminster Drollery*, p. 6; ditto to *Merry Drol-*

lery Compleat, pp. 38, 39, 40; and that to our present volume, foot-note in section third), a few letters have been necessarily suppressed in this piece of coarse humour. Verse fourth, on p. 33, refers to Ben Jonson's loss of valuable manuscripts by fire, and his consequent "Execration upon Vulcan," before June, 1629; an event deeply to be regretted: also to the whimsical account of the fire on London Bridge (see *Merry Drollery, Compleat*, pp. 87, 369, and Additional Note in present volume, tracing the poem to 1651, and the event to 1633).

An amusing poem was written, by Thomas Randolph, on the destruction of the Mitre Tavern at Cambridge, about 1630; it begins, " Lament, lament, you scholars all." (See *A Crew of kind London Gossips*, 1663, p. 72).

Page 38. *In Eighty Eight, ere I was born*.

Also given later, in *Merry Drollery*, 1661, p. 77, and *Ditto, Compleat*, p. 82 and 369. Compare the Harleian MS. version, No. 791, fol. 59, given in our Appendix to *Westminster Drollery*, p. 38, with note. The romance of "*the Knight of the Sun* is mentioned by Sir Tho. Overbury in his *Characters*, as fascinating a Chambermaid, and tempting her to turn lady-errant. "The book is better known under the title of *The Mirror of Princely Deedes and Knighthood*, wherein is shewed the worthinesse of The Knight of the Sunne, &c. It consists of nine parts, which appear to have been published at intervals between 1585, and 1601." *(Lucasta*, &c., edit. 1864, p. 13.)

Page 40. *And will this Wicked World*, &c.

We never met this elsewhere: it was probably written either in 1605, or almost immediately afterwards. Among Robert Hayman's *Quodlibets*, 1628, in Book Second, No. 49, is an Epigram (p. 27):—

Of the Gunpowder Holly-day, the 5th
of November.

The Powder-Traytors, Guy Vaux, *and his mates,*
Who by a Hellish plot sought Saints estates,

Haue in our Kalendar vnto their shame,
A ioyful Holy-day *cald by their Name.*

Jeremiah Wells has among his *Poems on Several Occasions*, 1667, one, at p. 9, "On Gunpowder Treason," beginning "*Hence dull pretenders unto villany*," which solemnly conjures up a picture of what might have ensued if (what even Baillie Nicol Jarvie would call) the "awfu' bleeze" had taken place. [The same rare volume is interesting, as containing a Poem on the Rebuilding of London, after the fire of 1666, p. 112, beginning "What a Devouring Fire but t'other day!"]

With Charles Lamb, we have always regretted the failure of the Gunpowder Plot. It would have been a magnificent event, fully equal to Firmillian's blowing up the Cathedral of St. Nicholas, at Badajoz; and the loss of life to all the Parliament Members would have been a cheap price, if paid, for such a remembrance. The worst of all is, that, having been attempted, there is no likelihood of any subsequent repetition meeting with better success. *Hinc illæ lachrymæ!* Faux, Vaux, or Fawkes must have been a noble, though slightly misguided, enthusiast; for he had intended to perish, like Samson, with his victims. All good Protestants now admire the Nazarite, although they bon-fire-raise poor Guido. But then he failed in his work, while the other slayer of Philistines attained success: which perhaps accounts for the different apotheosis. As Lady Macbeth puts it: "The attempt, *and not the deed*, confounds us!"

Page 44. *A Maiden of the Pure Society.*

A version of this epigram is among the MSS. at end of a volume of "Various Poems," in the British Museum: Press-mark, Case 39. a. These have been printed by Fred. J. Furnival, Esq., for the Ballad Society, as "Love Poems and Humorous Ones," 1874. "A Puritane with one of hir societie," is No. 26, p. 22.

Page 52. *He that a Tinker,* &c.

This re-appears in the *Antidote against Melancholy*, 1661 p. 65; and, with music, in the 1719 *Pills to p. Mel.*, iii. 52

U

Page 55. *Idol of our Sex!* &c.

This Lady Carnarvon was the wife of Robert Dormer, second Baron Dormer, created Visc. Ascott, or Herld, and Earl of Carnarvon, 2d Aug., 1628. Obiit 1643. He fell at the Battle of Newbury, 20th Sept. (See Clarendon's *History of the Rebellion*, Book vii. p. 350, edit. 1720, where his merits are recognized.) Her name was Anna-Sophia, daughter of Philip, Earl of Pembroke. The child mentioned in the poem was their son, Charles Dormer, who died in 1709, when the Viscounty and Earldom became extinct. The poem was written at his birth, on January 1st.

Page 57. *Uds bodykins! Chill work no more.*

We find this, a year earlier, (an inferior version, lacking third verse, but longer,) as *Cockbodykins, chill*, &c., in *Wit's Interpreter*, p. 143, 1655; and p. 247, 1671. It is a valuable, because trustworthy and graphic, record of the troubles falling upon those who tried to labour on, despite the stir of civil war. 4th verse, "that a vet," seems corruption of that is fetched; horses *in a hole (W. Int.)*; vange thy note, is *take thy note. (do)*. Prob. date, 1647.

The Second Part.

THen straight came ruffling to my dore,
    Some dozens of these rogues, or more:
        So zausie they be grown.
Facks[,] if they come, down they sit,
They'l never ask me leave one whit,
        They'l take all for their own.

Then ich provision straight must make,
And from my Chymney needs must take,
        And vlitch both pure and good. [a flitch]
Oh! 'twould melt a Christians heart to see,
That such good Bacon spoil'd should be,
        'Twas as red as any blood.

But in it would, whether chud or not,
Together with Beans into the pot,
        As sweet as any viggs.

And when chave done all that I am able,
They'l slat it down all under table,
    And zwear they be no Pigs.

Then Ize did intreat their worships to be quiet,
And ich would strive to mend their diet,
    And they shall have finer feeding,
They zwear goddam thee for a boor,
Wee'l gick thee raskal out a door,
    And teach thee better breeding.

Then on the fire they [do] put on
A piece of beef, or else good mutton,
    No, no, this is no meat.
Forsooth they must have finer food,
A good vat hen with all her brood ;
    And then perhaps they'l eat.

But of late ich had a crew together,
They were meer devils, ich ask'd them whether
    That they were not of our nation.
Good Lord defend us from all zuch,
They zaid they were wild Irish, *or else* Dutch,
    They were of the Devils generation.

And when these raskals went away,
What e're you thing they did me repay
    Ich will not you deceive.
Facks[,] just as folks go to a vaire,
They vaidled up my goods and ware,
    And so they took their leave.

O what a clutter they did make
Our house for Babel *they did take,*
    We could not understand a jot.
Yet they did know what did belong
To drink and zwear in our own tongue,
    Such language they had a got.

Nor home ich any zafe aboad,
If that Ise chance to go abroad,
    These rogues will come to spy me ;

Then zurrah, zurrah, quoth they, tarry,
We know false letters you do carry,
  And so they come to try me.

For as swift as any lightning goes
Straight all their hand into my hose,
  There out they pull my purse.
O zurrah, zurrah, this is it,
Your Letters are in silver writ ;
  You may go take your course.

A Trouper t'other day did greet me,
[.   .   .   .   Lost line.]
  But could you guesse the reason,
Thou art, quoth he, a rebel, Knave,
And zo thou dost thy zelf behave,
  For thou doest whistle treason.

Nor was this raskal much to blame,
For all his mates zwore just the zame,
  That ich was fain to do.
Ich humble pardon of him sought,
And gave him money for my fault,
  And glad I could scape so too.

(*Wits Interpreter*, 250, 1671 ed.)

This is, veritably, a "document in madness" of such civil wars and military licence. It reads like the genuine narratives of Prussian brutality and outrage during the occupation of Alsace and Lorraine: which is hereafter to be bitterly avenged.

Page 60. *I keep my horse, I keep*, &c.

This lively ditty is sung by Latrocinio in the comedy of "The Widow," Act iii. sc. 1, produced about 1616, and written by JOHN FLETCHER, Ben Jonson, and Thomas Middleton. The song bears trace of Fletcher's hand (more, we believe, than of Jonson's). It has a rollicking freedom that made it a favourite. We meet it in *Wit's Interpreter*, 1655, p. 69; 1671, p. 175; and elsewhere. See Dyce's *Middleton*, iii. 383, and *Dodsley's Old Plays*, 1744, vi. 34.

Page 61. *There is not halfe so warm a fire.*

This re-appears, with variations and twelve additional lines (inferior), in *Westminster-Drollery*, 1671, i. 102; where is the corrupt text "*and* daily *pays us with what is.*" Our present text gives us the true word, "*dully.*"

Page 62. Fuller *of wish, than hope,* &c.

Fuller's book, "A *Pisgah sight of Palestine,*" was published about 1649. The epitaph "Here lies Fuller's earth," is well known. He died in 1661.

Page 63. Cloris, *now thou art fled away.*

The author of this song was DR. HENRY HUGHES. Henry Lawes gives the music to it, in his "*Ayres,*" 1669, Bk. iii. p. 10. It is also in J. P.'s *Sportive Wit*, 1656, p. 15; the *Loyal Garland* (Percy Soc. Reprint of 1686 edit. xxix. 67); *Pills to p. Mel.*, 1719, iii. 331. Sometimes attributed to Sir R[obert] A[ytoun].

In *Sportive Wit* there are variations as well as an Answer, which we here give. The different title seems consequent on the Answer presupposing that *Amintas* has not died, merely disappeared. It is "A Shepherd fallen in Love : A Pastoral." The readings are : *Lambkins follow ; They're gone, they're ;* Dog *howling* lyes, *While* he *laments with woful* cryes ; Oh *Cloris, Cloris, I decay,* And *forced am to cry well, &c.* Sixth verse there omitted. It has, however, on p. 16 :—

The Answer.

[1656.]

CLoris, *since thou art gone astray,*
Amyntas *Shepherd's fled away ;*
And all the joys he wont to spye
I' th' pretty babies of thine eye,
Are gone ; and she hath none to say
But who can help what will away, will away ?

*The Green on which it was her [? his] chance
To have her hand first in a dance,
Among the merry Maiden-crue,
Now making her nought but sigh and rue
The time she ere had cause to say*   [p. 17.]
Ah, who can help what will away, will away?

*The Lawn with which she wont to deck
And circle in her whiter neck;
Her Apron lies behind the door;
The strings won't reach now as before:
Which makes her oft cry well-a-day:
But who can help what* will away?

*He often swore that he would leave me,
Ere of my heart he could bereave me:
But when the Signe was in the tail,
He knew poor Maiden-flesh was frail;
And laughs now I have nought to say,
But who can help what* will away.

*But let the blame upon me lie,
I had no heart him to denie:
Had I another Maidenhead,
I'd lose it ere I went to bed:
For what can all the world more say,
Than who can help what* will away?
        (*Sportive Wit; or, The Muses' Merriment.*)

Page 68.   *I tell you all, both great and small.*

Also in Captain William Hickes' *London Drollery*, 1673, p. 179, where it is entitled "Queen Elizabeth's Song." The dance tune *Sallanger's* (or more commonly *Sellenger's*) *Round* is given in Chappell's Pop. Music, O. T., p. 69. The name is corrupted from *St. Leger's Round;* as in Yorkshire the Doncaster race is called the Sillinger, or Sellenger, to this day.

Page 70.   *When* James *in Scotland first began.*

Not yet found elsewhere, in MS. or print. The sixth

verse refers to King James the First making so many Knights, on insufficient ground, that he incurred ridicule. Allusions are not infrequent in dramas and ballads. Here is the most noteworthy of the latter. It is in Additional MS. No. 5,832, fol. 205, British Museum.

Verses upon the order for making Knights of such persons who had £46 *per annum* in King *James* I.'s time.

Come all you farmers out of the country,
    Carters, plowmen, hedgers and all,
Tom, Dick and Will, Ralph, Roger and Humfrey,
    Leave off your gestures rusticall.
Bidd all your home-sponne russetts adue,
And sute your selves in fashions new ;
    Honour invites you to delights :
    Come all to Court and be made Knights.

2.

He that hath fortie pounds per annum
    Shalbe promoted from the plowe :
His wife shall take the wall of her grannum,
    Honour is sould soe dog-cheap now.
Though thow hast neither good birth nor breeding,
If thou hast money, thow art sure of speeding.

3.

Knighthood in old time was counted an honour,
    Which the best spiritts did not disdayne :
But now it is us'd in so base a manner,
    That it's noe creditt, but rather a staine :
Tush, it's noe matter what people doe say,
The name of a Knight a whole village will sway.

4.

Shepheards, leave singing your pastorall sonnetts,
    And to learne complements shew your endeavours :
Cast of [ʃ] for ever your two shillinge bonnetts,
    Cover your coxcombs with three pound beavers.
Sell carte and tarrboxe new coaches to buy,
    Then, "Good your Worship," the vulgar will cry.

5.

And thus unto worshipp being advanced,
  Keepe all your tenants in awe with your frownes ;
And let your rents be yearly inhaunced,
  To buy your new-moulded maddams new gowns.
Joan, Sisse, *and* Nell *shalbe all ladified,*
Instead of hay-carts, in coaches shall ryde.

6.

Whatever you doe, have a care of expenses,
  In hospitality doe not exceed :
Greatnes of followers belongeth to princes :
  A Coachman and footmen are all that you need :
And still observe this, let your servants meate lacke,
  To keep brave apparel upon your wives backe.

[Additional stanza from Mr. Hunter's MS.]

7.

Now to conclude, and shutt up my sonnett,
  Leave of the Cart-whip, hedge-bill and flaile,
This is my counsell, think well upon it,
  Knighthood and honour are now put to saile.
Then make haste quickly, and lett out your farmes,
And take my advice in blazing your armes.
  Honor invites, &c.

(Shakespeare Soc., 1846, pp. 145-6, J. O. Halliwell's Commentary on Merry Wives of Windsor, Act. ii. sc. 1, "These Knights will hack." Also his notes in Tallis's edit., of the same, n. d., pp. 122-3. William Chappell, in *Pop. Music O. T.*, p. 327, gives the tune.)

Page 72. *The Chandler drew near his end.*

Another tolerable Epigram on a Chandler meets us, beginning "How might his days end that made weeks [wicks]?" among the Epitaphs of *Wits Recreations,* 1640-5 (Reprint, p. 271).

Page 73. *Farre in the Forrest of Arden.*

This is one of MICHAEL DRAYTON'S Pastorals, printed in 1593, in the Third Eclogue, and entitled *Dowsabell.* See *Percy's Reliques*, vol. i. bk. 3, No. 8, 2nd edit. 1767, for remarks on variations, amounting to a remodelling, of this charming poem. We are glad to know that Mr. James Russell Smith is preparing a new edition of Michael Drayton's voluminous works, to be included in the *Library of Old Authors.* Drayton suppressed his couplet poem of " Endimion and Phœbe :" *Ideus Latmvs.* It has no date, but was cited by Lodge in 1595, and has been reprinted by J. P. Collier ; one of his handsome and carefully printed quartos, a welcome boon.

Page 78. *On the twelfth day of* December.

This ballad, a very early example of the *Down down derry* burden, is not yet found elsewhere   It refers to the expedition against Scotland (then in alliance with Henry II. of France) made by the Protector, Edward, Duke of Somerset, in 1547, the first (not " fourth ") year of Edward VIth's reign.   The battle was fought on the "Black Saturday, as it was long remembered, the tenth day of September (not of " December," as the ballad mis-states it to have been).   Terrible and remorseless was the slaughter of the ill-armed Scots, after they had imprudently abandoned their excellent hilly position, by the well-appointed English horsemen.   The prisoners taken amounted to about fifteen hundred ("we found above twenty of their villains to one of their gentlemen," says Patten), among whom was the Earl of Huntley, Lord Chancellor of Scotland, who on the previous day had sent a personal challenge to Somerset, asking to decide the contest by single combat : an offer which was not unreasonably declined, the Protector declaring that he desired no peace but such as he might win by his sword. "And thou, trumpet," he told Huntley's herald, " say to thy master, he seemeth to lack wit to make this challenge to me, being of such estate by the sufferance of God as to have so weighty a charge of so precious a jewel, the government of a King's person, and then the protection of all his realms." We learn that the Scots slain were tenfold the number of the prisoners taken. This battle of "Muskleburgh Field" (nearly the same locality as the battle of Prestonpans, wherein Prince Charles Edward in 1745 defeated Colonel Gardiner and his English troops), known also as of Fawside Brae, or of Pinkie, is described with unusual precision by an eye-witness: See *The Expedition into Scotland of the most worthily-fortunate Prince Edward Duke of Somerset*, uncle to our most noble Sovereign Lord the King's Majesty Edward the VI., &c., made in the first year of his Majesty's most prosperous reign, and set out by way of Diary, by W. Patten, Londoner. First published in 1548, this was reprinted in Dalyell's *Fragments of Scottish History*, Edinburgh, 1798. This old ballad is not included by Dalyell, who probably knew not of its existence.

Page 80. *In* Celia['*s face*] *a question did arise*.
By THOMAS CAREW, written before 1638. In Addit. MSS. No. 11,811, fol. 10; No. 22,118, fol. 43; also in *Wits Recreations* (Repr., p. 19); Roxb. Libr. Carew, p. 6, &c.

Page 81. *Blacke Eyes, in your dark Orbs doe lye*.
By JAMES HOWELL, Historiographer to Charles II., and author of the celebrated *Epistolæ Ho-Elianæ*, 1645, 1647, 1650, and 1655. He died in November, 1666; according to Anthony à Wood, (whose account of him in the *Athenæ Oxonienses*, iii. 744, edit. 1817, is given by Edward Arber in his excellent *English Reprints*, vol. viii, 1869, with a welcome promise of editing the said *Epistolæ*). This poem of " Black eyes," &c., occurs among Howell's poems collected by Sergeant-Major Peter Fisher, p. 68, 1663; again re-issued (the same sheets) as "*Mr. Howell's Poems upon divers Emergent Occasions;* Printed by James Cottrel, and dated 1664. It is also found in C. F.'s *Wit at a Venture; or*, Clio's *Privy Garden*, containing Songs and Poems on Several Occasions,

Never before in Print" (which statement is incorrect, as usual). Our text is the earliest we know in type. The only variations, in *Howell's Poems*, are: 1st line, *doth lie*; 4th verse, And by *those spells I am* possest.

Page 83. *We read of Kings, and Gods, &c.*

This is another of the charming poems by THOMAS CAREW, always a favourite with his own generation (few MS. or printed Collections being without many of them), and deserving of far more affectionate perusal in our own time than he generally meets. It is in Addit. MS. No. 11, 811, fol. 6b., entitled there "His Love Neglected." Elsewhere, as "A Cruel Mistress."

Page 84. *What ill luck had I, Silly Maid,* &c.

Although closely resembling the Catch "*What Fortune had I, poor Maid as I am*," *of* 1661 *Antidote ag. Melancholy*, p, 74, and *Merry Drollery* ii. 152 (equal to p. 341 of editions 1670 and 1691), this song is virtually distinct, and probably was the earlier version in date. One has been evidently borrowed or adapted from the other.

Page 85. *I never did hold all that glisters,* &c.

This vigorous expression of opinion from a robust nature, uncorrupted amid a conventionalized, treacherous, and selfishly-cruel community, is a valuable record of the true Cavalier "all of the olden time." We have never met it elsewhere. He has no half-likings, no undefined suspicions, and admits of no paltering with the truth, or shirking of one's duty. As we read we behold the honest man before us, and remember that it was such as he who made our England what she is:—

> *Pride in their port, defiance in their eye,*
> *I see the Lords of human kind pass by.*

The contemplation of such brave spirits may help to nerve fresh readers to emulate their virtues, despite the sickly fancies or grovelling politics and social theories of degenerate days. The singer may be somewhat overbearing in announcement of his preferences :

> ———*Just this*
> *Or that in you disgusts me ; here you miss,*
> *Or there exceed the mark,*—

But, if he errs at all, it is on the safe side.

Page 88. *No Gypsie nor no Blackamore.*

Composers and arrangers of such collections as this Drollery seem to have often chosen pieces simply for contrast. Thus, after the manly directness of "The Doctor's Touchstone," we find the vilely mercenary husband here exhibited, and followed by the truthful description (justifiable, although coarsely outspoken) of "The baseness of Whores." Such were they of old: such are they ever.

Page 92. *Let not Sweet Saint,* &c.

Like the three preceding poems, not yet found elsewhere, but worthy of preservation.

Page 93. *How happy's that Prisoner.*

Written "by a Person of Quality:" whom we suspect to have been Sir Francis Wortley, but without evidence to substantiate the guess. This is the earliest appearance in print, known to us, of this characteristic outburst of Cavalier vivacity, which re-appears as the Musician's Song, in "*Cromwell's Conspiracy,*" 1660, Act iii. sc. 2; and *Merry Drollery,* 1661, p. 101. (See also *M. D. C.,* pp. 107, 373). As to the introduction of the several ancient philosophers (referred to in former Appendix, p. 373), compare the delightful *Chanson a Boire,*

> *Je cherche en vin la vérité,*
>   *Si le vin n'aide à ma foiblesse,*
> *Toute la docte antiquité*
>   *Dans le vin puisa la sagesse,*

> Oui c'est par le bon vin que le bon sens éclate,
> *J'en atteste* Hypocrate,
>   Qui dit qu'il fait a chaque mois
>   Du moins s'enivrer une fois, &c.

(The other twelve verses are given complete in *"Brallaghan; or, the Deipnosophists,"* 1845, pp. 198-203, with a clever verse-translation, by the foremost of linguistic scholars now alive—the friend of Talfourd and of Dr. W. Maginn—at whom many nowadays presume to scoff, and whom Benchers defame and banish themselves from.)

Page 97. *Fire! Fire! O how I burn, &c.*

Also in *Windsor Drollery*, 1672, p. 126, as " Fire! Fire! *lo here* I burn in my desire," &c. And in Henry Bold's *Latine Songs*, 1685, p. 139, where it is inserted, to be alongside of this parody on it by him, song xlvii., or a

MOCK.

1.

Fire, Fire,
  Is there no help for thy desire?
Are tears all spent? Is Humber *low?*
Doth Trent *stand still? Doth* Thames *not flow?*
Though all these can't thy Feaver cure,
  Yet Tyburn *is a Cooler lure,*
And since thou can'st not quench thy Fire,
Go hang thy self, and thy desire!

2.

Fire, fire,
Here's one [*still*] *left for thy desire,*
  Since that the Rainbow in the skye,
  Is bent a deluge to deny,
As loth for thee a God should Lye.
    Let gentle Rope come dangling down,
    One born to hang shall never drown,
And since thou can'st not quench the Fire,
Go hang thy self, and thy desire!
            (*Latine Songs*, 1685, p. 140.)

Page 98. *'Tis not how witty, nor how free.*

A year earlier, this had appeared in *Wit's Interpreter*, 1655, p. 4 (1671, p. 108), entitled "What is most to be liked in a Mistress." Robt. Jamieson quotes it, from *Choyce Drollery*, in his *Pop. Bds.*, 1806, ii. 309. We believe it to be by the same author as the poem next following, and regret that they remain anonymous. Both are of a stately beauty, and recall to us those Cavalier Ladies with whose portraits Vandyck adorned many family mansions.

Page 99. *She's not the fairest of her name.*

One clue, that may hereafter guide us to the authorship, we know the lady's name. It was FREEMAN. This poem also had appeared a year earlier, at least, in *Wit's Interpreter*, 1655, p. 55 (; 1671 ed., p. 161). Also in *Wit and Drollery*, 1661, p. 162; in *Oxford Drollery*, part ii. 1671, p. 87; and in *Loyal Garland*, 1686, as "The Platonick Lover" (reprinted by Percy Soc., xxix. 64). There should be a comma in fifth line, after the word Constancy. Various readings:—Verse 2, *meanest* wit; and *yet* a; 3, His *dear* addresses; walls be *brick* or stone.

Page 100. *'Tis late and cold, stir up the fire.*

This Song, by JOHN FLETCHER, in his *Lover's Progress*, Act iii. sc. 1., before 1625. The music is found in Additional MS. No. 11,608 (written about 1656), fol. 20; there called "Myne Ost's Song, sung in *ye Mad Lover* [wrong: a different play], set by Robt. Johnson." It re-appears in *Wit and Drollery* 1661, p. 212; in the *Academy of Complements*, 1670, p. 175, &c. It is the Song of the Dead Host, whose return to wait upon his guests and ask their aid to have his body laid in consecrated ground, is so humorously described. His forewarnings of death to Cleander are, to our mind, of thrilling interest. These scenes were Sir Walter Scott's favourites; but Leigh Hunt, perversely, could see no merit in them. We believe that the tinge of sepulchral dullness in Mine Host enhances the vividness of the incidents, like the taciturnity of Don Guzman's stony statue in Shadwell's "Libertine."

Thus the hundred-paged volume of *Choyce Drollery*, 1656,—" Delicates served up by frugall Messes, as aiming at thy satisfaction not saciety,"—comes to an end, with Beaumont and Fletcher. On them remembrance loves to rest, as the fitting representatives of that class of courtly gentlemen, poets, wits, and scholars, who were, to a great extent, even then, fading away from English society. To them had been visible no phase of the Rebellion, and they probably never conceived that it was near. Beaumont, with his statelier reserve, and his tendency to quiet musing, fostered "under the shade of melancholy boughs" at Grace-Dieu, had early passed away, honoured and lamented; a month before his friend Shakespeare went to rest: Shakespeare, who, having known half a century of busy life, felt contented, doubtless, to fulfil the wish that he had long before expressed, himself, almost prophetically:—

> " *Let me not live,*"—
> *Thus his good melancholy oft began,* . . . .
> "*After my flame lacks oil, to be the snuff*
> *Of younger spirits, whose apprehensive senses*
> *All but new things disdain ; whose judgments are*
> *Mere fathers of their garments ; whose constancies*
> *Expire before their fashions :*"—*this he wished.*

Fletcher survived nine years, and battled on with somewhat of spasmodic action; at once widowed and orphaned by the death of his close friend and work-fellow; winning fresh triumphs, it is true, and leaving many a trace of his bright genius like a gleam of heaven's own light across the sadness and corruption of an imaginary world, that was not at all unreal in heroism or in wickedness. He also passed away while young; a few months later than the time when Charles the First came to the throne, suddenly elevated by the death of his father James, bringing abruptly to a consummation that marriage with the

French Princess which did so much to lead him and his country into ruin. The year 1625 was the separating date between the autumnal ripeness and the chill of fruitless winter. A sunny glow remains on Fletcher to the last. With him it fades, and the world that he had known is changed.

[End of Notes to *Choyce Drollery*.]

APPENDIX

APPENDIX. PART 2.

ANTIDOTE AGAINST MELANCHOLY. 1661.

Gratiano.—" Why should a man, whose blood is warm within,
  Sleep when he wakes, and creep into the jaundice
  By being peevish ? I tell thee what, Antonio,—
  I love thee, and it is my love that speaks ;—
  There are a sort of men, whose visages
  Do cream and mantle like a standing pond,
  And do a wilful stillness entertain,
  With purpose to be dress'd in an opinion
  Of wisdom, gravity, profound conceit ;
  As who should say, ' I am Sir Oracle,
  And, when I ope my lips, let no dog bark !' "
          (*Merchant of Venice*, Act i. sc. 1.)

WE have already, in a brief Introduction, (pp. 105-110), explained our reason for adding all that was necessary to complete this work ; a large portion having been anticipated in *Merry Drollery* of the same year, 1661. In the Postscript (pp. 161-165), we endeavoured to trace the authorship of the entire collection ; leaving to these following notes, and those attached to *M. Drollery, Compleat*, the search for separate poems or songs. Also, on pp. 166-175, we traced the history of "Arthur o' Bradley," delaying the important song of his Wedding (from an original of the date 1656), unto Part IV. of our *Appendix*.

x

To no other living writer are we lovers of old literature more deeply indebted than to the veteran John Payne Collier, who is now far advanced in his eighty-seventh year, and whose intellect and industry remain vigorously employed at this great age: one proof of the fact being his new edition of Shakespeare (each play in a separate quarto, issued to private subscribers), begun in January, 1875, and already the Comedies are finished, in the third volume. Among his numerous choice reprints of rare originals, his series of the more than *"Seven Early Poetical Miscellanies"* was a work of greatest value. To these, with his new *"Shakespeare,"* the interesting *"Old Man's Diary,"* his *"Bibliographical and Critical Account of the Rarest Books in the English Language,"* his *"Annals of the Stage,"* *"The Poetical Decameron,"* his charming *"Book of Roxburghe Ballads,"* 1847, his *"Broadside Black-Letter-Ballads,"* 1868, and other labours, no less than to his warmth of heart and friendly encouragement by letters, the present Editor owes many happy hours, and for them makes grateful acknowledgment.

About the year 1870, J. P. Collier issued to private subscribers his very limited and elegant Reprint, in quarto, of *"An Antidote against Melancholy,"* 1661. This is already nearly as unattainable as the original.

J. P. Collier gave no notes to his Reprint of the "Antidote," but, in the brief Introduction thereunto, he mentioned that :—" This poetical tract has been selected for our reprint on account of its rarity, the excellence of the greater part of its contents, the high antiquity of some of them, and from the fact that many of the ballads and humorous pieces of versification are either not met with elsewhere, or have been strangely corrupted in repetition through the press. Two or three of them are used by Shakespeare, and the word 'incarnadine' [see our p. 148] is only found in 'Macbeth' (A. ii., sc. 2), in Carew's poems, and in this tract : here we have it as the name of a red wine ; and nobody hitherto has noticed it in that sense.

"When Ritson published his 'Robin Hood' in 1795, he relied chiefly upon the text of the famous ballad of

'Arthur o' Bradley,' as he discovered it in the miscellany before us [See our *Merry Drollery, Compleat*, pp. 312, 399; also, in present volume, p. 166, and Additional Note]; but, learned in such matters as he undoubtedly was, he was not aware of the very early period at which 'Arthur o' Bradley' was so popular as to be quoted in one of our Old Moralities, which may have been in existence in the reigns of Henry VI. or Henry VII., which was acted while Henry VIII. or Edward VI. were on the throne, and which is contained in a manuscript bearing the date of 1579.

"The few known copies of 'An Antidote against Melancholy' are dated 1661, the year after the Restoration, when lawless licence was allowed both to the press and in social intercourse; and, if we permitted ourselves to mutilate our originals, we might not have reproduced such coarseness; but still no words will be found which, even a century afterwards, were not sometimes used in private conversation, and which did not even make their appearance at full length in print. Mere words may be said to be comparatively harmless; but when, as in the time of Charles II, they were employed as incentives to vice and laxity of manners, they become dangerous. The repetition of them in our day, in a small number of reprints, can hardly be offensive to decorum, and unquestionably cannot be injurious to public morals. We always address ourselves to the students of our language and habits of life."

Page 113 (original, p. 1). *Not drunken, nor sober, &c.*

Joseph Ritson gave this Bacchanalian chant in the second volume of his "English Songs," p. 58, 1783. Forty-six verses, out of the seventy, had been repeated in the "Collection of Old Ballads," 1723-25, (which Ambrose Philips and David Mallet may have edited,) "The Ex-Aletation of Ale" is in vol. iii. p. 166. Part, if not all, must have been in existence fully ten years before it appeared in the "Antidote," as we find "O Ale *ab alendo*, thou Liquor of life!" with music by John Hilton, in his "Catch that Catch Can," p. 5, 1652. It is also in *Wit's Merriment; or, Lusty Drollery*, 1656, p. 118; eight verses only. These are: 1. Not drunken; 2. But yet to commend it; 3. But yet, by your leave; 4. It makes a man merry; 5. The old wife whose teeth; 6. The Ploughman, the Lab'rer; 7. The man that hath a black blous to his wife; 8. With that my friend said, &c.   Still earlier, the poem had appeared, imperfectly, in a four-paged quarto pamphlet, dated 1642 (along with The Battle fought between the Norfolk Cock and the Wisbeach Cock," see *M. D. C.*, p. 242) as by THOMAS RANDALL, i.e. RANDOLPH. Accordingly, it has been included (34 verses only) in the 1875 edition of his Works, p. 662. We personally attach no weight to the pamphlet's ascription of it to Randolph, (who died in March, 1634-5). It is far more likely to have been the work of SAMUEL ROWLANDS, in whose *Crew of Kind London Gossips*, 1663, we meet it, p. 129-141, and whose style it more closely resembles. Some poems duly assigned to Randolph are in the same volume, but the "Exaltation of Ale" is *not* thus distinguished. There are seventy-two verses given, and the motto is *Tempus edax rerum, &c.* We have not been able to consult an earlier edition of S. Rowland's *"Crew,"* &c., about 1650.

So long afterwards as 1788, we find an abbreviated copy of the song, six verses, in Lackington's " British Songster," p. 202, entitled "A Tankard of Ale." The first verse runs thus:—

> *"Not drunk, nor yet sober, but brother to both,*
> *I met with a man upon Aylesbury Vale,*
> *I saw in his face that he was in good case*
> *To go and take part of a tankard of ale."*

Omitting all sequence of narrative, the other verses are adapted from the *Antidote's* 21st, 19th, 10th, 26th, and 50th; concerning the hedger, beggar, widow, clerk, and amicable conclusion over a tankard of ale. In a *Convivial Songster*, of 1807, by Tegg, London, these six are given with addition of another as fifth:—

> *The old parish Vicar, when he's in his liquor,*
> *Will merrily at his parishioners rail,*

"*Come, pay all your tithes, or I'll kiss all your wives,*"
   When once he shakes hands with a tankard of ale.

It had appeared in a Chap-book (circa 1794, according to Wm. Logan; see his amusing "Pedlar's Pack," pp. 224-6), with other five verses inserted before the Finale. We give them to complete the tale :—

There's the blacksmith by trade, a jolly brisk blade,
   Cries, "Fill up the bumper, dear host, from the pail;"
So cheerful he'll sing, and make the house ring,
   When once he shakes hands with a tankard of ale.
      Laru la re, laru, &c.   So cheerful, &c.

There's the tinker, ye ken, cries "old kettles to mend,"
   With his budget and hammer to drive in the nail;
Will spend a whole crown, at one sitting down,
   When once he shakes hands with a tankard of ale.
      Laru, &c.

There's the mason, brave John, *the carver of stone,*
   The Master's grand secret he'll never reveal;
Yet how merry is he with his lass on his knee,
   When once he shakes hands with a tankard of ale.
      Laru, &c.

You maids who feel shame, pray me do not blame,
   Though your private ongoings in public I tell;
Young Bridget *and* Nell *to kiss will not fail*
   When once they shake hands with a tankard of ale.
      Laru, &c.

There's some jolly wives, love drink as their lives,
   Dear neighbours but mind the sad thread of my tale;
Their husbands they'll scorn, as sure's they were born,
   If once they shake hands with a tankard of ale.
      Laru, &c.

From wrangling or jangling, and ev'ry such strife,
   Or anything else that may happen to fall;
From words come to blows, and sharp bloody nose,
   But friends again over a tankard of ale.
      Laru, &c.

Notice the characteristic mention of William Elderton, the Ballad-writer (who died before 1592), in the thirty-third verse (our p. 119) :—

> For ballads Elderton *never had peer ;*
> *How went his wit in them, with how merry a gale,*
> *And with all the sails up, had he been at the cup,*
> *And washed his beard with a* pot of good ale.

William Elderton's "New Yorkshire Song, intituled *Yorke, Yorke, for my Monie,*" (entered at Stationers' Hall, 16 November, 1582, and afterwards "Imprinted at London by Richard Iones; dwelling neere Holbourne Bridge : 1584)," has the place of honour in the Roxburghe Collection, being the first ballad in the first volume. It consequently takes the lead in the valuable "Roxburghe Bds." of the Ballad Society, 1869, so ably edited by William Chappell, Esq., F.S.A. It also formed the commencement of Ritson's *Yorkshire Garland :* York, 1788. It is believed that Elderton wrote the "excellent Ballad intituled The Constancy of Susanna" (Roxb. Coll., i. 60; Bagford, ii. 6; Pepys, i. 33, 496). A list of others was first given by Ritson ; since, by W. C. Hazlitt, in his *Handbook,* p. 177. Elderton's "Lenton Stuff ys come to the town" was reprinted by J. O. Halliwell, for the Shakespeare Society, in 1846 (p. 105). He gives Drayton's allusion to Elderton in Notes to Mr. Hy. Huth's "79 Black-Letter Ballads," 1870, 274 (the "Praise of my Ladie Marquess," by W. E., being on pp. 14-16). Elderton had been an actor in 1552 ; his earliest dated ballad is of 1559, and he had ceased to live by 1592. Camden gives an epitaph, which corroborates our text, in regard to the "thirst complaint" of the balladist :—

> *Hic situs est sitiens, atque ebrius Eldertonus—*
> *Quid dico—Hic* situs *est ? hic potius* sitis *est.*

Thus freely rendered by Oldys :—

> Dead drunk here Elderton *doth lie ;*
> *Dead as he is, he still is dry ;*
> *So of him it may well be said,*
> *Here he, but not his thirst, is laid.*

A MS., time of James I., possessed by J. P. Collier, mentions, in further confirmation:

> Will Elderton's *red nose is famous everywhere,*
> *And many a ballet shows it cost him very dear;*
> *In ale, and toast, and spice, he spent good store of coin,*
> *You need not ask* him *twice to take a cup of wine.*
> *But though his nose was red, his hand was very white,*
> *In work it never sped, nor took in it delight;*
> *No marvel therefore 'tis, that white should be his hand,*
> *That ballets writ a score, as you well understand.*

(See Wm. Chappell's Popular Music of the Olden Time, pp. 107, 815; and J. P. Collier's Extracts from Reg. Stat. Comp., *passim*, Indices, art. Elderton; and his Bk. of Roxb. Bds., p. 139.)

Page 125 (orig. 14).   *With an old Song, made by, &c.*

The fashion of disparaging the present, by praising the customs and people of days that have passed away, is almost as old as the Deluge, if not older. Homer speaks of the degeneracy in his time, and aged Israel had long earlier lamented the few and evil days to which his own life extended, in comparison with those patriarchs who had gone before him. Even as we know not the full value of the Mistress or the friend whose affection had been given unto us, until separated from them, for ever, by estrangement or the grave, so does it seem to be with many customs and things. Robert Browning touchingly declares:—

> *And she is gone; sweet human love is gone!*
> *'Tis only when they spring to heaven that angels*
> *Reveal themselves to you; they sit all day*
> *Beside you, and lie down at night by you*
> *Who care not for their presence, muse or sleep,*
> *And all at once they leave you, and you know them!*

Modified in succeeding reigns, the ballad of "The Queen [Elizabeth]'s Old Courtier, and A New Courtier of the King [James]" has already known two hundred and fifty years' popularity. The earliest printed copy was probably issued by T. Symcocke, by or after 1626. We find it in several books about the time of the Restoration, when parodies became frequent. It is in *Le Prince d'Amour*, 1660, p. 161; *Wit and Drollery*, 1682 (not in 1656, 1661 edits.), p. 278, "With an old Song," &c; *Wit and Mirth*, 1684, p. 43; *Dryden's Misc. Poems* (ed. 1716, IV. 108); with the Music, in *Pills*, iii. 271; in *Philomel*, 130, 1744; Percy's *Reliques*, ii. Bk. 3, No. 8, 1767; Ritson's *English Sgs.*, ii. 140, and Chappell's *Pop. Music*, p. 300, to which refer for a good introduction, with extract from Pepys Diary of 16th June, 1668. Accompanying a Parody by T. Howard, Gent. (beginning similarly, "An Old Song made of an old aged pate"), it meets us in the Roxburghe Coll., iii. 72, printed for F. Coles (1646-74).

Among other parodies may be mentioned one entitled "An Old Souldier of the Queen's" (in *Merry Drollery, Compleat*, 31, and in *Wit and Drollery*, 248, 1661); another, "The New Souldier" *(Wit and Drollery*, 282, 1682), beginning :—

> With a new Beard but lately trimmed,
> With a new love-lock neatly kemm'd,
> With a new favour snatch'd or nimm'd,
> With a new doublet, French-*like trimm'd* ;
> And a new gate, as if he swimm'd ;
>   Like a new Souldier of the King's,
>   And the King's new Souldier.
>
> *With a new feather in his Cap;*
> *With new white bootes, without a strap;* &c.

In the same edition of *Wit and Drollery*, p. 165, is yet another parody, headed *"Old Souldiers,"* which runs thus (see *Westminster-Drollery*, ii. 24, 1672,) :—

> *Of Old Souldiers the song you would hear,*
> *And we old fiddlers have forgot who they were.*

John Cleveland had a parody on the Queen's Courtier, about 1648, entitled The Puritan, beginning "With face and fashion to be known, For one of sure election."

Another, called The Tub-Preacher, is doubtfully attributed to Samuel Butler, and begins similarly, "With face and fashion to be known: With eyes all white, and many a groan" (in his *Posthumous Works*, p. 44, 3rd edit., 1730). The political parody, entitled "Saint George and the Dragon, *anglicé Mercurius Poeticus*," to the same tune of "The Old Courtier," is in the Kings Pamphlets, XVI., and has been reprinted by T. Wright for the Percy Soc., iii. 205. It bears Thomason's date, 28 Feb., 1659-[60], and is on the overthrow of the Rump, by General Monk. It begins thus :—

> *News! news! here's the occurrences and a new*
> *Mercurius,*
> *A dialogue between* Haselrigg *the baffled and*
> Arthur *the furious;*
> *With* Ireton's *readings upon legitimate and spurious,*
> *Proving that a Saint may be the Son of a Wh*——,
> *for the satisfaction of the curious.*
> *From a Rump insatiate as the Sea,*
> Libera nos, Domine, &c.

Old songs have rarely, if ever, been modernized so successfully as "The Queen's Old Courtier," of which "The Fine Old English Gentleman" is no unworthy representative. Popular though it was, thirty or forty years ago, it is not easily met with now; thus we may be excused for adding it here :—

THE FINE OLD ENGLISH GENTLEMAN.

I'LL sing you a good old song, made by a good old pate,
  Of a fine old English gentleman, who had an old
    estate,
And who kept up his old mansion, at a bountiful old
    rate;
With a good old porter to relieve the old poor at his gate.
Like a fine old English gentleman, all of the olden time.

His hall so old was hung around with pikes, and guns,
    and bows,
And swords, and good old bucklers, that had stood
    against old foes;

*'Twas there "his worship" held his state in doublet and
  trunk hose,
And quaff'd his cup of good old Sack, to warm his good
  old nose:
    Like a fine old English gentleman, &c.*

*When Winter's cold brought frost and snow, he open'd
  house to all;
And though three-score and ten his years, he featly led
  the ball;
Nor was the houseless wanderer e'er driven from his hall,
For, while he feasted all the great, he ne'er forgot the
  small:
    Like a fine old English gentleman, &c.*

*But time, though sweet, is strong in flight, and years
  roll swiftly by;
And autum's falling leaves proclaim'd, the old man—
  he must die!
He laid him down right tranquilly, gave up life's latest
  sigh;
While a heavy stillness reign'd around, and tears
  dimm'd every eye.
    For this good old English gentleman, &c.*

*Now surely this is better far than all the new parade
Of theatres and fancy balls, "At Home," and masquer-
  ade;
And much more economical, when all the bills are paid:
Then leave your new vagaries off, and take up the old
  trade
    Of a fine old English gentleman, &c.*

A series of eight Essays, each illustrated with a design by R. W. Buss, was devoted to "The Old and Young Courtier" in the *Penny Magazine* of the Society for Diffusion of Useful Knowledge, in 1842.

Charles Matthews used to sing (was it in "Patter *versus* Clatter"?) an amusing version of "The Fine Young English Gentleman," of whom it was reported that,

> *He kept up his vagaries at a most astounding rate,*
> *And likewise his old Landlady,—by staying out so late,*
> *Like a fine young English gentleman, one of the*
>   *present time, &c.*

T. R. Planché wrote a parody to the same tune, in his "Golden Fleece," on the "Fine Young Grecian Gentleman," Iason, as described by his deserted wife Medea: it begins, "I'll tell you a sad tale of the life I've been led of late." In Dinny Blake's "*Sprig of Shillelah*," p. 3, is found "The Rale Ould Irish Gintleman," (5 verses) beginning, "I'll sing you a dacent song, that was made by a Paddy's pate," and ending thus:—

> *Each Irish boy then took a pride to prove himself a man,*
> *To serve a friend, and beat a foe it always was the plan*
>   *Of a rale ould Irish Gintleman, the boy of the*
>   *olden time.*

(Or, as Wm. Hy. Murray, of Edinburgh, used to say, in his unequalled "Old Country Squire," "A smile for a friend, a frown for a foe, and a full front for every one!")

At the beginning of the Crimean War appeared another parody, ridiculing the Emperor Nicholas, as "The Fine Old Russian Gentleman" (it is in Berger's *Red, White, and Blue*, 467); and clever Robert B. Brough, in one of his more bitter moods against "The Governing Classes," misrepresented the "Fine Old English Gentleman" (*Ibid*, p. 733), as splenetically as Charles Dickens did in *Barnaby Rudge*, chapter 47.

Page 20 (original). Pan *leave piping, &c.*

Given already, in our Appendix to the *Westminster Drollery*, p. liv., with note of tune and locality. See Additional Note in Part 3 of present Appendix.

Page 129 (orig. 26). *Why should we boast of* Arthur, *&c.*

There are so many differences in the version printed in the *Antidote agt. Melancholy* from that already given in *Merry Drollery, Compleat*, p. 309, (cp. Note, p. 399), that we give the former uncurtailed.

Along with the music in *Pills to p. Mel.*, iii. 116, 1719, are the extra verses (also in *Wit and Mirth*, 1684, p. 29?) agreeing with the *Antidote;* as does the version in *Old Bds.*, i. 24, 1723.

Another old ballad, in the last-named collection, p. 153, is upon "King Edward and Jane Shore; in Imitation, and to the Tune of, St. *George* and the *Dragon.*" It begins (in better version): —

Why should we boast of Lais *and her knights,*
Knowing such Champions entrapt by Whorish Lights?
Or why should we speak of Thais *curled Locks,*
Or Rhodope, *&c.*

Roxb. Coll., iii. 258, printed in 1671. Also in *Pills*, with music, iv. 272. The authorship of it is ascribed to SAMUEL BUTLER, in the volume assuming to be his "Posthumous Works" (p. iii., 3rd edition, 1730); but this ascription is of no weight in general.

In Edm. Gayton's *Festivous Notes upon Don Quixot*, 1654, p. 231, we read:—"'Twas very proper for these Saints to alight at the sign of St. *George*, who slew the Dragon which was to prey upon the Virgin: The truth of which story hath been abus'd by his own country-men, who almost deny all the particulars of it, as I have read in a scurrilous Epigram, very much impairing the credit and Legend of St. *George;* As followeth,

T*Hey say there is no* Dragon,
 Nor no Saint George *'tis said.*
Saint George *and* Dragon *lost,*
 Pray Heaven there be a Maid!

But it was smartly return'd to, in this manner,

S*Aint* George *indeed is dead,*
 And the fell Dragon *slaine;*
The Maid *liv'd so and dyed,—*
 She'll ne'r do so againe."

Somewhat different is the earlier version, in *Wit's Recreations*, 1640-45. (Reprint, p. 194, which see, "To save a maid," &c.) The Answer to it is probably Gayton's own.

Page 133 (orig. 29). *Come hither, thou merriest, &c.*
Issued as a popular broadsheet, printed at London for Thomas Lambert, probably during the lifetime of Charles I., we find this lively ditty of "Blew Cap for Me!" in the Roxburghe Coll., i. 20, and in the Bd. Soc. Reprint, vol. i. pp. 74-9. Mr. Chappell mentions that the tune thus named "is included in the various editions of *The Dancing Master* from 1650 to 1690; and says, the reference to 'when our good king was in Falkland town,' [in the *Antidote* it reads " our good *knight*," line 13] may supply an approximate date to the composition." We believe that it must certainly have been before the Scots sold their king for the base bribe of money from the Parliamentarians, in 1648, when " Blew caps" became hateful to all true Cavaliers. The visit to Falkland was in 1633, so the date is narrowed in compass. From the Black-letter ballad we gain a few corrections: *drowne*, for dare, in 4th line; long *lock'd*, 26th line; for *further exercises*, 28th; *Mistris* (so we should read *Maitresse*, not *a metrel*), 29th; *Pe gar* me do love you (not " Dear"), 30th; *she* replide. The First Part ends with the Irishman. The Second Part begins with two verses not in the *Antidote* :—

A Dainty spruce Spanyard, with haire black as jett,
  long cloak with round cape, a long Rapier and Ponyard;
Hee told her if that she could Scotland forget,
  hee'd shew her the Vines as they grow in the Vineyard.
    " *If thou wilt abandon*
      this Country so cold,
    I'll show thee faire Spaine,
      and much Indian gold."
    But stil she replide, " *Sir,*
      I pray let me be ;
    Gif ever I have a man,
      Blew-cap for me."

A haughty high German of Hamborough towne,
  a proper tall gallant, with mighty mustachoes ;

He weepes if the Lasse vpon him doe but frowne,
  yet he's a great Fencer that comes to ore-match vs.
    But yet all his fine fencing
      Could not get the Lasse;
    She deny'd him so oft,
      that he wearyed was;
    For still she replide, "Sir,
      I pray let me be;
    Gif ever I have a man,
      Blew-cap for me.

In the Netherland Mariner's Speech we find for the fifth line of verse, "*Isk* will make thee," *said* he, "sole Lady," &c. Another verse follows it, before the conclusion:—

These sundry Sutors, of seuerall Lands,   [4]
  did daily solicite this Lasse for her fauour:
And euery one of them alike vnderstands
  that to win the prize they in vaine did endeauour:
    For she had resolued
      (as I before said)
    To haue bonny Blew-cap,
      or else bec a maid.
    Vnto all her suppliants
      still replyde she,
    " Gif ever I have a man,
      Blew-cap for me."

At last came a Scottish-man (*with a blew-cap*),
  and he was the party for whom she had tarry'd;
To get this blithe bonny Lasse 'twas his gude hap,—
  they gang'd to the Kirk, & were presently marry'd.
    I ken not weele whether
      it were Lord or Leard; [Laird]
    They caude him some sike
      a like name as I heard;
    To chuse him from au
      She did gladly agree,—
    And still she cride, " Blew-cap,
      th'art welcome to mee."

The song is also reprinted for the Percy Society, (Fairholt's *Costume*), xxvii. 130, as well as in Evans' *O. Bds.*, iii. 245. Compare John Cleavland's "Square Cap,"— "Come hither, *Apollo's* bouncing girl."

Page 135 (orig. 30). *The Wit hath long beholden been.*

In Harleian MS. No. 6931, where it is signed as by DR. W. STRODE.

The tune of this is "The Shaking of the Sheets," according to a broadside printed for John Trundle (1605-24, before 1628, as by that date we believe his widow's name would have been substituted). We find it reprinted by J. P. Collier in his *Book of Roxburghe Ballads*, p. 172, 1847, as "The Song of the Caps." In an introductory note, we gather that "This spirited and humorous song seems to have been founded, in some of its points, upon the 'Pleasant Dialogue or Disputation between the Cap and the Head,' which prose satire went through two editions, in 1564 and 1565: (see the Bridgewater Catalogue, p. 46.) It is, however, more modern, and certainly cannot be placed earlier than the end of the reign of Elizabeth. It may be suspected that it underwent some changes, to adapt it to the times, when it was afterwards reprinted; and we finally meet with it, but in a rather corrupted state, in a work published in 1656, called 'Sportive Wit: the Muses Merriment, a new Spring of Lusty Drollery,' &c." [p. 23.] It appears, with the music, in *Pills*, iv. 157; in Percy Society's "Costume," 1849, 115, with woodcuts of several of the caps mentioned.

In *Sportive Wit*, 1656, p. 23, is a second verse (coming before "The Monmouth Cap," &c.) :—

> 2.—*The Cap doth stand, each man can show,*
> *Above a Crown, but Kings below:*
> *The Cap is nearer heav'n than we;*
> *A greater sign of Majestie:*
> *When off the Cap we chance to take,*
> *Both head and feet obeysance make;*
>   For any Cap, &c.

In our 3rd verse, it reads :—ever *brought*, The *quilted*, Furr'd ; *crewel* ; 4th verse, line 6, of *(some say)* a horn. 5th verse, crooked *cause aright ; Which, being round and endless, knows* ǁ *To make as endless any cause* [A better version]. 6th, *findes* a mouth ; 7th, The *Motley Man* a Cap ; [for lines 3, 4, compare Shakespeare, as to it taking a wise man to play the fool,] like *the Gyant's* Crown. 8th, Sick-*mans ;* When *hats in Church* drop off apace, *This Cap ne'er leaves the* head *uncas'd*, Though he be *ill ;* [two next verses are expanded into three, in *Sp. Wit.*] 11th, none but *Graduats* [N.B.] ; *none* covered are ; But *those that* to ; *go* bare. *This* Cap, *of all the Caps that be,* Is *now ; high* degree.

Page 139 (orig. 37). *Once I a curious eye did fix.*

This is in THOMAS WEAVER'S *Songs and Poems of Love and Drollery,* p. 16, 1654. Elsewhere attributed to JOHN CLEVELAND (who died in 1658), and printed among his Poems "*J. Cleavland Revived*" p. 106, 3rd edit. 1662), as "The Schismatick," with a trashy fifth verse (not found elsewhere) :—

> *I heard of one did touch,*
> *He did tell as much,*
> *Of one that would not crouch*
>   *At* Communion ;
> *Who thrusting up his hand*
>   *Never made a stand*
> *Till he came where her f—— had union ;*
> *She without all terrour,*
> *Thought it no errour,*
> But did laugh till the tears down did trickle,
> Ha, ha, ha, Rotundus, Rotundus, 'tis you that my spleen doth tickle.

It is likewise in the *Rump* collection, i. 223, 1662 ; *Loyal Sgs.,* i. 131, 1731.

Page 139 (orig. 47), *I's not come here to tauk of* Prut.

By BEN JONSON. This is the song of the Welshmen,

Evan, Howell, and Rheese, alternately, in Praise of Wales, sung in an Anti-Masque "For the Honour of Wales," performed before King James I. on Shrove Tuesday, 1618-19. The final verse is omitted from the *Antidote against Melancholy*. It is this (sung by Rheese) :—

*Au, but what say yow should it shance too,
That we should leap it in a dance too,
And make it you as great a pleasure,
If but your eyes be now at leisure ;
As in your ears s'all leave a laughter,
To last upon you six days after?
Ha ! well-a-go to, let us try to do,
As your old* Britton, *things to be writ on.*

CHORUS.—*Come, put on other looks now,
And lay away your hooks now ;
And though yet yow ha' no pump, sirs,
Let 'em hear that yow can jump, sirs,
Still, still, we'll toudge your ears,
With the praise of her thirteen s'eeres.*

(See Col. F. Cunningham's "Mermaid" Ben Jonson, iii. 130-2, for Gifford's Notes.) With a quaint old woodcut of a strutting Welshman, in cap and feather, the song re-appears in *"Recreations for Ingenious Head-pieces,* 1645 *(Wits Recreations,* Reprint, p. 387).

Page 143. *Old Poets Hipocrin admire.*

This is attributed to THOMAS RANDALL, or RANDOLPH (died 1634-5), in *Wit and Mirth,* 1684. p. 101 : But to N. N., along with music by Hy. Lawes, in his *Ayres,* Book ii. p. 29, 1655. It is also in *Parnassus Biceps,* 1656, p. 158, *"All* Poets," &c., and in *Sportive Wit,* p. 60.

Page 144. *Hang the Presbyter's Gill.*

With music in *Pills,* vi. 182; title, "The Presbyter's Gill :" where we find three other verses, as 4th, 5th, and 7th :—

4.

The stout-brested Lombard, *His brains ne'er incumbred,*
  With drinking of Gallons three ;
Trycongius *was named, And by* Cæsar *famed,*
  Who dubb'd him Knight Cap-a-pee.

5.

If then Honour be in't, Why a Pox should we stint
  Ourselves of the fulness it bears ?
H' has less Wit than an Ape, In the blood of a Grape,
  Will not plunge himself o'er Head and Ears.

7.

See the bold Foe appears, May he fall that him Fears,
  Keep you but close order, and then
We will give him the Rout, Be he never so stout[,]
  And prepare for his Rallying agen.

8 (Final).

Let's drain the whole Cellar, &c.

The accumulative progression, humourously exaggerated, is to be seen employed in other Drinking Songs; notably in "Here's a Health to the Barley-Mow, my brave boys!" (still heard at rural festivals in East Yorkshire, and printed in J. H. Dixon's *Bds. & Sgs. of the Peasantry,* Bell's annotated edit., p. 159) and "Bacchus Overcome," beginning "My Friend and I, we drank," &c. (in *Coll. Old Bds.,* iii. 145, 1725.)

Page 145.   *'Tis Wine that inspires.*

With music by Henry Lawes, in his Select Ayres, i. 32, 1653, entitled "The Excellency of Wine:" the author was "LORD BROUGHALL" [query, Broghill?].

(Page, in original, 55.)   *Let the bells ring.*

See Introduction to our *Westminster-Drollery* Reprint, pp. xxxvii-viii. Although not printed in the first edition of his "Spanish Curate," it is so entirely in the spirit of JOHN FLETCHER that we need not hesitate to assign it to him: and he died in 1625.

Page 146. *Bring out the [c]old Chyne.*

With music, by Dr. John Wilson, in John Playford's *Select Ayres*, 1659, p. 86, entitled Glee to the Cook. A poem attributed to Thomas Flatman, 1655, begins, "A Chine of Beef, God save us all!"

Page 147. *In Love? away! you do me wrong.*

Given, with music by Henry Lawes, in his *Select Ayres*, Book iii. p. 5, 1669. The author of the words was Dr. HENRY HUGHES. We do not find the burden, "Come, fill's a Cup," along with the music.

(Page 65, orig.) *He that a Tinker, a Tinker &c.*

See *Choyce Drollery*, 52, and note on p. 289.

Page 149, line 8th, *Now that the Spring, &c.*

This was written by WILLM. BROWNE, author of "Britannia's Pastorals," and therefore dates before 1645. See Additional Note, late in Part IV., on p. 296 of *M. D. C.*

Page 149. *You Merry Poets, old boys.*

Given, with music by John Hilton, in his *Catch that Catch Can*, 1652, p. 7. Also in Walsh's *Catch-Club*, ii. 13, No. 24.

Page 150. *Come, come away, to the Tavern, I say.*

By Sir JOHN SUCKLING, in his unfinished tragedy "The Sad One," Act iv. sc. 4, where it is sung by Signior Multecarni the Poet, and two of the actors; but without the final couplet, which recalls to memory Francis's rejoinder in Henry IV., pt. i. Suckling was accustomed to introduce Shakesperian phrases into his plays, and we believe these two lines are genuine. We find the Catch, with music by John Hilton in that composer's *Catch that Catch Can*, 1652, p. 15. (Also in Playford's *Musical Companion*, 1673, p. 24.)

Captain William Hicks has a dialogue of Two Parliamentary Troopers, beginning with the same first line, in *Oxford Drollery*, i. 21, 1671. Written before 1659, thus:

> Come, come away, to the Tavern, I say,
>   Whilst we have time and leisure for to think;
> I find our State lyes tottering of late,
>   And that e're long we sha'n't have time to drink.
>   Then here's a health to thee, to thee and me,
>   To me and thee, to thee and me, &c.

Page 151. *There was an Old Man at* Walton *Cross*.

This should read "*Waltham* Cross." By RICHARD BROME, in his comedy of "The Jovial Crew," Act ii., 1641, wherein it is sung by Hearty, as "t'other old song for that" [the uselessness of sighing for a lass]; to the tune of "Taunton Dean," (see Dodsley's *Old Plays*, 1st edit., 1744, vi. 333). With music by John Hilton, it is given in J. H.'s *Catch that Catch Can*, 1652, p. 31. It is also in Walsh's *Catch Club* (about 1705) ii. 17, No. 43.

Page 151. *Come, let us cast dice, who shall drink.*

In J. Hilton's *Catch that Catch Can*, 1652, p. 55, with music by William Lawes; and in John Playford's *Musical Companion*, 1673, p. 24.

Page 151. *Never let a man take heavily, &c.*

With music by William Lawes, in Hilton's *Catch that Catch Can*, 1652, p. 38.

Page 152. *Let's cast away care, and merrily sing.*

With music by William Lawes, in Hilton's *Catch that*

Catch Can, 1652, p. 37. Wm. Chappell gives the words of four lines, omitting fifth and sixth, to accompany the music of Ben Jonson's "Cock Lorrell," in *Pop. Mus. of O. T.*, 161 (where date of the *Antidote* is accidentally misprinted 1651, for 1661).

Page 152. *Hang sorrow, and cast away care.*

With music by William Lawes, in Hilton's *Catch that Catch Can*, 1652, p. 39. The words alone in *Windsor Drollery*, 140, 1672. Richard Climsall, or Climsell, has a long ballad, entitled "Joy and Sorrow Mixt Together," which begins,

> *HAng Sorrow! let's cast away care,*
>   *for now I do mean to be merry;*
> *Wee'l drink some good Ale and strong Beere,*
>   *With Sugar, and Clarret, and Sherry.*
> *Now Ile have a wife of mine own:*
>   *I shall have no need for to borrow;*
> *I would have it for to be known*
>   *that I shall be married to morrow.*
> Here's a health to my Bride that shall be!
>   come, pledge it, you coon merry blades;
> The day I much long for to see,
>   we will be as merry as the Maides.

Poor fellow! he soon changes his tune, after marriage, although singing to the music of "Such a Rogue would be hang'd,"—better known as "Old Sir Simon the King." Printed by John Wright the younger (1641-83), it survives in the Roxburghe Collection, i. 172, and is reprinted for the Bd. Soc., i. 515. As may be seen, it is totally different from the Catch in Hilton's volume and the *Antidote*; which is also in *Oxford Drollery*, Pt. 3, p. 136, there entitled "A Cup of Sack:—" *Hang Sorrow, cast,*" &c.

It there has two more verses:—

2.

Come Ladd, here's a health to thy Love, [p. 136.]
  Do thou drink another to mine,

> I'le never be strange, for if thou wilt change
>   I'le barter my Lady for thine:
> She is as free, and willing to be
>   To any thing I command,
> I vow like a friend, I never intend
>   To put a bad thing in thy hand:
> Then be as frollick and free   [p. 137.]
>   With her as thou woul'st with thine own,
> But let her not lack good Claret and Sack,
>   To make her come off and come on.
>
> 3
>
> Come drink, we cannot want Chink,
>   Observe how my pockets do gingle,
> And he that takes his Liquor all off
>   I here do adopt him mine ningle:
> Then range a health to our King,
>   I mean the King of October,
> For Bacchus is he that will not agree
>   A man should go to bed sober:
> 'Tis wine, both neat and fine,
>   That is the faces adorning,
> No Doctor can cure, with his Physick more sure,
>   Than a Cup of small Beer in the morning.

This shows how a great man's gifts are undervalued. Christopher Sly was truly wise (yet accounted a Sot and even a Rogue, though "the Slys are no rogues: look in the chronicles! We came in with Richard Conqueror!") when, with all the wealth and luxury of the Duke at command, he demanded nothing so much as "a pot o' the smallest ale." He had good need of it.

Page 152. *My Lady and her Maid, upon a merry pin.*

This meets us earlier, in Hilton's *Catch that Catch Can*, 1651, p. 64, with music by William Ellis. The missing first verse reappears (if, indeed, not a later addition) in *Oxford Drollery*, 1674, Part iii. p. 163, as "made at Oxford many years since:—

> My Lady and her Maid
> Were late at Course-a-Park :
> The wind blew out the candle, and
> She went to bed in the dark,
>
> My Lady, &c. [as in *Antidote ag. Mel.*]

It was popular before December, 1659; allusions to it are in the *Rump*, 1662, i. 369; ii. 62, 97.

Page 153. *An old house end.*

Also in *Windsor Drollery*, 1672, p. 30.

Same p. 153. *Wilt thou lend me thy Mare.*

With music by Edmund Nelham, in John Hilton's *Catch that Catch can*, 1652, p. 78. The Answer, here beginning "Your Mare is lame," &c., we have not met elsewhere. The Catch itself has always been a favourite. In a world wherein, amid much neighbourly kindness, there is more than a little of imposition, the sly cynicism of the verse could not fail to please. Folks do not object to doing a good turn, but dislike being deemed silly enough to have been taken at a disadvantage. So we laugh at the Catch, say something wise, and straightway let ourselves do good-natured things again with a clear conscience.

Page 154. *Good* Symon, *how comes it, &c.*

With music by William Howes, in Hilton's *Catch that Catch can*, 1652, p. 84. Also in Walsh's *Catch-Club*, ii. 77. We are told that the *Symon* here addressed, regarding his Bardolphian nose, was worthy Symon Wadloe,— "Old *Sym*, the King of Skinkers," or Drawers. Possibly some jocular allusion to the same reveller animates the choice ditty (for which see the *Percy Folio MS.*, iv. 124, and *Pills*, iii. 143),

> *Old Sir* Simon *the King!*
> *With his ale-dropt hose,*
> *And his malmesy nose,*
> *Sing hey ding, ding a ding ding.*

We scarcely believe the ascription to be correct, and that "Old Symon the King" originally referred to Simon Wadloe, who kept the "Devil and St. Dunstan" Tavern, whereat Ben Jonson and his comrades held their meetings as The Apollo Club; for which the *Leges Conviviales* were written. Seeing that Wadloe died in 1626, or '27, and there being a clear trace of "Old Simon the King" in 1575, in Laneham's *Kenilworth Letter* (Reprinted for Ballad Society, 1871, p. cxxxi.), the song appears of too early a date to suit the theory. *Tant pis pour les faits.* But consult Chappell's *Pop. Mus.*, 263-5, 776-7.

Same p. 154. *Wilt thou be fatt? &c.*

In 1865 (see his *Bibliog. Account*, i. 25), J. P. Collier drew attention to the mention of Falstaff's name in this Catch; also to the other *Shakesperiana*, viz., the complete song of "Jog on, jog on the footpath way," (p. 156), and the burden of "Three merry boys," to "The Wise-men were but Seven" (*M. D. C.*, p. 232), which is connected with Sir Toby Belch's joviality in *Twelfth Night*, Act ii. 3.

Page 155. *Of all the birds that ever I see.*

With the music, in Chappell's *Pop. Mus. O. T.*, p. 75. This favourite of our own day dates back so early, at least, as 1609, when it appeared in (Thomas Ravenscroft's?) *Deuteromelia; or, the Second Part of Musick's Melodie, &c.*, p. 7. We therein find (what has dropped out, to the damage of our *Antidote* version), as the final couplet:—

Sinamont and ginger, nutmegs and cloves,
And that gave me my jolly red nose.

Of course, it was the spice deserved blame, not the liquor (as Sam Weller observed, on a similar occasion, "Somehow it always *is* the salmon"). Those who remember (at the Johnson in Fleet Street, or among the Harmonist Society of Edinburgh) the suggestive lingering over the first syllable of the word "gin-ger," when "this song is well sung," cannot willingly relinquish the half-line. It is a genuine relic, for it also occurs in Beaumont and Fletcher's Knight of the Burning Pestle," about 1613, Act i. sc. 3; where chirping Old Merrythought, " who sings with never a penny in his purse," gives it thus, while " singing and hoiting " [i.e., skipping] :—

> *Nose, nose, jolly red nose,*
> *And who gave thee this jolly red nose?*
> *Cinnamon and ginger, nutmegs and cloves,*
> *And they gave me this jolly red nose.*

And we know, by *A Booke of Merrie Riddles*, 1630, and 1631, that it was much sung :

> *—then Ale-Knights should*
> *To sing this song not be so bold,*
> *Nutmegs, Ginger, Cinamon and Cloves,*
> *They gave us this jolly red nose.*

Same p. 155. *This Ale, my bonny lads, &c.*

Like Nos. 4, 21, 24, 31, &c., not yet found elsewhere.

Page 156. *What! are we met? Come. &c.*

With music by Thomas Holmes, in Hilton's *Catch that Catch can*, 1652, p. 46.

Same p. 156. *Jog on, jog on the foot path-way.*

The four earliest lines of this ditty are sung by Autolycus the Pedlar, and "picker up of unconsidered trifles," in Shakespeare's *Winter's Tale* (about 1610), Act iv. sc. 2. Whether the latter portion of the song was also by him (nay, more, whether he actually wrote, or merely quoted even the four opening lines), cannot be determined. We prefer to believe that from his hand alone came the fragment, at least—this lively snatch of melody, with good philosophy, such as the Ascetics reject, to their own damage. No wrong is done in accepting the remainder of the song as genuine. The final verse is orthodox, according to the Autolycusian rule of faith. It is in *Windsor Drollery*, p. 30; and our Introduction to *Westminster-Drollery*, p. xxxv.

Page 157. *The parcht earth drinks,* &c.

Compare, with this lame paraphrase of Anacreon's racy Ode, the more poetic version by Abraham Cowley, printed in *Merry Drollery, Compleat*, p. 22 (not in 1661 ed. *Merry D.*) All of Cowley's Anacreontiques are graceful and melodious. He and Thomas Stanley fully entered into the spirit of them, *arcades ambo.*

Same, p. 157. *A Man of Wales,* &c.

We meet this, six years earlier, in *Wits Interpreter*, 1655 edit., p. 285; 1671, p. 290. Our text is the superior.

Page 158. *Drink, drink, all you that think.*

Also found in *Wit and Mirth*, 1684, p. 113.

Page 159. *Welcome, welcome, again to thy wits.*

By JAMES SHIRLEY, (1590-1666) in his comedy, "The Example," 1637, Act v. sc. 3, where it is the Song of Sir Solitary Plot and Lady Plot. Repeated in the *Academy of Complements*, 1670, p. 209. Until after that date, for nearly a century, almost all the best songs had been written for stage plays. It forms an appropriate finale, from the last Dramatist of the old school, to the Restoration merriment, the *Antidote against Melancholy,* of 1661.

In one of the later "Sessions of the Poets" *(vide postea* Part 4, § 2)—probably, of 1664-5,—Shirley is referred to, ungenerously. He was then aged nearly seventy:—

Old Shirley *stood up, and made an Excuse,*
  Because many Men before him had got;
He vow'd he had switch'd and spur-gall'd his Muse,
  But still the dull Jade kept to her old trot.

He is also mentioned, with more reverence implied, by George Daniel of Beswick; and we may well conclude this second part of our Appendix with the final verses from the Beswick MS. (1636-53); insomuch as many Poets are therein mentioned, to whom we return in Section Fourth :—

> *The noble* Overburies *Quill has left*   [verse 20]
> *A better Wife then he could ever find:*
> *I will not search too deep, lest I should lift*
> *Dust from the dead: Strange power, of womankind,*
>   *To raise and ruine; for all he will claime,*
>   *As from that sex; his Birth, his Death, his Fame.*
>
> *But I spin out too long: let me draw up*
> *My thred, to honour names, of my owne time*
> *Without their Eulogies, for it may stop*
> *With Circumstantiall Termes, a wearie Rhime:*
>   *Suffice it if I name 'em; that for me*
>   *Shall stand, not to refuse their Eulogie.*
>
> *The noble* Falkland, Digbie, Carew, Maine,
> Beaumond, Sands, Randolph, Allen, Rutter, May,*
> *The devine* Herbert, *and the* Fletchers *twaine,*
> Habinton, Shirley, Stapilton; *I stay*   [N.B.]
>   *Too much on names; yet may I not forget*
>   Davenant, *and* Suckling, *eminent in witt.*
>
> Waller, *not wants, the glory of his verse;*
> *And meets, a noble praise in every line;*
> *What should I adde in honour? to reherse,*
> *Admired* Cleveland? *by a verse of mine?*
>   *Or give ye glorious Muse of* Denham *praise?*
>   *Soe withering Brambles stand, to liveing Bayes.*
>
> *These may suffice; not only to advance*
> *Our* English *honour, but for ever crowne*

* [In margin, a later-inserted line reads:
   "Godolphin, Cartwright, Beaumont, Montague."]

Poesie, 'bove the reach of Ignorance;
Our dull fooles unmov'd, admire their owne
   Stupiditie; and all beyond their sphere
   As Madnes, and but tingling in the Eare.

[Final Verse.]

Great Flame! whose raies at once have power to peirce
The frosted skull of Ignorance, and close
The mouth of Envie; if I bring a verse
Unapt to move; my admiration flowes
   With humble Love and Zeale in the intent
   To a cleare Rapture, from the Argument.

(G. D.'s "*A Vindication of Poesie.*")

End of Notes to *Antidote.*

APPENDIX. PART 3.

§ 1.—EXTRA SONGS IN THE
WESTMINSTER-DROLLERY, 1674.

"A living Drollery!" (Shakespeare's *Tempest*, Act iii. sc. 3.)

BEFORE concluding our present series, *The Drolleries of the Restoration*, we have gladly given in this volume the fourteen pages of Extra Songs contained in the 1674 edition of *Westminster-Drollery*, Part 1st. Sometimes reported as amounting to "nearly forty" (but, perhaps, this statement referred to the Second Part inclusive), it is satisfactory to have joined these six to their predecessors; especially insomuch that our readers do not, like the original purchasers, have to pay such a heavy price as losing an equal number of pages filled with far superior songs. For, the 1671 Part First contained exactly 124 pages, and the 1674 edition has precisely the same number, neither more nor less. The omissions are not immediately consecutive, (as are the additions, which are gathered in one group in the final sheet, pp. 111-124.) They were selected, with unwise discrimination, throughout the volume. Not fourteen pages of objectionable and relinquishable *facetiæ;* but ten songs, from among the choicest of the poems. Our own readers are in better case, therefore: they gain the additions, without yielding any treasures of verse in exchange.

We add a list of what are thus relinquished from the 1674 edition, noting the pages of our *Westm. D.* on which they are to be found :—

P.   5. Wm. Wycherley's, *A Wife I do hate* - 1671
— 10. Dryden's, *Phillis* Unkind: *Wherever I am* do.
— 15. Unknown, *O you powerful gods,* - - ? do.
— 28. T. Shadwell's, *Thus all our life long,* - 1669
— 30. Dryden's, Cellamina, *of my heart,* - - 1671
— 31. Ditto, *Beneath a myrtle shade,* - - - do.
—116. Ditto, Ditto (almost duplicate), - do.
— 47. Ditto, *Make ready, fair Lady,* - - - 1668
— —. Etherege's, *To little or no purpose,* - - do.
— 91. T. Carew's, *O my dearest, I shall,* &c., bef. 1638
—100. Ditto, or Cary's, *Farewell, fair Saint,* bef. 1652

Thus we see that most of these were quite new when the *Westminster-Drollery* first printed them (in four cases, at least, before the plays had appeared as books): they were rejected three years later for fresh novelties. But the removal of Carew's tender poems was a worse offence against taste.

Except the odd Quakers' Madrigall of "Wickham Wakened" (on p. 120; our p. 188), which is not improbably by Joe Haynes, we believe the whole of the other five new songs of 1674 came from one work. We are unable at once to state the name and author of the drama in which they occur. The five are given (severely mutilated, in two instances) in *Wit at a Venture; or,* Clio's *Privy-Garden,* of the same date, 1674. Here, also, they form a group, pp. 33-42; with a few others that probably belong to the same play, viz., "Too weak are human eyes to pry;" "Oh that I ne'er had known the power of Love;" "Must I be silent? no, and yet forbear;" "Cease, wandering thought, and let her brain" (this is Shirley's, in the "Triumph of Beauty," 1645); "How the vain world ambitiously aspires;" "Heaven guard my fair *Dorinda:*" and, perhaps, "Rise, golden Fame, and give thy name or birth." Titles are added to most of these.

Page 179. *So wretched are the sick of Love*, is, on p. 37 of *Wit at a Venture*, entitled Distempered Love. The third verse is omitted.

Page 181. *To Arms! To Arms! &c.*, on p. 39, entitled The Souldier's Song; 13th line reads "Where *we* must try."

Page 182. *Beauty that it self can kill*, on p. 35; reading, in 20th line, "When the fame and virtue falls ‖ Careless courage, &c.

Page 183. *The young, the fair, &c.*, on p. 33, is entitled *The Murdered Enemy;* reading *Clarissa* for *Camilla;* and giving lines 17th and 19th, "Her beauties" and "Fierce Lions," &c. Line 23rd is "And not to check it in the least."

Page 184. *How frailty makes us to our wrong.*

Called A Moral Song in *Wit at a Venture*, p. 41, which rightly reads "grovel," not "gravel," in line 6; but omits third verse, and all the Chorus.

Page 188. *The Quaker and his Brats.*

We have not seen this elsewhere. Attributed to "the famous actor, JOSEPH HAINES," or "Joe Haynes,"

Who, while alive, in playing took great pains,
Performing all his acts with curious art,
Till Death appear'd, and smote him with his dart.

His portrait, as when riding on a Jack-ass, in 1697, is extant. He died 4th April, 1701, and was mourned by the Smithfield muses.

§ 2—ADDITIONAL NOTES

To the 1671-72 Editions of

WESTMINSTER-DROLLERY.

Page 81. *Is she gone? let her go.*

This is a parody or mock on a black-letter ballad in the Roxburghe Collection, ii. 102, entitled "The Deluded Lasses Lamentation : or, the False Youth's Unkindness to his Beloved Mistress." Its own tune. Printed for P. Brooksby, J. Deacon, J. Blare, J. Black. In four-line verses, beginning :—

> *Is she gone? let her go, I do not care,*
> *Though she has a dainty thing, I had my share :*
> *She has more land than I by one whole Acre,*
> *I have plowed in her field, who will may take her.*

Part I., p. 105. *Hic jacet*, John Shorthose.

The music to this is in Jn. Playford's *Musical Companion*, 1673, p. 34 (as also to "Here lyes a woman," &c. See Appendix to *Westm. Droll.*, p. lviii).

Part I., p. 106. *There is not half so warm, &c.*

See *Choyce Drollery*, 1656, p. 61, *ante*; and p. 293, for note correcting "daily" to "dully" in ninth line.

Part II., p. 74 (App. p. lv.) *As* Moss *caught his Mare.*

Not having had space at command, when giving a short Addit. Note on p. 408 of *M. D. C.*, we now add a nursery rhyme (we should gladly have given another, which mentions catching the mare "Napping up a tree"). Perhaps the following may be the song reported as being sung in South Devon :—

M OSS *was a little man, and a little mare did buy,*
 For kicking and for sprawling none her could come nigh;
She could trot, she could amble, and could canter here and there,
But one night she strayed away—so Moss *lost his Mare.*

Moss *got up next morning to catch her fast asleep,*
And round about the frosty fields so nimbly he did creep.
Dead in a ditch he found her, and glad to find her there,
So I'll tell you by and bye, how Moss *caught his mare.*

Rise! stupid, rise! he thus to her did say,
Arise you beast, you drowsy beast, get up without delay,
For I must ride you to the town, so don't lie sleeping there,
He put the halter round her neck—so Moss *caught his mare.*

As that prematurely wise young sceptic Paul Dombey declared, when a modern-antique Legend was proffered to him, "I don't believe that story!" It is frightfully devoid of *ærugo*, even of *æruca*. It may do for South Devon, and for Aylesbury farmers over their "beer and bacca," but not for us. The true Mosse found his genuine mare veritably "napping" (not dead), up a real tree.

In John Taylor's "*A Swarme of Sectaries and Schismatiqves,*" 1641, his motto is (concerning Sam Howe lecturing from a tub),

The Cobler preaches and his Audience are
As wise as Mosse *was, when he caught his Mare.*

Part II., page 89. *Cheer up, my mates, &c.*

(See Appendix to *Westm. Droll.*, p. lxii.) The author of this frollicsome ditty was no other than ABRAHAM COWLEY (1618-67), dear to all who know his choice "Essays in Prose and Verse," his unlaboured letters, the best of his smaller poems, or the story of his stainless life and gentleness. It is that noble thinker and poet, Walter Savage Landor, who writes, and in his finest mood :—

Appendix.

> *Time has been*
> *When* Cowley *shone near* Milton, *nay, above !*
> *An age roll'd on before a keener sight*
> *Could separate and see them far apart.*
> (*Hellenics*, edit. 1859, p. 258.)

Yet while we yield unquestioningly the higher rank as Poet to John Milton, we hold the generous nature of his rival, Cowley, in more loving regard. He was not of the massive build in mind, or stern unflinching resolution needed for such times as those wherein his lot was cast. When the weakest goes to the wall, amid universal disturbance and selfish warring for supremacy, his was not the strong arm to beat back encroachment. Gentle, affectionate, and truthful, exceptionally pure and single-minded, although living as Queen Henrietta's secretary in her French Court, where impurity of thought and lightness of conduct were scarcely visited with censure, the uncongenial scenes and company around him help to enhance the charm of his mild disposition. Heartless wits might lampoon him, stealthy foes defame him, lest he should gain one favour or reward that they were hankering after. To us he remains the lover of the "Old Patrician trees," the friend of Crashaw and of Evelyn, the writer of the most delightful essays and familiar letters: alas! too few.

The "Song" in *Westminster-Drollery*, ii. 89, set by Pelham Humphrey, is the opening verse of Cowley's "ODE : Sitting and Drinking in the Chair made out of the Reliques of Sir Francis Drake's Ship." [The chair was presented to the University Library, Oxford.]

Corrections: *dull men* are those *who* tarry; and spy *too*. Three verses follow. Of these we add the earliest, leaving uncopied the others, of 21 and 18 lines. They are to be found on p. 9 of Cowley's "Verses written on Several Occasions," folio ed., 1668. The idea of the shipwreck "in the wide Sea of Drink" had been early welcomed by him, and treated largely, Feb. 1638-9, in his *Naufragium Joculare*.

2.

What do I mean: What thoughts do me misguide?
As well upon a staff may Witches ride
  Their fancy'd Journies in the Ayr,
As I sail round the Ocean in this Chair:
  'Tis true; but yet this Chair which here you see,
For all its quiet now and gravitie,
Has wandred, and has travail'd more
Than ever Beast, or Fish, or Bird, or ever Tree before.
In every Ayr, and every Sea 't has been,
'T has compas'd all the Earth, and all the Heavens
  't has seen.
Let not the Pope's it self with this compare,
This is the only Universal Chair.

It must have been written before 1661, as it appears among the "*Choyce Poems, being Songs, Sonnets, &c.*, printed for Henry Brome, (who ten years afterwards published *Westm. Droll.*) at the Gun in Ivie Lane, in that year. It is in the additional opening sheet, p. 13; not found in the 1658 editions of *Choyce Poems*.

· *Westminster-Drollery* Appendix, p. liv. "*The Green Gown,*" Pan, *leave piping, &c.*

Under the title "The Fetching Home of May," we meet an early ballad-form copy in the Roxburghe Collection, i. 535, printed for J. Wright, junior, dwelling at the upper end of the Old Bailey. It begins " Now *Pan* leaves piping," and is in two parts, each containing five verses. Three of these are not represented in the *Antidote* of 1661. Wm. Chappell, the safest of all guides in such matters, notes that "the publisher [of the broadside] flourished in and after 1635. No clue remains to the authorship." (*Bd. Soc.* reprint, iii. 311, 1875.)

As in the case of the companion-ditty, "Come, Lasses and Lads" (*Westm. Droll.*, ii. 80), we may feel satisfied that this lively song was written before the year 1642. No hint of the Puritanic suppression of Maypoles can be discerned in either of them. Such sports were soon afterwards prohibited, and if ballads celebrating their past delights had then been newly written, the author must have yielded to the temptation to gird at the hypocrites and despots who desolated each village green. We cannot regard the *Roxburghe Ballad* as being superior to the *Antidote* version : But they mutually help one another in corrections. We note the chief : first verse, So lively *it* passes; *Good lack*, what paines; 2, *Thus* they so much; 3 (our 4), Came very *lazily*. It is after the five verses that differences are greatest. Our 6th verse is absent, and our 7th appears as the 8th; with new 6th, 7th, 9th, and 10th, which we here give, but print them to match our others :

THE FETCHING HOME OF MAY.
(The Second Part.)

6.

This Maying so pleased || Most of the fine lasses,
    That they much desired to fetch in May flowers,
For to strew the windows and such like places,
    Besides they'l have May bows, fit for shady bowers.
But most of all they goe || To find where Love doth growe,
Each young man knowes 'tis so, || Else hee's a clowne :
For 'tis an old saying, || "There is great joying,
When maids go a Maying," || *They'll have a greene gowne*.

7.

Maidens and young men goe, || As 'tis an order old,
    For to drink merrily and eat spiced cakes;
The lads and the lasses their customs wil hold,
    For they wil goe walk i' th' fields, like loving mates :
Em calls for *Mary*, || And *Ruth* calls for *Sarah*,
Iddy calls for *Har[r]y* || To man them along :
Martin calls *Marcy*, || *Dick* calls for *Debary*,
Then they goe lovingly || *All in a throng.*

8. (*Westm. Droll.*, 7.)

The bright *Apollo* || Was all the while peeping
    To see if his *Daphne* had bin in the throng,

And, missing her, hastily downward was creeping,
  For [*Thetis*] imagined [he] they tarri'd too long.
Then all the troope mourned ‖ And homeward returned,
For *Cynthia* scorned ‖ To smile or to frowne :
Thus did they gather May ‖ All the long summer's day,
And went at night away, ‖ *With a green gowne*.

9.

Bright *Venus* still glisters, Out-shining of *Luna* ;
  Saturne was present, as right did require ;
And he called *Jupiter* with his Queen *Juno*,
  To see how Dame *Venus* did burn in desire :
Now *Jove* sent *Mercury* ‖ To *Vulcan* hastily,
Because he should descry [decoy] Dame *Venus* down :
Vulkan came running, On *Mars* he stood frowning,
Yet for all his cunning, ‖ *Venus had a greene gowne*.

10.

Cupid shootes arrowes At *Venus* her darlings,
  For they are nearest unto him by kind :
Diana he hits not, nor can he pierce worldlings,
  For they have strong armour his darts to defend :
The one hath chastity, And *Cupid* doth defie ;
The others cruelty ‖ makes him a clowne :
But leaving this I see, From *Cupid* few are free,
And ther's much courtesie *In a greene gowne*.

FINIS.

We have a firm conviction that these verses (not including "The bright Apollo") were unauthorized additions by an inferior hand, of a mere ballad-monger. We hold by the *Antidote*.

Part II., 100, Appendix, p. lxviii. Here is the old ballad mentioned, from our own black-letter copy. Compare it with *W. D.* :—

The Devonshire Damsels' Frollick.

Being an Account of nine or ten fair Maidens, who went one Evening lately, to wash themselves in a pleasant River, where they were discovered by several Young Men being their familiar Acquaintances, who took away their Gowns and Petticoats, with their Smocks and Wine and good Chear; leaving them a while in a most melancholly condition.

To a pleasant New Play-house Tune [music is given]: Or, Where's my Shepherd ?
This may be Printed. R[obt]. P[ocock, 1685-8].

TOm *and* William *with* Ned *and* Ben,
   In all they were about nine or ten ;
Near a trickling River endeavour to see
   a most delicate sight for men ;
Nine young maidens they knew it full well,
   Sarah, Susan, *with bonny* Nell,
      and all those others whose names are not here,
      intended to wash in a River clear.
Simon *gave out the report*
   the rest resolving to see the sport   [,]
The Young freely repairing declaring
   that this is the humours of Venus *Court*   [,]
In a Bower those Gallants remaine
   seeing the Maidens trip o're the plain   [:]
They thought no Body did know their intent
   as merrily over the Fields they went

Nell *a Bottle of Wine did bring*
   with many a delicate dainty thing   [,]
Their Fainting Spirits to nourish and cherish
   when they had been dabbling in the Spring   [:]
They supposing no Creature did know
   to the River they merrily goe,
When they came thither and seeing none near   [,]
   Then under the bushes they hid their chear.

Then they stripping of all their Cloaths
  their Gowns their Petticoats Shooes & Hose [,]
Their fine white smickits then stripping & skipping[,]
  no Body seeing them they suppose [,]
Sarah enter'd the River so clear
  and bid them follow they need not fear [,]
For why the Water is warm they replyed [,]
  then into the River they sweetly glide.

Finely bathing themselves they lay
  like pretty Fishes they sport and play [,]
Then let's be merry[,] *said* Nancy, *I fancy,*
  it's seldom that any one walks this way [.]
Thus those Females were all in a Quill
  and following on their Pastime still [,]
All naked in a most dainty trim
  those Maidens like beautifull Swans did swim.

Whilst they followed on their Game [,]
  out came sweet William *and* Tom *by name.*
They took all their Clothing and left nothing [t' 'em:]
  Maids was they not Villains and much to blame[?]
Likewise taking their Bottle of Wine [,]
  with all their delicate Dainties fine [:]
Thus they were rifled of all their store,
  was ever poor Maidens so serv'd before.

From the River those Maidens fair
  Return'd with sorrow and deep despair [;]
When they seeing, brooding[,] *concluding*
  that somebody certainly had been there [,]
With all their Treasure away they run [,]
  Alas [!] *said* Nelle[,] *we are undone,*
Those Villains I wish they were in the Stocks,
  that took our Petticoats Gowns and Smocks.

Then Sweet Sarah *with modest* Prue
  they all was in a most fearful Hue [,]
Every Maiden replying and crying
  they did not know what in the world to do [.]

> *But what laughing was there with the men*
> * in bringing their Gowns and Smocks again* [,]
> *The Maidens were modest & mighty mute* [,]
> * and gave them fine curtsies and thanks to boot.*

Printed for P. Brooksby at the Golden Ball in Pye Corner [1672-95.]

Part II., pp, 120, 123 (App. p. lxxii.) *O Love if e'er, &c.* There is a parody or "Mock" to this, beginning "O Mars, if e'er thoult ease a blade,'' and entitled "The Martial Lad,' in Wm. Hicks' *London Drollery*, 1673, p. 116.

End of Notes to *Westminster-Drollery*.

APPENDIX. PART 4.

§ 1.—EXTRA SONGS IN THE

MERRY DROLLERY, 1661.

(Not repeated in the 1670 and 1691 Editions.)

Falstaff.—" If Sack and Sugar be a fault, Heaven help the wicked."   (*Henry IV.*, Pt. 1, Act ii. Sc. 4.)

COLLECTIONS of Songs, depending chiefly on the popularity of such as are already in vogue, or of others that promise fairly to please the reader, are necessarily of all books the most liable to receive alterations when re-issued. Thus we ourselves possess half-a-dozen editions of *the Roundelay*, and also of the *Bullfinch*, both undated eighteenth-century songsters ; each copy containing a dozen or more of Songs not to be found in the others. Our *Merry Drollery* is a case in point. As already mentioned, there is absolutely no difference between the edition of 1670 and 1691 of *Merry Drollery, Compleat,* except the title-page. It was a well-understood trade stratagem, to re-issue the unsold sheets, those of 1670, with a freshly-dated title-page, as in 1691; so to catch the seekers after novelty by their most tempting lure. Even the two pages of "List of New Books" (reprinted conscientiously by ourselves in *M. D., C.*, pp. 358, 359) are identical in both !

We take credit beforehand for the readers' satisfaction at our providing such a *Table of First Lines*, as we hereafter give, that may enable him easily and convincedly to understand the alterations made from the 1661 edition of *Merry Drollery*, both parts, when it was re-issued in a single volume, paged consecutively, in 1670 and 1691. It is more difficult to understand *why* the changes were made, than thus to see what they were. 1. It could not have been from modesty: although some objectionable pieces were omitted, others, quite as open to censure, were newly admitted instead. 2. Scarcely could it have been that as political satires they were out of date (except in the case of the Triumph over The Gang—England's Woe —and Admiral Dean's Funeral: our pp. 198, 218, 206); for in the later volume are found other songs on events contemporary with these, which, being rightly considered to be of abiding interest, were retained. 3. It was not that the songs rejected were too common, and easily attainable; for they are almost all of extreme rarity, and now-a-days not procurable elsewhere. 4. It must have been a whim that ostracised them, and accepted novelties instead! At any rate, here they are! As in the case of the sheet from *Westminster-Drollery*, 1674 (see p. 177), readers possess the Extra Songs of both early and late editions, along with all that are common to both, and this without confusion.

Almost all of these *Merry Drollery* Extra Songs were written before the Restoration; of a few we know the precise date, as of 1653, 1650, 1623, &c. These are chiefly on political events, viz. the Funeral of Admiral Dean, so blithely commented on, with forgetfulness of the man's courage and skill while remembering him only as an associate of rebels; the story of England's Woe (certainly published before the close of 1648), with scorn against the cant of Prynne and Burton; the noisy, insensate revel of the song on the Goldsmith's Committee (1647, p. 237), where we can see in the singers such unruly cavaliers as those who brought discredit and ruin; as also in the coarser "Letany" (on our page 241); and in the still earlier description of New England (before 1643), which forms a most important addition to the already rich material gathered from these contemporary records, shewing the views entertained of the nonconforming and irreconcileable zealots who held close connection with the discontented Dutchmen. Although caricatured and maliciously derisive, it is impossible to doubt that we have here a group of portraits sufficiently life-like to satisfy those who beheld the originals. As to the miscellaneous pieces, the Sham-Tinker, who comes to "Clout the Cauldron," has genuine mirth to redeem the naughtiness. Dr. Corbet's (?) "Merrie Journey into France" is crammed full of pleasantry, and while giving a record of sights that met the traveller, enlivens it with airy gaiety that makes us willing companions. This, with variations, may be met with elsewhere in print; but not so the delightfully sportive invitation of The Insatiate Lover to his Sweetheart, "Come hither, my own Sweet Duck" (p. 247). To us it appears among the best of these thirty-five additions: musical and fervent, without coarseness, the song of an ardent lover, who fears nothing, and is ripe for any adventure that war may offer. One of Rupert's reckless Cavaliers may have sung this to his Mistress. Of course it would be unfair to blame him for not being awake to the higher beauty of such a sentiment as Montrose felt and inspired :—

> But if thou wilt prove faithful, then,
>   And constant of thy word,
> I'll make thee glorious by my pen,
>   And famous by my sword :
> I'll serve thee in such noble ways
>   Was never heard before;
> I'll crown and deck thee all with bays,
>   And love thee more and more.

Or, as Lovelace nobly sings :—

> Tell me not, sweet, I am unkinde,
>   That from the nunnerie
> Of thy chaste breast and quiet minde
>   To warre and armes I flie.

> True : a new Mistresse now I chase,
>   The first foe in the field;
> And with a stronger faith embrace
>   A sword, a horse, a shield.

> Yet this inconstancy is such
>   As you too shall adore;
> I could not love thee, dear, so much,
>   Lov'd I not Honour more.

C'est magnifique! mais ce n'est pas—L'amour. At least, and we imply no more, Lovelace and those who act on such high principles, find their *Lux Casta* marrying some neighbouring rival. But we may be sure that the singer of our *Merry Drollery* ditty won *his* Lass, literally in a canter.

Part I., p. 2 [our p. 195.] *A Puritan of late.*

Compare John Cleveland's "Zealous Discourse between the Independent-Parson and Tabitha," "Hail Sister," &c. (*J. C. Revived*, 1662, p. 108); and also the superior piece of humour, beginning, "I came unto a Puritan to wooe," *M. D., C.,* p. 77. The following description of the earlier sort of Precisian, ridiculous but not yet dangerous, is by Richard Brathwaite, and was printed in 1615:—

To the Precisian.

> *F*Or the Precisian that dares hardly looke,
>   (Because th' art pure, forsooth) on any booke,
> Save Homilies, and such as tend to th' good
> Of thee and of thy zealous brother-hood:
> Know my Time-noting lines ayme not at thee,
> For thou art too too curious for mee.
> I will not taxe that man that's wont to slay
> " His Cat for killing mise on th' Sabbath day: ["]
> No ; know my resolution it is thus,
> I'de rather be thy foe then be thy pus:
> And more should I gaine by't: for I see,
> The daily fruits of thy fraternity:
> Yea, I perceiue why thou my booke should shun,
> " Because there's many faultes th' art guiltie on :"

Therefore with-drawe, by me thou art not call'd,
Yet do not winch (good iade) when thou art gall'd,
I to the better sort my lines display,
I pray thee then keep thou thy selfe away.
    (*A Strappado for the Diuell*, 1615.)

The sixth line offers another illustration of what has been ably demonstrated by J. O. Halliwell, commenting on the *"too-too* solid flesh" of *Hamlet*, Act i. sc. 2, in Shakespeare Soc. Papers, i. 39-43, 1844.

By it being printed within double quotational commas, we see that the reference to a Puritan hanging his cat on a Monday, for having profanely caught a mouse on the Sabbath-Sunday, was already an old and familiar joke in 1615. James Hogg garbled a ballad in his *Jacobite Relics*, 1819, i. 37, as "*There was a* Cameronian *Cat, Was hunting for a prey,*" &c., but we have a printed copy of it, dated 1749, beginning "*A Presbyterian Cat sat watching of her prey.*" Also, in a poem "On Lutestrings, Cat-eaten," we read :—

Puss, I will curse thee, maist thou dwell
With some dry Hermit in a Cel,
Where Rat ne're peep'd, where Mouse ne'er fed,
And Flies go supperlesse to bed:
Or with some close par'd Brother, where
Thou'lt fast each Sabbath in the yeare,
Or else, profane, be hang'd on Monday,
For butchering a Mouse on Sunday, &c.
    (*Musarum Deliciæ*, 1656, *p.* 53.)

John Taylor, the Water-Poet, so early as 1620, writes of a Brownist :—

The Spirit still directs him how to pray,
Nor will he dress his meat the Sabbath day,
Which doth a mighty mystery unfold ;
His zeale is hot, although his meat be cold.
Suppose his Cat on Sunday kill'd a rat,
She on the Monday must be hang'd for that.
    (J. P. C.'s *Bibl. Acc.*, ii. 418.)

Page 11 [our 197]. *I dreamt my Love, &c.*

In the *Percy Folio MS.* (about 1650) p. 480 ; E. E. T. S., iv. 102, with a few variations, one of which we have noted in margin of p. 181. The industrious editors of the printed text of the *Percy Folio MS.* were not aware of the fact that many of the shorter pieces were already to be found in print; but this is no wonder. They are not easy to discover (see next p. 352), and although we ourselves note occasionally " not found elsewhere," it is with the remembrance that a happy " find" may yet reward a continuous search hereafter. We do not despair of recovering even the lost line of " The Time-Poets."

Page 12 [our 198]. *Now* Lambert's *sunk, &c.*

In the 1662 edit. of the *Rump,* i. 330, and in *Loyal Sgs.,* 1731, i. 219. It may have been written so early as Jan. 15th, 1659-60, when Col. Lambert had submitted to the Parliament, on finding the troops disinclined to support him unanimously. Another ballad made this inuendo :—

> John Lambert *at* Oliver's *Chair did roare,*
> *And thinks it but reason upon this score,*
> *That* Cromwell *had sitten in his before ;*
>   Still blessed Reformation.   (*Rump,* ii. 99.)

Fairfax had returned to his house, and to Monk were given the thanks of the rescued Parliament. As M. de Bordeaux writes of him to Card. Mazarin, at this exact date, " he is now the most powerful subject in the whole nation. Fleetwood, Desborough, and all the others of the same faction are entirely out of employment" (Guizot's *Monk,* 1851, p. 156). Although no mention or definite allusion seems made in the ballad to Monk's attack on the London defences, Feb. 9th, we incline to think this may be nearer to the true date : if it refers to the oath of abjuration, of Feb. 4th, which was offered to Monk, as on March 1st. "Arthur's Court" is an allusion to Sir Arthur Haselrig, "a rapacious, head-strong, and conceited agitator" (*Ibid,* p. 37). Monk had not publicly declared himself for the King until May; but he was seen to be opposed to the Rump by 11th Feb., when its effigies were enthusiastically burnt. Richard Cromwell's abdication had been, virtually, April 22nd, 1659.

Page 32 [204]. *A young man walking all alone.*

This is another of the songs contained in the *Percy Folio MS.* (p. 460; iv. 92 of print); wrongly supposed to be otherwise lost, but imperfect there, our fourth and fifth verses being absent. We cannot accept *"if that I may thy favour haue, thy bewtye to behold,"* as the true reading; while we find *"If that thy favour I may win With thee for to be bold:"* which is much more in the Lover's line of advance. Yet we avail ourselves of the "I am so *mad*" in 3rd verse, because it rhymes with "maidenhead," in *M. D.*, though not suiting with the "honestye" of the *P. F. MS.* The final half-verse is different.

Page 56 [206].   Nick Culpepper *and* Wm. Lilly.

Also in 1662 edition of the *Rump*, i. 308; and *Loyal Songs*, 1731, i. 192. The event referred to happened in June, 1653, the engagement between the English and Dutch fleets commencing on the 2nd, renewed the next day. Six of the Dutch ships were sunk, and twelve taken, with thirteen hundred prisoners. *Blake*, *Monk*, and *Dean* were the English commanders, until *Dean* was killed, the first day. Monk took the sole command on the next. Clarendon gives an account of the battle, and says: "*Dean*, one of the *English* Admirals, was killed by a cannon-shot from the Rear-Admiral of the *Dutch*," before night parted them. "The loss of the *English* was greatest in their General *Dean*. There was, beside him, but one Captain, and about two hundred Common Sea-men killed: the number of the wounded was greater; nor did they lose one Ship, nor were they so disabled but that they followed with the whole fleet to the coast of *Holland*, whither the other fled; and being got into the *Flie* and the *Texel*, the English for some time blocked them up in their own Harbors, taking all such Ships as came bound for those parts. (*His. Reb.*, B. iii. p. 487, ed. 1720.)

Verse 1. Nicholas Culpeper, of Spittle Fields, near London, published his *New Method of Physick*, and Alchemy, in 1654.

As to William Lilly, "the famous astrologer of those times, who in his yearly almanacks foretold victories for the Parliament with so much certainty as the preachers did in their sermons," consult his letter written to Elias Ashmole, and the notes of Dr. Zachary Gray to Butler's *Hudibras*, Part ii. Canto 3. " He lived to the year 1681, being then near eighty years of age, and published predicting almanacks to his death." He was one of the close committee to consult about the King's execution *(Echard)*. He lost much of his repute in 1652; in 1655 he was indicted at Hickes Hall, but acquitted. He dwelt at Hersham, Walton-on-Thames, and elsewhere. Henry Coley followed him in almanack-making, and John Partridge next. In the Honble. Robt. Howard's Comedy, " The Committee," 1665, we find poor Teague has been consulting Lilly:—

> "*I will get a good Master, if any good Master wou'd Get me; I cannot tell what to do else, by my soul, that I cannot; for I have went and gone to one* LILLY'S; *He lives at that house, at the end of another house, By the* May-pole *house; and tells every body by one Star, and t'other Star, what good luck they shall have. But he cou'd not tell nothing for poor Teg.*"
> (*The Committee*, Act i.)

Verse 12. The Master of the Rolls. This was Sir Dudley Digges, builder of Chilham Castle, near Canterbury, Kent, who had in 1627 moved the impeachment of the Duke of Buckingham, and been rewarded with this Mastership.

Verse 18. Alludes to the rigorous suppression of the Play-houses (*vide ante* p. 285, for a descriptive Song); and as we see from verse 17, the Bear-garden, like Rope-dancers and Tumblers, met more tolerance than actors (except from Colonel Pride). Not heels were feared, but heads and hands. Bears, moreover, could not stir up men to loyalty, but tragedy-speeches might. One Joshua Gisling, a Roundhead, kept bears at Paris Garden, Southwark.

23. "Goodman *Lenthall*," "neither wise nor witty," ("that creeps to the house by a back door," *Rump*, ii. 185,) the Speaker of the Commons from 1640 to 1653; Alderman *Allen*, the dishonest and bankrupt goldsmith, both rebuked by *Cromwell*, when he forcibly expelled the Rump. (See the ballad on pp. 62-5 of *M. D., C.*, verses 9 and 10, telling how "*Allen* the coppersmith was in great fear. He had done as [i.e. *us*] much hurt," &c.; also 2, 15, for the dumb-foundered "Speaker without his Mace.") This Downfall of the Rump had been on April 20th, 1653, not quite three months before the funeral of *Dean*. Whoever may have been the writer of this spirited ballad, we believe, wrote the other one also : judging solely by internal evidence.

24. *Henry Ireton*, who married Bridget Cromwell in January, 1646-7, and escaped from the Royalists after having been captured at Naseby, proved the worst foe of Charles, insatiably demanding his death, died in Ireland of the plague, 15th November, 1651. His body was brought to Bristol in December, and lay in state at Somerset House. Over the gate hung the "hatchment" with "*Dulce et decorum est pro patria mori*"—which one of the Cavaliers delightedly translated, "Good it is for his country that he is dead." Like Dean's, two years later, Ireton's body was buried with ostentatious pomp in Henry VII.'s Chapel, (Feb. 6 or 7;) to be ignominiously treated at Tyburn after the Restoration. The choice of so royal a resting-place brought late insult on many another corpse. His widow was speedily married to Charles Fleetwood, before June, 1652.

In verse 26, we cannot with absolute certainty fill the blank. Yet, in the absence of disproof, we can scarcely doubt that the name suppressed was neither *Sexby*, "an active agitator," who, in 1658, employed against Cromwell "all that restless industry which had formerly been exerted in his favour" (Hume's *Hist. Engd.*, cap. lxi.);

nor "Doomsday Sedgwick;" not *Sidney*, staunch Republican, Algernon Sidney, whose condemnation was in 1687 secured most iniquitously, and whose death more disgracefully stains the time than the slaughter of Russell, although sentimentalism chooses the latter, on account of his wife. Sidney was "but a young member" at the Dissolution of 20th April, 1653. Probably the word was *Say*, the notorious "Say and Seale," "Crafty Say," of whom we read :—

> *There's half-witted* Will Say *too,*
> *A right Fool in the Play too,*
> *That would make a perfect Ass,*
>   *If he could learn to Bray too.*

("Chips of the Old Block," 1659; *Rump*, ii. 17.)

Page 64 [213]. *I went from* England, &*c.*

A MS. assertion gives the date of this *"Cantilena de Gallico itinere* as 1623. There seems to us no good reason for doubting that the author was DR. RICHARD CORBET (1582-1635), Bishop of Oxford, afterwards of Norwich. It is signed Rich. Corbett in Harl. MS. No. 6931, fol. 32, *reverso,* and appears among his printed poems, 3rd edit. 1672, p. 129. In *Wit and Mirth,* 1684, p. 76, it is entitled "Dr. Corbet's Journey," &c. But it is fair to mention that we have found it assigned to R. GOODWIN, by the epistolary gossip of inaccurate old Aubrey (see Col. Franc. Cunningham's *"Mermaid edit."* *of Ben Jonson,* i. Memoirs, p. lvii. first note). In a recent edition of Sir John Suckling's Works, 1874, it is printed as if by him ("There is little doubt that it is his"), i. 102, without any satisfactory external evidence being adduced in favour of Suckling. In fact, the external evidence goes wholly against the theory. The very MS. Harl. 367, which is used as authority, is both imperfect and corrupt throughout, as well as anonymous (*ex. gratiæ,* misreading the *Bastern,* for Bastile), and the date on it, 1623, will not suit Suckling at all : though Sir Hy. Ellis is guessed (by his supposed handwriting,) to have attributed it to him. Could it be possible that he was otherwise unacquainted with the poem?

At earlier date than our own copy we find it, by Aug. 30th, 1656, in *Musarum Deliciæ*, p. 17, and in *Parnassus Biceps*, also 1656, p. 24. From this (as well as Harl. MS. 367) we gain corrections printed as our *marginalia*, pp. 214-6: *deserv'd*, for received; *statue* stairs, At *Nôtre Dame;* prate, *doth* please, &c. Harl. MS. 367 reads "The Indian *Roc* [probably it is correct]; and "As great and wise as Luisuè" [Luines, who died 1622]. *Parnassus Biceps* has an extra verse, preceding the one beginning "His Queen," (and Harl. 367 has it, but inferior) :—

> The people don't dislike the youth,
> Alleging reasons. For in truth
> Mothers should honoured be.
> Yet others say, he loves her rather
> As well as ere she loved his father,
> And that's notoriously.

(A similar scandal meets us in other early French reigns: Diana de Poictiers had relations with Henry II., as well as with his father, Francis I., &c.) Compare *West. Droll.*, i. 87, and its Appendix, pp. xxv-vi.

It may be a matter of personal taste, but we cannot recognize the genial Bishop in the "R. C., Gent.," who wrote "The Times Whistle." A reperusal of the E. E. T., 1871, almost *convinces* us that they were not the same person. We must look elsewhere for the author.

In MS., on fly leaf, prefixed to 1672 edition of Dr. Corbet's poems, in the Brit. Mus. (press mark, 238, b. 56), we read :—

> *IF flowing wit, if Verses wrote with ease,*
> *If learning void of pedantry can please,*
> *If much good humour, join'd to solid sense,*
> *And mirth accompanied by Innocence,*
> *Can give a Poet a just right to fame,*
> *Then* CORBET *may immortal honour claim.*
> *For he these virtues had, & in his lines*
> *Poetick and Heroick spirit shines.*

Tho' bright yet solid, pleasant but not rude,
With wit and wisdom equally endued.
Be silent Muse, thy praises are too faint,
Thou want'st a power this prodigy to paint,
At once a Poet, Prelate, and a Saint.
      Signed, John Campbell.

Page 85 [218]. *I mean to speak of* England's, &c.

In the 1662 *Rump*, i. 39; and in *Loyal Songs*, 1731, i. 12. It is also in *Parnassus Biceps* so early as 1656, p. 159, where we obtain a few peculiar readings; even in the first line, which has "of England's fate;" "Prin *and* Burton;" "*wear* Italian *locks for their abuse* (instead of "Stallion locks for a bush"); They'll only have private *keyes* for their use," &c. We are inclined to accept these as correct readings, although our text (agreeing with the *Rump*) holds an intelligible meaning. But those who have inspected the curiosities preserved in the Hôtel de Cluny, at Paris, can scarcely have forgotten "the Italian [pad-] Locks" which jealous husbands imposed upon their wives, as a preservative of chastity, whenever they themselves were obliged to leave their fair helpmates at home; and the insinuation that Prynne and Burton intended to introduce such rigorous precautions, nevertheless retaining "private keyes" for their own use, has a covert satire not improbable to have been intentional. Still, remembering the persistent war waged by these intolerant Puritans against "the unloveliness of love-locks," there are sufficient claims for the text-reading: in their denunciation of curled ringlets "as Stallion locks" hung out "for a bush," or sign of attraction, such as then dangled over the wine-shop door (and may still be seen throughout Italy), although "good wine needs no bush" to advertise it. Instead of "The brownings," (i.e. *The Brownists*, a sect that arose in the reign of Elizabeth, founded by Robt. Browne), in final verse, *Parnassus Biceps* reads "The Roundheads." The poem was evidently written between 1632 and 1642.

Strengthening the probability of "Italian locks" being the correct reading, we may mention in one of the *Rump* ballads, dated 26 January, 1660-1, we find "The Honest Mens Resolution" is to adopt this very expedient :—

> "*But what shall we do with our Wives*
> *That frisk up and down the Town,* ...
> *For such a Bell-dam,*
> *Sayes* Sylas *and* Sam,
> *Let's have an* Italian *Lock !*
> (*Rump* Coll., 1662, ii. 199.)

Page 88 [220]. *Hang Chastity, &c.*

Probably refers to the New Exchange, at Durham House stables (see Additional Note to page 134 of *M. D., C*). Certainly written before 1656. Lines 15 and 32 lend some countenance, by similarity, to the received version in the previous song's sixth verse.

Page 95 [222]. *It was a man, and a jolly, &c.*

With some trifling variations, this re-appears as "The Old Man and Young Wife, beginning "*There was an old man, and a jolly old man, come love me,*" &c., in *Wit and Mirth*, 1684, p. 17. The tune and burden of "The Clean Contrary Way" held public favour for many years. See *Pop, Mus. O. T.*, pp. 425, 426, 781. In the 1658 and 1661 editions of *Choyce Poems* [by John Eliot, and others], pp. 81, are a few lines of verse upon "The Fidler's that were committed for singing a song called, "*The Clean Contrary Way*" :—

> *THe Fidlers must be whipt the people say,*
>   *Because they sung* the clean contrary way ;
> *Which if they be, a Crown I dare to lay*
> *They then will sing* the clean contrary way.
> *And he that did these merry Knaves betray,*
> *Wise men will praise,* the clean contrary way :
> *For whipping them no envy can allay,*   [p. 82.]
> *Unlesse it be* the clean contrary way.
>   *Then if they went the Peoples tongues to stay,*
>   *Doubtless they went* the clean contrary way.

Page 134 [223]. *There was a Lady in this Land.*
Re-appears in *Wit and Drollery*, 1682, p. 291 (not in the 1656 and 1661 editions), as "The Jovial Tinker," but with variations throughout, so numerous as to amount to absolute re-casting, not by any means an improvement: generally the contrary. Here are the second and following verses, of *Wit and Drollery* version :—

> *But she writ a letter to him,*
> *And seal'd it with her hand,*
> *And bid him become a Tinker*
> *To clout both pot and pan.*
>
> *And when he had the Letter,*
> *Full well he could it read;*
> *His Brass and eke his Budget,* [p. 292.]
> *He streight way did provide,*
>
> *His Hammer and his Pincers*
> *And well they did agree*
> *With a long Club on his Back*
> *And orderly came he.*
>
> *And when he came to the Lady's Gates*
> *He knock'd most lustily,*
> *Then who is there the Porter said,*
> *That knock'st thus ruggedly?*
>
> *I am a Jovial Tinker, &c.*

The words of a later Scottish version of "Clout the Cauldron," beginning "Hae ye ony pots or pans, Or ony broken Chandlers?" (attributed by Allan Cunningham to one Gordon) retouched by Allan Ramsay, are in his *Tea-Table Miscellany*, 1724, Pt. i. (p. 96 of 17th edit., 1788.) Burns mentions a tradition that the song " was composed on one of the Kenmure family in the Cavalier time." But the disguised wooer of the later version is repulsed by the lady. Ours is undoubtedly the earlier.

Page 148 [230]. *Upon a Summer's day.*
The music to this is given in Chappell's *Pop. Music of Olden Time* [1855], p. 255, from the *Dancing Master*,

1650-65, and *Musick's Delight on the Cithern*, 1666, where the tune bears the title "Upon a Summer's day." In Pepy's Collectiom, vol. i. are two other songs to the same tune.

Page 153 [Suppl. 3]. *Mine own sweet honey, &c.*
Evidently a parody, or "Mock" of "Come hither, my own," &c., for which, and note, see pp. 247, 367.

Second Part of *Merry Drollery*, 1661.

Page 22 [235]. *You that in love, &c.*
A different version of this same song, only half its length, in four-line stanzas, had appeared in J. Cotgrave's *Wit's Interpreter*, 1655. p. 124. It is also in the 1671 edition, p. 229; and in *Wit and Drollery*, 1682 edit., 287, entitled "The Tobacconist." We prefer the briefer version, although bound to print the longer one; bad enough, but not nearly so gross as another On Tobacco, in *Jovial Drollery*, 1656, beginning "When I do smoak my nose with a pipe of Tobacco."

In the Collection of Songs by the Wits of the Age, appended to *Le Prince d'Amour*, 1660, (but on broadsheet, 1641) we find the following far-superior lyric on

TOBACCO.

TO feed on Flesh is Gluttony,
 It maketh men fat like swine.
But is not he a frugal Man
 That on a leaf can dine !

He needs no linnen for to foul,
 His fingers ends to wipe,
That hath his Kitchin in a Box,
 And roast meat in a Pipe.

The cause wherefore few rich mens sons
 Prove disputants in Schools,
Is that their fathers fed on flesh,
 And they begat fat fools.

This fulsome feeding cloggs the brain,
And doth the stomack cloak;
But he's a brave spark that can dine
With one light dish of smoak.

Audi alterem partem! Five years earlier (May 28th, 1655), William Winstanley had published "A Farewell to Tobacco," beginning :—

FArewell thou Indian smoake, Barbarian vapour,
  Enemy unto life, foe to waste paper,
Thou dost diseases in thy body breed,
And like a Vultur on the purse doth feed.
Changing sweet breaths into a stinking loathing,
And with 3 pipes turnes two pence into nothing;
Grim Pluto *first invented it, I think,*
To poison all the world with hellish stink, &c.

(18 lines more. *The Muses' Cabinet,* 1655, p. 13.)

The three pipes for two-pence was a cheapening of Tobacco since the days, not a century before, when for price it was weighed equally against gold. Our early friend Arthur Tennyson wrote in one of our (extant) Florentine sketch-books the following *impromptu* of his own :—

I Walk'd by myself on the highest of hills,
  And 'twas sweet, I with rapture did own;
As fish-like I opened unto it my gills
And gulp'd it in ecstasy down;
To feel it breathe over my bacca-boiled tongue,
That so much of its fragrance did need,
And brace up completely a system unstrung
For months with this Devil's own Weed.

But even so early as 1639, Thomas Bancroft had printed, (written thirteen years before) in his *First Booke of Epigrammes,* the following,

ON TOBACCO TAKING.

THe Old Germans, that their Divinations made
  From Asses heads upon hot embers laid,
Saw they but now what frequent fumes arise
From such dull heads, what could they prophetize

> *But speedy firing of this worldly frame,*
> *That seemes to stinke for feare of such a flame.*
>
> (*Two Bookes of Epigrammes*, No. 183, sign. E 3.)

We need merely refer to other Epigrams On Tobacco, as "Time's great consumer, cause of idlenesse," and "Nature's Idea," &c., in *Wit's Recreations*, 1640-5, because they are accessible in the recent Reprint (would that it, *Wit Restored* and *Musarum Deliciæ* had been carefully edited, as they deserved and needed to be; but even the literal reprint of different issues jumbled together pell-mell is of temporary service): see vol. ii., pp. 45, 38; and 96, 97, 139, 161, 227, 271. Also p. 430, for the "Tryumph of Tobacco over Sack and Ale," attributed to F. Beaumont, (if so, then before 1616) telling

> *Of the Gods and their symposia;*
> *But Tobacco alone,*
> *Had they known it, had gone*
> *For their Nectar and Ambrosia;*

and vol. i. p. 195, on "A Scholler that sold his Cussion" to buy tobacco. It is but an imperfect version on ii. 96, headed "A Tobacconist" (eight lines), of what we gave from *Le Prince d'Amour*: it begins "All dainty meats I doe defie, || Which feed men fat as swine." Answered by No. 317, "On the Tobacconist," p. 97. By the way: "Verrinus" in *M. D., C.*, pp. 10, 364, consult *History of Signboards*, p. 354—"*Puyk van Verinas en Virginia Tabac;*" Englished, "Tip-Top Varinas," &c.

Page 27 [237]. *Come Drawer, some Wine.*

Probably written by THOMAS WEAVER, and about 1646-8. It is in his collection entitled *Love and Drollery*, 1654, p. 13. Also in the 1662 *Rump*, i. 235; and the *Loyal Garland*, 1686 (Percy Soc. Reprint, xxix. 31). Compare a similar Song (probably founded on this one) by Sir Robt. Howard, in his Comedy, "The Committee," Act iv., "Come, Drawer, some Wine, Let it sparkle and shine,"—or, the true beginning, "Now the Veil is thrown off," &c. The Committee of Sequestration of Estates belonging to the Cavaliers sat at Goldsmith's Hall, while Charles was imprisoned at Carisbrook, in 1647. A ballad of that year, entitled Prattle your pleasure under the Rose," has this verse :—

> *Under the rose be it spoken, there's a damn'd Committee,*
> *Sits in hell* (Goldsmith's Hall) *in the midst of the City,*
> *Only to sequester the poor Cavaliers,—*
> *The Devil take their souls, and the hangmen their ears.*

(As Hamlet says, " You pray not well ! "—but such provocation transfers the blame to those who caused the anger.)

Again, in another Ballad, " I thank you twice," dated 21st August, same year, 1647 :—

> *The gentry are sequestered all ;*
> *Our wives we find at* Goldsmith's Hall,
> *For there they meet with the devil and all,*
>   *Still, God a-mercy, Parliament !"*

On our p. 239, it is amusing to find reference to "the Cannibals of Pym," remembering how Lilburn and others of that party indulged in similar accusations of cannibalism, with specific details against " Bloody Bones, or Lunsford " (*Hudibras*, Pt. iii. canto 2), who was killed in 1644. Thus, " From *Lunsford* eke deliver us, ‖ That eateth up children" (Rump i. 65) ; and Cleveland writes, " He swore he saw, when *Lunsford* fell, ‖ A child's arm in his pocket " (J. C. *Revived, Poems*, 1662, p. 110).

Page 32 [240]. *Listen, Lordings, to my story.*

With the music, this reappears in *Pills to p. Mel.*, 1719, iv. 84, entitled " The Glory of all Cuckolds." Variations few, and unimportant : " The Man in Heaven's " being a very doubtful reading. In the Douce Collection, iv. 41, 42, are two broadsides, A New Summons to Horn Fair, beginning " You horned fumbling Cuckolds, In City, court, or Town," and (To the women) " Come, all you merry jades, who love to play the game," with capital wood-cuts: Jn Pitts, printer. They recal Butler's description of the Skrimmington. The joke was much relished. Thus, in *Lusty Drollery*, 1656, p. 106, is a Pastorall Song, beginning:—

> *A silly poor sheepherd was folding his sheep,*
> *He walked so long he got cold in his feet,*
> *He laid on his coales by two and by three,*
> *The more he laid on*
>   *The Cu-colder was he.*

Three verses more, with the recurring witticism; repeated finally by his wife.

Page 33 [Supp. 6]. *Discourses of late, &c.*

Also, earlier in *Musarum Deliciæ*, 1656, (Reprint, p. 48) as "The Louse's Peregrinations," but without the sixth verse. *Breda*, in the Netherlands, was beseiged by Spinola for ten months, and taken in 1625. *Bergen*, in our text, is a corrupt reading.

Page 38 [241]. *From* Essex-*Anabaptist Lawes*.

We do not understand whence it cometh that the most bitter non-conformity and un-Christian crazes of enthusiasm seem always to have thriven in Essex and the adjacent Eastern coast-counties, so far as Lincolnshire, but the fact is undeniable. Whether (before draining the fens, see "The Upland people are full of thoughts," in *A Crew of kind London Gossips*, 1663, p. 65) this proceeded from their being low-lying, damp, dreary, and dismal, with agues prevalent, and hypochondria welcome as an amusement, we leave others to determine. Cabanis declared that Calvinism is a product of the small intestines; and persons with weak circulation and slow digestion are seldom orthodox, but incline towards fanaticism and uncompromising dissent. Your lean Cassius is a pre-ordained conspirator. Plain people, whether of features or dwelling-place, think too much of themselves. Mountaineers may often hold superstitions, but of the elemental forces and higher worship. They possess moreover a patriotic love of their native hills, which makes them loth to quit, and eager to revisit them, with all their guardian powers: the *nostalgia* and *amor patriæ* are strongest in Highlanders, Switzers, Spanish muleteers, and even Welsh milkmaids. It was from flat-coasted Essex that most of the "peevish Puritans" emigrated to Holland, and thence to America, when discontented with every thing at home.

The form of a Le'tanty or Litany, for such mock-petitions as those in our text (not found elsewhere), and in *M.D.,C.*, p. 174, continued in favour from the uprise of the Independents (simply because they hated Liturgies), for more than a century. In the King's Pamphlets, in the various collections of *Loyal Songs, Songs on affairs of State*, the *Mughouse Diversions, Pills to purge State Melancholly, Tory Pills*, &c., we possess them beyond counting, a few being attributed to Cleveland and to Butler. One, so early as 1600, " Good Mercury, defend us!" is the work of Ben Johnson.

Verse 1.—The " Brownist's Veal " refers to Essex calves, and the scandal of one Green, who is said to have been a Brownist. 4.—"From her that creeps up Holbourne hill:" the cart journey from Newgate to the "tree with three corners" at Tyburn. *Sic itur ad astra*. When, Oct. 1654, Cromwell was thrown from the coach-box in driving through Hyde park, a ballad on " The Jolt on Michaelmas Day, 1654," took care to point the moral:—

> *Not a day nor an hour*
> *But we felt his power,*
>   *And now he would show us his art;*
> *His first reproach*
> *Is a fall from a coach,*
>   And his last will be from a cart.
>   (*Rump* Coll. i. 362.)

Thus also in *M.D.,C.* p. 255:
   Then *Oliver, Oliver*, get up and ride, ...
   Till thou plod'st along to the *Paddington tree*.

5.—" Duke Humphrey's hungry dinner " refers to the tomb popularly supposed to be of "the good Duke"

Humphrey of Gloucester (murdered 1447), but probably of Sir John Beauchamp (Guy of Warwick's son), in Paul's Walk, where loungers whiled away the dinner-hour if lacking money for an Ordinary, and "dined with Duke Humphrey." See Dekker's *Gulls Horn Book*, 1609. cap. iv. And Robt. Hayman writes :—

> *Though a little coin thy purseless pockets line,*
> *Yet with great company thou'rt taken up ;*
> *For often with Duke* Humfray *thou dost dine,*
> *And often with Sir* Thomas Gresham *sup.*
> (R. H.'s *Quodlibets*, 1628.)

"An old Aunt"—this term used by Autolycus, had temporary significance apart from kinship, implying loose behaviour; even as "nunkle" or uncle, hails a mirthful companion. In Roxb. Coll., i. 384, by L[aur.] P[rice], printed 1641-83," is a description of three Aunts, "seldom cleanly," but they were genuine relations, though "the best of all the three" seems well fitted by the *Letany* description: which *may* refer to her.

Page 46 [Supp. p. 7]. *If you will give ear.*

A version of this, slightly differing, is given with the music in *Pills to p. Mell.*, iv. 191. It has the final couplet; which we borrow and add in square brackets.

Page 61 [Supp. 9]. *Full forty times over.*

Earlier by six years, but without the Answer, this had appeared in *Wit and Drollery*, 1656, p. 58; 1661, p. 60. It is also, as "written at Oxford," in second part of *Oxford Drollery*, 1671, p. 97.

Page 62 [Supp. 11]. *He is a fond Lover,* &c.

This, and the preceding, being superior to the other reserved songs might have been retained in the text but for the need to fill a separate sheet. This Answer is in *Love and Mirth* (i.e. *Sportive Wit*) 1650, p. 51.

Merry Drollery, 1661.

Page 64 [Supp. 12]. *If any one do want a House.*
Virtually the same (from the second verse onward) as "A Tenement to Let," beginning "I have a Tenement," &c., in *Pills to p. Mel.*, 1720, vi. 355; and *The Merry Musician* (n. d. but about 1716), i. 43. Music in both.

Page 81 [Supp, 13]. *Fair Lady, for your New, &c,*
Resembling this is "*Ladies, here I do present you, With a dainty dish of fruit,*" in *Wit and Drollery*, 1656, p. 103.

Page 103 [244]. *Among the Purifidian Sect.*
In Harl. MS. No. 6057, fol. 47. There it is entitled "The Puritans of New England."

Page 106 [248]. *Come hither, my own sweet Duck.*
We come delightedly, as a relief, upon this racy and jovial Love-song, which redeems the close of the volume. It has the gaiety and *abandon* of John Fletcher's and Richard Brome's. We have never yet met it elsewhere. It was probably written about 1642. The reserved song in Part i., p. 153 (Supplement, p. 3), seems to be a vile parody on it, in the coarse fashion of those persons who disgraced the cause of the Cavaliers. The rank and file were often base, and their brutality is evidenced in the songs which we have been obliged to degrade to the Supplement.

It was certainly popular before 1659, for we find it quoted as furnishing the tune to "A proper new ballad (25 verses) on the Old Parliament," beginning "Good Morrow, my neighbours all," with a varying burden :—

> *Hei ho, my hony,*
> *My heart shall never rue,*
> *Four and twenty now for your Mony,*
> *And yet a hard penny worth too.*
> (*Rump*, 1662 ii, 26.)

The music is in Playford's *English Dancing Master*, 1686.

Page 116 [Supp. 14].   *She lay up to, &c.*

Five years earlier, in *Wit and Drollery*, 1656, p. 56; 1661, p. 58. With the original, in *M. D., C.*, p. 300, compare the similar disappointment, by Cleveland, "The Myrtle-Grove" (*Poems*, p. 160, edit. 1661.)

Page 149 [253].   *If that you will hear, &c.*

This is the same, except a few variations, as "Will you please to hear a new ditty?" in our *Westminster-Drollery*, 1671, i. 88; Appendix to ditto, pp. xxxvi-vii (compare the coarser verses, p. 368 in present volume, and "Upon the biting of Fleas," in *Musarum Deliciæ*, 1656; Reprint, p. 64.)

[We here close our Notes to the "Extra Songs" of *Merry Drollery*, 1661. But we have still some Additional Notes, on what is common to the editions of 1661, 1670, and 1691 (as promised in *M. D., C.*, p. 363).]

MERRY DROLLERY,
Complete.
OR,
A COLLECTION
Of { Jovial POEMS,
    Merry SONGS,
    Witty DROLLERIES,

Intermixed with Pleasant *Catches*.

The First Part.

Collected by
W.N. C.B. R.S. J.G.
LOVERS of WIT

LONDON,
Printed for *Simon Miller*, at the Star, at
the West End of St. *Pauls*, 1670.

B B

APPENDIX. PART 4.

§ 2.—ADDITIONAL NOTES TO THE
MERRY DROLLERY, COMPLEAT.
(Common to all editions, 1661, '70, '91, and 1875.)
"A pretty slight Drollery."
(*Henry IV.*, pt. 2. Act ii. Sc. 1.)

Title-page to 1670 Edition.

WE here give the title-page of the 1670 Edition of *Merry Drollery, Compleat*, Part 1st. As mentioned on our p. 231, the 1670 edition was re-issued as a new edition in 1691, but with no alteration except the fresh title-page, with its date and statement of William Miller's stock in trade.

Of the four "Lovers of Wit," 1661, we believe we have unearthed one, viz. "R. S.," in RALPH SLEIGH, who wrote a song beginning, "*Cupid, Cupid,* makes men stupid; I'll no more of such boys' play ;" *(Sportive Wit,) Jovial Drollery,* 1656, p. 22.

M. D., C., p. 11 [13]. Verse 6. "Mahomet's pidgeon," that was taught to pick seeds from out his ear, so that it might be thought to whisper to him. The "mad fellow clad alwaies in yellow," i.e., in his military Buff-coat—"And somewhat his nose is blew, boys," certainly alludes to Oliver Cromwell: His being "King and no King," to his refusing the Crown offered by the notables whom he had summoned in 1657. As the "New Peers," his sons Henry and Richard among them, insulted and contemned by the later and mixed Parliament of January 20th, 1658, were "turned out" along with their foes the recalcitrant Commons, on Feb. 4th, we have the date of this ballad established closely.

Page 29. Nonsense. *Now Gentlemen, if, &c.*

Two other "Messes of Nonsense" may be found in *Recreations for Ingenious Headpieces*, 1645 (Reprint, *Wit's Recreations*, pp. 400, 401); beginning "When *Neptune's* blasts," and "Like to the tone of unspoke speeches." The latter we believe to have been written by Bishop Corbet. In *Wit's Merriment* (i.e. *Sportive Wit*), 1656, is the following: A FANCY:—

> WHen Py crust first began to reign,
>   Cheese parings went to warre.
> Red Herrings lookt both blew and wan,
>   Green leeks and Puddings jarre.
> Blind Hugh went out to see
>   Two Cripples run a race,
> The Ox fought with the Humble Bee,
>   And claw'd him by the face.

Page 36, lines 21, 22. *"Honest Dick;"* and *"L."*

These lines furnish a clue to the date of this ballad, (and its "Answer" quickly followed): "Honest Dick" being Richard Cromwell, whose Protectorate lasted only eight months, beginning in September, 1658. "The name with an L—" refers to his unscrupulous rival Lambert; with his spasmodic attempts at supremacy, urged on by his own ambition and that of his wife (accustomed too long to rule Oliver himself, during a close intimacy, not without exciting scandal, while she insisted on displacing Lady Dysart). For an account of Lambert's twenty-one years of captivity, first at Guernsey and later at Plymouth, see *Choice Notes on History, from N. and Q.*, 1858, pp. 155-163. Lambert played a selfish game, lost it, and needs no pity for having had to pay the stakes. But for " Honest Dick," " Tumble down Dick," who had warmly pleaded with his father to save the king's life in the fatal January of 1649, we keep a hearty liking. Carlyle stigmatizes him as "poor, idle, trivial," &c., but let that pass. Had Richard been crafty or cruel, like those who removed him from power, his reign might have been prolonged. But "what a wounded name" he would have then left behind, compared with his now stainless character: and, in any case, his ultimate fall was certain.

Page 43, line 16th, "*Call for a constable blurt.*"

An allusion to Middleton's Comedy, "Blurt, Master Constable," 1602.

Page 62, 368. *Will you hear a strange thing.*

The important event here described took place April 20th, 1653, and the ballad immediately followed. (Compare "Cheer up, kind country men," by S. S., "Rebellion hath broken up house," and "This Christmas time," in the Percy Soc. Pol. Bds., iii. 126; 180 *Loyal Songs*, 149, 1694; *Rump*, ii. 52.) At this date the strife between the fag-end of the Rump and Oliver, who was supported by his council of officers, came to open violence. Fearing his increased power, it was proposed to strengthen the Parliamentarians by admitting a body of "neutrals," Presbyterians, to act in direct opposition against the army-leaders. With a pretence of dissolving themselves there would have ensued a virtual extension of rule. Anxious and lengthy meetings had been held by Cromwell's adherents at Whitehall, one notably on the 19th, and continued throughout the night. Despite a promise, or half promise, of delay made to him, the Rump was meantime hurrying onward the objectionable measure, clearly with intention of limiting his influence: among the leaders being Sir Hy. Vane, Harry Marten, and Algernon Sidney. They knew it to be a struggle for life or death. From the beginning, this Long Parliament cherished the mistaken idea that they were everything supreme: providence, strength, virtue, and wisdom, etc., etc. If mere empty talk could be all this, such representative wind-bags might deserve some credit. Their doom was sealed; not alone for their incompetence, but also for proved malignity, and the attempt to perpetuate their own mischief, destroying the only power that seemed able to bring order out of chaos.

Cromwell received intelligence, from his adherents within the house, of the efforts being made to hurry the measure for settling the new representation, and then to dissolve for re-election. Major Harrison talked against time; until Cromwell could arrive after breaking up the Whitehall meeting. Ingoldsby, as the second or third messenger, had shown to him the urgent need of action. Followed by Lambert and some half-dozen officers, the General took with him a party of soldiers, reached the house, and found himself not too soon. Surrounding the chamber, and guarding the doors, the troopers remained outside. Clad in plain black, unattended and resolute, Oliver entered, stood looking on his discomfitted foes, and then sat down, speaking to no one except "dusky tough St. John, whose abstruse fanaticisms, crabbed logics, and dark ambitions issue all, as was natural, in decided avarice" (Carlyle's *Cromwell*, iii. 168, 1671 edit). Vane must have felt the peril, but held on unflinchingly, imploring the house to dispense with everything that might delay the measure, such as engrossing. The Speaker had risen at last to put the question, before the General started up, uncovered, and began his address. Something of stately commendation for past work he gave them. Perhaps at first his words were uttered solely to obtain a momentary pause, the whilst he gathered up his strength, and measured all the chances, before he broke with them for ever. Soon the tone changed into that of anger and contempt. He heaped reproaches on them: Ludlow says: "He spoke with so much passion and discomposure of mind, as if he had been distracted." "Your time is come!" he told them : "The Lord has done with you. He has chosen other instruments for the carrying on his work, that are more worthy."

Vane, Marten, and Sir Peter Wentworth tried to interrupt him, but it was almost beyond their power. Wentworth could but irritate him by indignant censure. He crushed his hat on, sprang from his place, shouting that he would put an end to their prating, and, while he strode noisily along the room, railed at them to their face, not naming them, but with gestures giving point to his invectives. He told them to begone : " I say you are no Parliament! I'll put an end to your sitting. Begone! Give way to honester men." A stamp of his foot followed, as a signal; the door flies open, " five or six files of musqueteers" are seen with weapons ready. Resistance (so prompt, with less provocation, in 1642) is felt to be useless, and, except mere feminine scolding, none is attempted. Not one dares to struggle. Afraid of violence, their swords hang idly at their side. As they pass out in turn, they meet the scathing of Oliver's rebuke. His control of himself is gone. Their crimes are not forgotten. He denounces Challoner as a drunkard, Wentworth for his adultery, Alderman Allen for his embezzlement of public military money, and Bulstrode Whitelock of injustice. Harry Marten is asked whether a whoremaster is fit to sit and govern. Vane is unable to resist a feeble protest, availing nothing—" This is not honest: Yea! it is against morality and honesty." In the absence of such crimes or flagrant sins of his companions, as his own frozen nature made him incapable of committing, there are remembered against him his interminable harangues, his hair-splitting, his self-sufficiency; and all that early deliberate treachery in ransacking his father's papers, which he employed to cause the death of Strafford. To all posterity recorded, came the ejaculation of Cromwell : " Sir Harry Vane, Sir Harry Vane—the Lord deliver me from Sir Harry Vane!" And, excepting a few dissentient voices, the said posterity echoes the words approvingly. The "bauble" mace had been borne off ignominiously, the documents were seized, including that of the unpassed measure, the room was cleared, the doors were locked, and all was over. The Long Parliament thus fell, unlamented

Page 66. *I'le sing you a Sonnet.*

Written and published in 1659; as we see by the references to *"Dick (Oliver's* Heir) that pitiful slow-thing, Who was once invested with purple clothing,"—his retirement being in April, 1659. Bradshaw, the bitter Regicide (whose harsh vindictiveness to Charles I. during the trial has left his memory exceptionally hateful), died 22nd November, 1659. Hewson the Cobbler was one of Oliver's new peers, summoned in January, 1658.

Pages 69, 368. *Be not thou so foolish nice.*

The music to this, by Dr. John Wilson, is in his *Chearfull Ayres*, 1659-60, p. 126.

Pages 70, 369. *Aske me no more.*

Gule is misprint for "Goal," and refers to the Bishops who, having been molested and hindered from attending to vote among the peers, were, on 30th December, 1642, committed to the Tower for publishing their protest against Acts passed during their unwilling absence. Finch, Lord Keeper; who, to save his life, fled beyond sea, and did not return until after the Restoration.

Pages 72, 369. *A Sessions was held, &c.*

To avoid a too-long interruption, our Additional Note to the "Sessions of the Poets" is slightly displaced from here, and follows later as Section Third.

Pages 87, 369. *Some Christian people all, &c.*

We have traced this burlesque narrative of the Fire on London Bridge ten years earlier than *Merry Drollery*, 1661, p. 81. It appeared (probably for the first time in print) on April 28th, 1651, at the end of a volume of *facetiæ*, entitled *The Loves of Hero and Leander* (in the 1677 edition, following *Ovid de Arte Amandi*, it is on p. 142) The event referred to, we suspect, was a destructive fire which broke out on London Bridge, 13th Feb. 1632-3. It is thus described :—" At the latter end of the year 1632, viz., on the 13th Feb., between eleven and twelve at night, there happened in the house of one Briggs, a needle-maker, near St. Magnus Church, at the north end of the bridge, by the carelessness of a maid-servant, setting a tub of hot sea-coal ashes under a pair of stairs, a sad and lamentable fire, which consumed all the buildings before eight of the clock the next morning, from the north end of the bridge, to the first vacancy on both sides, containing forty-two houses; *water being then very scarce, the Thames being almost frozen over*. Beneath, in the vaults and cellars, the fire remained burning and glowing a whole week after. After which fire, the north end of the bridge lay unbuilt for many years ; only deal boards were set up on both sides, to prevent people's falling into the Thames, many of which deals were, by high winds, blown down, which made it very dangerous in the nights, although there were lanthorns and candles hung upon all the cross-beams that held the pales together." (Tho. Allen's *Hist. and Antiq. of London*, vol. ii. p. 468, 1828.) Details and list of houses burnt are given (as in *Gent. Mag.* Nov. 1824), from the MS. *Record of the Mercies of God; or, a Thankfull Remembrance*, 1618-1635 (since printed), kept by the Puritan Nehemiah Wallington, citizen and turner, of London, a friend of Prynn and Bastwick He gives the date as Monday, 11th February, 1633. Our ballad mentions the river being frozen over, and "all on the tenth of January;" but nothing is more common than a traditional blunder of the month, so long as the rhythm is kept. (Compare *Choyce Drollery*, p. 78, and Appendix p. 297).

Another Fire-ballad (in addition to the coarse squib in present vol., pp. 33-7,) is "Zeal over-heated;" telling of a fire at Oxford, 1642; tune, Chivey Chace; and beginning, "Attend, you brethren every one." It is not improbably by Thomas Weaver, being in his *Love and Drollery*, 1654, p. 21.

Page 92, 370.   *Cast your caps and cares away.*

Of this song, from Beaumont and Fletcher's "Beggar's Bush," bef. 1625, the music set by Dr. John Wilson is in his *Cheerfull Ayres*, 1659-60, p. 22.

Pages 97, 371.   *Come, let us drink.*

"Mahomet's Pigeon," a frequent allusion: compare *M. D. C.*, pp. 11, 192; and present appendix, p. 356.

Pages 100, 108 (App.) 371.   *Satires on Gondibert.*

See Additional Note in this vol. § 3, *post*, for a few words on D'Avenant.   Since printing *M. D. C.*, we have been enabled (thanks to W. F. Fowle, Esq., possessor of to consult the very rare Second Satire, 1655, mentioned on p. 371. It is entitled, "The Incomparable Poem GONDIBERT VINDICATED from the Wit-Combats of Four ESQUIRES, *Clinias, Dametas, Sancho*, and *Jack Pudding*." [With this three-fold motto:—]

Χοτέει καὶ ἀοίδ τω ἀοίδω.
Vatum quoque gratia rara est.
Anglicè,
One Wit-Brother ‖ *Envies another.*

Printed in the year 1655." It begins on p. 3, with a poetical address to Sir Willm. Davenant, asking pardon beforehand in case his "yet-unhurt Reputation" should suffer more through the champion than from the attack made by the four "Cyclops, or Wit-Centaurs," two of whom he unhesitatingly names as "Denham and Jack Donne," or "Jack Straw." But even thus early we notice the sarcasm against D'Avenant himself: when in reference to the never-forgotten "flaws" in his face, the Defender writes:—

Will *shew thy face* (be't what it will),
We'l push 'um yet a quill for quill.

The third poem, p. 8, again to the Poet, mocks him as well as his assailants' lines (our *M. D. C.*, p. 108) with twenty triplets :—

> *After so many poorer scraps*
> *Of Playes which nere had the mishaps*
> *To passe the stage without their claps, &c.*

Next comes a poem "Upon the continuation of Gondibert," "Ovid to Patmos pris'ner sent." (Later, we extract the chief lines for the "Sessions" Add. Note.) He is told,

> *Wash thee in* Avon, *if thou flie,*
> *My wary* Davenant *so high,*
> *Yet* Hypernaso *now you shall*
> *Ore fly this Goose so Capitall.*   (p. 14.)

After five others, came one Upon the Author, beginning,

> Daphne, *secure of the buff,*
>   *Prethee laugh,*
> *Yet at these four and their riff raff:*
>   *Who can hold*
>   *When so bold?*
> *And the trim wit of* Coopers *green hill*, .. ·

Ending thus :—

> Denham, *thou'lt be shrewdly shent*
>   *To invent*
> *Such Drawlery for merriment, &c. . . .*
> *A Drawing* Donne *out of the mire.*

A burlesque of Gondibert on same p. 18, as "Canto the Second, or rather Cento the first;" begins "*All in the Land of* Bembo *and of* Bubb." One stanza partly anticipates Sam. Butler :—

> *The Sun was sunk into the watery lap*
>   *Of her commands the waves, and weary there,*
> *Of his long journey, took a pleasing nap*
>   *To ease his each daies travels all the year.*

P. 23 gives "To *Daphne* on his incomparable (and by the Critick incomprehended) Poem, *Gondibert*," this consolation: "Chear up, dear friend, a *Laureat* thou must be," &c. Hobbes comes in for notice, on p. 24, and Denham with his Cooper's Hill has another slap. The final poem, on p. 27, is "Upon the Author's writing his name, as in the Title of his Booke, D'Avenant :"—

1.

"*Your Wits have further than you rode,*
You needed not to have gone abroad.
  D'avenant *from* Avon *comes,*
  Rivers are still the Muses Rooms.
Dort, *knows our name, no more Durt on't :*
An't be but for that D'avenant.

2.

And when such people are restor'd
(A thing belov'd by none that whor'd)
My noches then may not appeare,
The gift of healing will be near.   (*clowns*)
  Meane while Ile seeke some Panax *(salve of*
  Shall heal the wanton Issues and crackt Crowns.
I will conclude, Farewell Wit Squirty Fegos
And drolling gasmen Wal-Den-De-Donne-Dego.
(Finis.)"

Here, finally, are Waller, Denham, [Bro]de[rick], and Donne clearly indicated. They receive harder measure, on the whole, than D'avenant himself; so that the Second Volume of Satires, 1655, is neither by the author of "Gondibert," nor by those who penned the "Certain Verses" of 1653. Q. E. D.

Pages 101, 372. *I'll tell thee,* Dick, *&c.*

As already mentioned, the popularity of Suckling's "Ballad on a Wedding" (probably written in 1642) caused innumerable imitations. Some of these we have indicated. In *Folly in Print,* 1667, is another, "On a Friend's Wedding," to the same tune, beginning, "Now *Tom,* if *Suckling* were alive, And knew who *Harry* were to wive." In D'Urfey's *Pills to Purge Melancholy,* 1699, p. 81 ; ed. 1719, iii, 65, is a different "New Ballad upon a Wedding" [at Lambeth], with the music, to same tune and model, beginning, "The sleeping *Thames* one morn I cross'd, By two contending *Charons* tost." Like Cleveland's poem, as an imitation it possesses merit, each having some good verses.

Pages 111, 112.   *The Proctors are two.*

Among the references herein to Cambridge Taverns is one (3rd verse) to the Myter: part of which fell down before 1635, and was celebrated in verse by that "darling of the Muses," Thomas Randolph. His lines begin "Lament, lament, ye scholars all!" He mentions other Taverns and the Mitre-landlord, Sam :—

> *Let the* Rose *with the* Falcon *moult,*
> *While* Sam *enjoys his wishes;*
> *The* Dolphin, *too, must cast her crown:*
> *Wine was not made for fishes.*

Pages 115, 374.   '*Tis not the silver, &c.*

The mention, on pp. 116, of "our bold Army" turning out the "black Synod," refers less probably to Colonel "*Pride's Purge*" of the Presbyterians, on 6th December, 1648, than to the events of April 20, 1653; and helps to fix the date to the same year. In 6th verse the blanks are to be thus filled, "Arms of the *Rump* or the *King*;" "C. R., or O. P.;" the joke of "the breeches" being a supposed misunderstanding of the Commonwealth-Arms on current coin (viz., the joined shields of England and Ireland) for the impression made by Noll's posteriors. Compare "Saw you the States-Money," in *Rump* Coll., i. 289. On one side they marked "God with us!"

> " Common-wealth *on the other, by which we may guess* God *and the* States *were not both of a side.*"

Pages 121, 375.   *Come, let's purge our brains.*

This song is almost certainly by THOMAS JORDAN, the City-Poet. With many differences he reprints it later in his *London in Luster*, as sung at the Banquet given by the Drapers Company, October 29th, 1679; where it is entitled "The Coronation of Canary," and thus begins (in place of our first verse):—

D*Rink your wine away,*
    'Tis my Lord Mayor's day,
  Let our Cups and Cash be free.
Beer and Ale are both ‖ *But the sons of froth,*
  Let us then in wine agree.
To taste a Quart ‖ *Of every sort,*
  The thinner and the thicker;
That spight of Chance ‖ *We may advance,*
  The Nobler and the Quicker.
Who shall by Vote of every Throat
  Be crown'd the King of Liquor.

2.

Muscadel *Avant*, Bloody Alicant,
  Shall have no free vote of mine:
Claret *is a Prince, And he did long since*
  In the Royal order shine.
His face, &c, (as in M. D. C. p. 112.)

In sixth verse, "*If a* Cooper *we With a red nose see*," refers to Oliver Cromwell; and proves it to have been written before September, 1658.

Pages 125, 315. *Lay by, &c., Law lies a-bleeding.*

The date of this ballad seems to have been 1656, rather than 1658. The despotism of the sword here so powerfully described, was under those persons who are on p. 254 of *M. D. C.* designated "Oliver's myrmidons," meaning, probably, chiefly the major-generals of the military districts, into which the country was divided after Penruddock's downfall in 1655. They were Desborough, Whalley, Goffe, Fleetwood, "downright" Skippon, Kelsey, Butler, Worseley, and Berry; to these ten were added Barkstead. Compare Hallam's account: —"These were eleven in number, men bitterly hostile to the royalist party, and insolent to all civil authority.

They were employed to secure the payment of a tax of ten per cent., imposed by Cromwell's arbitrary will on those who had ever sided with the King during the late wars, where their estates exceeded £100 per annum. The major-generals, in their correspondence printed among Thurloe's papers, display a rapacity and oppression greater than their master's. They complain that the number of those exempted is too great; they press for harsher measures; they incline to the unfavourable construction in every doubtful case; they dwell on the growth of malignancy and the general disaffection. It was not indeed likely to be mitigated by this unparalleled tyranny. All illusion was now gone as to the pretended benefits of the civil war. It had ended in a despotism, compared to which all the illegal practices of former kings, all that had cost Charles his life and crown, appeared as dust in the balance. For what was Ship-money, a general burthen, by the side of the present decimation of a single class, whose offence had long been expiated by a composition and effaced by an act of indemnity? or were the excessive punishments of the Star Chamber so odious as the capital executions inflicted without trial by peers, whenever it suited the usurper to erect his high court of justice [by which Gerard and Vowel in 1654, Slingsby and Dr. Hewit in 1658 fell]? A sense of present evils not only excited a burning desire to live again under the ancient monarchy, but obliterated, especially in the new generation, that had no distinct remembrance of them, the apprehension of its former abuses." *(Constitutional Hist. England,* cap. x. vol. ii. p. 252, edit. 1872.) This from a writer unprejudiced and discriminating.

Pages 131, 376. *I'll tell you a story.*

TOWER HILL AND TYBURN. The date of this ferocious ballad is not likely to have been long before the execution of the regicides Harrison, Hacker, Cook, and Hew Peters, in October, 1660; some on the 13th, others on the 16th. Probably, shortly before the trial of Harry

Marten, on the 10th of the same month. The second verse indicates a considerable lapse of time since Monk's arrival and the downfall of the Rump (burnt in effigy, Febr. 11, 1659-60); so we may be certain that it was written late, about September, if not actually at beginning of October.

Sir Robert TICHBOURNE, Commissioner for sale of State-lands, Alderman, Regulator of Customs, and Lord Mayor in 1658, was named in the King's Proclamation, 6th June, 1660, as one of those who had fled, and who were summoned to appear within fourteen days, on penalty of being exempted from any pardon. His name occurs again, among the exceptions to the Act of Indemnity; along with those of Thos. Harrison, Hy. Marten, John Hewson, Jn. Cook, Hew Peters, Francis Hacker, and other forty-five. Nineteen of these fify-one surrendered themselves: Tichbourne and Marten among them. None of them were executed; although Scoop was, who also had yielded. The trial of the regicides commenced on 9th October, at Hick's Hall, Clerkenwell.

HUGH PETERS suffered, along with JOHN COOK (the Counsel against Charles I.) "that read the King's charge," on the 16th October,. He was depressed in spirits at the last, but there was dignity in his reply to one who insulted him in passing—"Friend, you do not well to trample on a dying man;" and his sending a token to his daughter awakens pity. Physically he had failed in courage, and no wonder, to face all that was arrayed to terrify him : or he might have justified anticipations and "made a pulpit of the place." His last sermon at Newgate is said to have been "incoherent."

HARRY MARTEN's private life is so generally declared to have been licentious (dozens of ballads refering to his "harem," "Marten's girl that was neither sweet nor sound," "Marten, back and leave your wench," &c.), and his old friend Cromwell when become a foe openly taxing him as a "whoremaster," that it is better for us to think of him with reference to his unswerving faithfulness in Republican opinions; his gay spirit (more resembling the reckless indifference of Cavaliers than his own associates can have esteemed befitting); his successful exertions on many occasions to save the shedding of blood; and his gallant bearing in the final hours of trial. The living death to which he was condemned, of his twenty years imprisonment at Chepstow Castle, has been recorded (mistakenly as *thirty*) by that devoted student Robert Southey, *clarum et venerabilem nomen!* in a poem which can never pass into oblivion, although cleverly mocked by Canning in the Anti-Jacobin, Nov. 20, 1797:—

> For twenty years secluded from mankind
> Here MARTEN lingered. Often have these walls
> Echo'd his footsteps, as with even tread
> He paced around his prison ; not to him
> Did Nature's fair varieties exist :
> He never saw the sun's delightful beams
> Save when through yon high bars it pour'd a sad
> And broken splendour.   Dost thou ask his crime?
> He had rebelled against his King, and sat
> In judgment on him : *&c.*

John Forster has written his memoir, and, in one of his best moments, Wallis painted him. Here are his own last words, sad yet firm, the old humour still apparent, if only in the choice of verse, it being the anagram of his name :—

> HERE, or elsewhere (all's one to you—to me !)
>   Earth, air, or water, gripes my ghostless dust,
> None knowing when brave fire shall set it free.
>   Reader, if you an oft-tried rule will trust,
>   You'll gladly do and suffer what you must.
>
> My life was worn with serving you and you,
> And death is my reward, and welcome too :
> Revenge destroying but itself.   While I
> To birds of prey leave my old cage and fly.
> Examples preach to th' eye—care, then, mine says,
> Not how you end, but how you spend your days.
>   (*Athenæ Oxonienses*, iii. 1243.)

As to Thomas HARRISON, fifth-monarchy enthusiast, firm to the end in his adversity, he who had been ruthless in prosperity, we have already briefly referred to his closing hours in our Introduction to *Merry Drollery, Compleat,* p. xxix.

JOHN HEWSON, Cobbler and Colonel, who had sat in the illegal mockery of Judgment on King Charles, was for the after years ridiculed by ballad-singers as a one-eyed spoiler of good leather. He escaped the doom of Tyburn by flight to Amsterdam, where he died in 1662. In default of his person, his picture was hung on a gibbet in Cheapside, 25th January, 1660-61. (See *Pepys' Diary* of that date.) His appearance was not undignified. One ballad specially devoted to him, at his flight, is "A Hymne to the Gentle Craft; or, *Hewson's* Lamentation :—

LISTEN a while to what I shall say
 Of a blind cobbler that's gone astray
Out of the Parliament's High-way,
 Good people, pity the blind!
          [verse 17.]
And now he has gone to the Lord knows whether,
He and this winter go together,
If he be caught he will lose his leather,
 Good people, pity the blind!
    (*Rump*, Coll. 1662 edit., ii. 151-4.)

Verse 14. Dr. John HEWIT with Sir Harry Slingsby had been executed for conspiracy against Cromwell, 8th June, 1658. The Earl of Strafford's death was May 12th, 1641; and that of Laud, January 10th, 1644.

Verse 15. DUN was the name of the Hangman at this time, frequently mentioned in the *Rump* ballads. Jack Ketch was his successor: Gregory had been Hangman in 1652.

Pages 134, 376. *I'll go no more to the Old Exchange.*

The *first* Royal Exchange, Sir Thomas Gresham's Bourse, was opened by Queen Elizabeth, January 23rd, 1570, and destroyed in the Great Fire of 1666. The *second* was commenced on May 6th, 1667, and burnt on January 10th, 1838. The present building, the *third*,

was opened by Queen Viotcria Oct., 28th, 1844. The
"Old Exchange," often referred to in ballads, was
Gresham's. But the "New Exchange" was one, erected
where the stables of Durham House in the Strand had
stood: opened April 11th, 1609, and removed in 1737.
King James I. had named it "Britain's Bourse." Built
on the model of the established Royal Exchange, it had
"cellars, a walk, and a row of shops, filled with milliners,
seamstresses, and those of similar occupations; and was
a place of fashionable resort. What, however, was intended to rival the Royal Exchange, dwindled into frivolity
and ruin, and the site is at present [1829] occupied by a
range of handsome houses facing the Strand" (T. Allen's
Hist. and Antiq. of London, iv. 254). In the ballad it is
sung of as "Haberdashers' Hall." Cp. Roxb. Coll., ii.,
230.

Pages 152, 378. *There is a certain, &c.*

This is an imperfect version of "A Woman's Birth,"
merely the beginning, four stanzas. The whole fifteen
(eleven following ours) are reprinted by Wm. Chappell,
in the Ballad Society's *Roxburghe Bds.*, iii. 94, 1875, from
a broadside in Roxb. Coll., i. 466, originally printed for
Francis Grove [1620-55]. 2nd verse reads:—Her husband *Hymen*; 4th. *Wandring* eye; *insatiate*. The gifts
of Juno, Flora, and Diana follow; with woman's employment of them.

Page 172. *Blind Fortune, if thou, &c.*

We find this in MS. Harleian, No. 6396, fol. 13. Also
two printed copies, in *Parnassus Biceps*, 1656, 124; and
in *Sportive Wit*, same year, p. 39. We gained the corrections, which we inserted as *marginalia*, from the MS.;
"*Ceres* in *hir* Garland" having been corrupted into
"*Cealus* in *his*." "*Aglaura*," Sir John Suckling's play,
(printed originally in 4to. 1639, with a broad margin of
blank, on which the wits made merry with epigrammes,
"By this wide margent," &c.), appeared on April 18th,

1638, and is here referred to. Probably the date of the poem is nearly as early. On p. 175 the "Pilgrimage up *Holborn* Hill" refers to a journey from Newgate to Tyburn. (See p. 365).

Pages 180, 379. *Heard you not lately of a man.*

The Mad-Man's Morrice; written by HUMFREY CROUCH: For the second part of the broad-sheet version we must refer readers to vol. ii. page 153, of the Ballad Society's reprint of the *Roxburghe Ballads* (now happily arrived at completion of the first massive folio vol. of Major Pearson's original pair; the bulky third and slim fourth vols. being afterwards added). We promised to give it, and gladly would have done so, if we had space: for it is a trustworthy picture of a Bedlamite's sufferings, under the harsh treatment of former days. Date about 1635-42.

To our enumeration of mad songs (*Westm. Droll.* App. p. 9) we may add Thomas Jordan's "I am the woefullest madman."

M. D., C., p. 198, lines 22, 23. *True Hearts.*

" I'll drink to thee a brace of quarts || Whose Anagram is called *True Hearts.*" The Anagram of True Hearts gives us "Stuart here!" which, like drinking "to the King—*over the water!*" in later days by the Jacobites, would be well understood by suspected cavaliers.

In March 1659-60 appeared the anagram "Charles Stuart: Arts Chast Rule. Later: Awld fool, Rob the Jews' Shop.

Pages 255, 287. *When I do travel in the night.*

Like "How happy 's the prisoner," *Ibid.* p. 107, we trace this so early as 1656. It is in *Sportive Wit*, p. 12, as "When I go to revel in the night," The Drunkard's Song.

Pages 153 (and Introduction, ix). *The best of Poets, &c.*

THE BOW GOOSE. We have found this, (15 verses of

our 18,) five years earlier, in *Sportive Wit*, 1656, p. 35. It there begins, "The best of Poets write of Hogs, And of *Ulysses* barking Dogs; Others of Sparrows, Flies, and Hogs." Our text, though later, seems to be the better, and has three more verses: "Frogs," in connection with "the Best of Poets," referring to Homer and to *Batrachomyomachia;* supposed to be his, and translated by George Chapman, about 1623 (of whom A. C. Swinburne has recently written so glowing a eulogium, coupling with it the noblest praise of Marlowe).

M. D., C., pp. 166, 376. *Now, thanks to, &c.*

Of course, the words displayed by dashes are *Crown, Bishop, King*. To this same tune are later songs (1659-60) in the *Rump*, ii. 193—200, "What a reprobate crew is here," &c. Wilkins prints an inferior version of 7th line in 3rd verse, as "Take *Prynne* and his clubs, or *Say* and his tubs," referring to William, Viscount "Say and Seal." Ours reads "club, or *Smec* and his tub," the allusion being to *Smectymnuus*, a name compounded, like the word *Cabal* in Charles II.'s time, of the initials of five personal names: Ste. Marshall, Edm. Calamy, Thos. Young, Matth. Newcomen, and Willm. Spurstow; all preachers, who united in a book against Episcopacy and the Liturgy. Milton, in 1641 published his *Animadversions upon the Remonstrants Defence against Smectymnuus*; and in 1642, *An Apology for Smectymnuus*. John Cleveland devotes a poem to "The Club Divines," beginning "Smectymnuus! the Goblin makes me start." *(Poems,* p. 38, 1661; also in the *Rump* Coll., i. 57.)

Pages 200, 382. *A Story strange, &c.*

Correction:—Instead of the words "*Choyce Drollery*, p. 31," in first line of note (M. D., C., p. 382), read "*Jovial Drollery* (i.e., *Sportive Wit*), p. 59." The same date, viz. 1656.

Pages 210-11, 384. "*To* Virginia *for Planters.*"

The reference here is to the proposed expedition of disheartened Cavaliers (among whom was Wm. D'Avenant) from France and England to the Virginian plantations. It was defeated in 1650, the vessels having been intercepted in the channel by the Commonwealth's fleet. By the way, the infamous sale into slavery of the royalist prisoners during the war in previous years by the intolerant Parliament, deserves the sternest reprobation.

Page 226. *"Sea-coal Lane."*

An appropriate dower, as Sea-coal Lane in the Old Bailey bore a similar evil repute to Turnball Street, Drury Lane, and Kent Street, for the *bona-roba* tribe : as "the suburbs" always did.

Pages 232, 390. *How poor is his spirit.*

Written when Oliver rejected the title of King, 8th May, 1657. (See next note, on p. 254.)

Pages 254, 393. Oliver, Oliver, *take up thy Crown.*

After Cromwell's designating the Battle of Worcester, 3rd September, 1651, his "crowning victory" many of his more uncompromising Republicans kept a stealthy eye upon him. Our ballad evidently refers itself to the date of the "purified" Parliament's "Petition and Advice," March 26, 1656, when Cromwell hesitated before accepting or declining the offered title of King; thinking (mistakenly, as we deem probable) that his position would become more unsafe, from the jealousy and prejudices of the army, than if he seemed contented with the name of Protector to the Commonwealth, while holding the actual power of sovereignty. His refusal was in April, 1657. Hallam thinks it was not until after Worcester fight that "he began to fix his thoughts, if not on the dignity of royalty, yet on an equivalent right of command. Two remarkable conversations, in which Whitelock bore a part, seem to place beyond controversy the nature of his designs. About the end of 1651, Whitelock himself,

St. John, Widdrington, Lenthall, Harrison, Desborough, Fleetwood, and Whalley met Cromwell, at his own request to consider the settlement of the nation," &c. *(Constit. Hist. England,* cap. x. p. 237, edit. 1872.) "Twelve months after this time in a more confidential discourse with Whitelock alone, the general took occasion to complain both of the chief officers of the army and of the parliament," &c. (*Ibid.* p. 238). The conference not being satisfactory to Cromwell, on each occasion ended abruptly; and Whitelock (if we may trust his own account, which perhaps is asking too much) was little consulted afterwards. When they had conferred the title of Lord Protector, the right of appointing his successor was added on 22nd May.

Pages 255, 393. *When I do travel, &c.*

"With upsie freeze I line my head," of our text, is in the play "Cromwell's Coronation" printed "With *tipsy frenzie.*" But we often find the other phrase; sometimes, as in the ballad of "The Good Fellow's Best Beloved" (i.e. strong drink) varied thus, "With good *ipse he,*" (about 1633). See Bd. Soc. *Roxb. Bds.* iii. 248, where is W. Chappell's note, quoting Nares:—"It has been said that *op-zee,* in Dutch, means 'over sea,' which comes near to another English phrase for drunkenness, being 'half-seas over.' But *op-zyn-fries* means, 'in the Dutch fashion,' or *à la mode de Frise,* which perhaps is the best interpretation of the phrase." In Massinger and Dekker's "Virgin Martyr," 1622, Act ii. sc. 1, we find the vile Spungius saying, " *Bacchus,* the God of brewed wine and sugar, grand patron of rob-pots, *upsie freesie* tipplers, and *super-naculum* takers," &c. Probably Badham's conjecture is right, and in Hamlet, i. 4, we should read not "up-spring," but

" *Keeps wassail, and the swaggering* upsy freeze."

Cambr. Essays, 1656; *Cambr. Shakesp.* viii. 30). T. Caldecott had so early as 1620 (in *Spec. new edit. Shakesp.* Hamlet) anticipated the guess, but not boldly.

He brings forward from T. Lodge's *Wit's Miserie*, 4to, 1596, p. 20, " Dance, leap, sing, drink, *upsefrize*." And again :—

> For Upsefreeze *he drunke from four to nine,*
> *So as each sense was steeped well in wine :*
> *Yet still he kept his* rouse, *till he in fine*
> *Grew extreame sicke with hugging* Bacchus *shrine.*
> [*The Shrift.*]

A new Spring shadowed in sundrie pithie Poems by *Musophilus*, 4to. 1619, signat. l. b., where "*Upsefreese*" is the name of the frier. Like "Wassael" and "Trinkael," the phrase upsie-friese, or vrijster, seems to have been used as a toast, perhaps for "To your sweetheart."

Pages 259, 354. *If none be offended.*

The exact date of this ballad's publication was 31st December, 1659 : in *Thomason Collection*, Numero xxii., folio, Brit. Mus.

Page 270. *Pray why should any, &c.*

Probably written in 1659-60, when Monk was bridling the Commons. "Cooks" alludes to John Cook, the Solicitor for the Commonwealth, who at the trial of Charles Ist. exhibited the charge of high treason. After the Restoration, Cook was executed along with Hugh Peters, 16th Oct., 1660, at Charing Cross.

Pages 283 (line 22), 395. *I have the finest Nonperel.*

"*Hyrens*" (as earlier printed in *Wit and Drollery*, 1656, p. 26), instead of "Syrens" of our text, is probably correct. Ancient Pistol twice asks "Have we not *Hirens* here?" *(Henry* IV., Part 2nd, Act ii. sc. 4). George Peele had a play, now lost, on "The Turkish Mahomet and Hiren the fair Greek" [1594?] In the *Spiritual Navigator*, 1615, we learn, is a passage, "There be Syrens in the sea of the world. *Syrens? Hirens*, as they are now called. What a number of these syrens, hirens, cockatrices, courteghians—in plain English, harlots—swimme amongst us!"

Page 287. Title, "*Oxford Jeasts.*"

An unfortunate misprint crept in, detected too late: for "*Feasts*" read properly "*Jeasts:*" the old fashioned initial *J* being barred across like *F*.

Page 293, line 11. "*Heresie in hops.*"

This must have been an established jest. (Compare Introd. to *M. D. C.*, pp. xxxi-ii. and T. Randolph's "Fall of the Mitre Tavern," Cambridge, before 1635,

The zealous students of that place
Change of religion bear :
That this mischance may soon bring in ||*A heresy of beer.*"

Page 295, line 24. "*A hundred horse.*"

"He that gave the King a hundred horse," refers, no doubt, to Sir John Suckling and his loyal service in 1642. See introduction to *M. D., C.*, pp. xix. xx. The Answer to "I tell thee, Jack, thou gavest the King," there mentioned, and probably referring to Sir John Mennis, a carping rival although a Cavalier, has a smack of Cleveland about it (it certainly is not Suckling's) :—

I *Tell thee, fool, who ere thou be,*
  That made this fine sing-song of me,
    Thou art a riming sot :
These very lines do thee betray,
This barren wit makes all men say
  'Twas some rebellious Scot.

But it's no wonder if you sing
Such songs of me, who am no King,
  When every blew-cap swears
Hee'l not obey King James his Barn,
That huggs a Bishop under's Arme,
  And hangs them in his ears.

> Had I been of your Covenant,
> You'd call me th' son of John of Gaunt,
> > And give me t great renown;
> But now I am John [f]or the King,
> You say I am but poor Suckling,
> > And thus you cry me down.
>
> Well, it's no matter what you say
> Of me or mine that run away;
> > I hold it no good fashion
> A Loyal subjects blood to spill,
> When we have knaves enough to kill
> > By force of Proclamation.
>
> Commend me unto Lesley stout,
> And his Pedlers him about,
> > Tell them without remorse   [p. 151.]
> That I will plunder all their packs
> Which they have got with their stoln knick knacks,
> > With these my hundred horse.
>
> This holy War, this zealous firke
> Against the Bishops and the Kirk
> > Is a pretended bravery;
> Religion, all the world can tell,
> Amongst Highlanders nere did dwell,
> > Its but to cloak your knavery.
>
> Such desperate Gamesters as you be,
> I cannot blame for tutoring me,
> > Since all you have is down,
> And every Boor forsakes his Plow,
> And swears that he'l turn Gamester now
> > To venture for a Crown.
> > (Le Prince d'Amour, 1660, pp. 150, 151.)

Pages 296, 398 (Cp. this vol. p. 149, line 8).   *Now that the Spring.*

This is by WILLM. BROWNE, author of "Britannia's Pastorals." The date is probably about fifteen years before 1645. It is one among the "Odes, Songs, and

Sonnets of Wm. Browne," in the Lansdowne MS. 777, fol. 4 *reverso* and 5, with extra verses not used in the Catch.

A Rounde. [1st verse sung by] All.

N *Ow that the Spring hath fill'd our veynes*
　With kinde and actiue fire,
And made green Liu'ryes for the playnes,
　and euery grove a Quire,
Sing we a Song of merry glee
　and Bacchus fill the bowle :
1. *Then heres to thee ;*　2. *And thou to mee*
　and euery thirsty soule.

Nor Care nor Sorrow ere pay'd debt
　nor never shall doe myne ;
I haue no Cradle goeing yet,
[? 2.] *nor I, by this good wyne.*
No wyfe at home to send for me,
　noe hoggs are in my grounde,
Noe suit at Law to pay a fee,
　Then round, old Jockey, round.

All.

Sheare sheepe that haue them, cry we still,
　But see that noe man scape
　To drink of the Sherry
　That makes us so merry
and plumpe as the lusty Grape.
　　　　　　　　(Lansdowne MS., No. 777.)

" Noe hoggs are in my grounds " may refer to the Catch (if it be equally old) :—

W *Hose three Hogs are these, and whose three Hoggs*
　are these,
They are John Cook's, *I know by their look, for I found*
　them in my pease.
Oh ! pound them : oh pound them ! But I dare not, for my
　life ;
For if I should pound John Cook's *Hoggs, I should never*
　kiss John Cook's *wife, &c.*
　　　　　　　　(Catch Club, 1705, iii. 46.)

Pages 293, 358. *Fetch me* Ben Jonson's *scull.*

In 1641 this was printed separately and anonymously as "*A Preparative to Studie; or, the Vertue of Sack*," 4to. Ben Jonson had died in August, 1637. Line 9 reads: dull *Hynde*; 21, Genius-making; 28, Welcome, by; after the word "scapes" these additional lines:—

> *I would not leave thee, Sack, to be with* Jove,
> *His Nectar is but faign'd, but I doe prove*
> *Thy more essentiall worth; I am (methinks), &c.*

Line 46, instead of "long since," reads "*of late*" (referring to whom?); 38, tempt a *Saint;* 44, *farther* bliss; 53, against thy *foes* (N.B.); That *would;* and, additional, after "horse," in line 56, this historical allusion to David Lesley, of the Scotch rebellion:—

> *I'me in the North already,* Lasley's *dead,*
> *He that would rise, carry the King his head,*
> *And tell him (if he aske, who kill'd the* Scot)
> *I knock't his Braines out with a pottle pot.*
> *Out ye Rebellious vipers; I'me come back*
> *From them againe, because there's no good Sack,*
> *T'other odd cup, &c.*

By this we are guided to the true date: between May, 1639, and August, 1640.

Pages 309, 399. *Why should we boast.*

Compare pp. 129, 315, of present volume, for the *Antidote* version and note upon it. Brief references must suffice for annotation here. See Mallory's "*Morte d'Arthur*," the French *Lancelot du Lac*, and *Sir Tristram*. Three MSS., the Auchinlech, Cambridge University, and Caius College, preserve the romance of *Sir Bevis of Hamptoun*, with his slaying the wild boar; his sword *Morglay* is often mentioned, like Arthur's *Excalibur:* Ascapard, the thirty-feet-long giant, who after a fierce battle becomes page to Sir Bevis. Caius Coll. MS. and others have the story *Richard Cœur de Leon*, but the street-ballad served equally to keep alive his fame among the populace, *Coll. Old Bds.* iii. 17. Wm. Ellis gives abstracts of romances on Arthur, Guy of Warwick, Sir Bevis, Richard Lion-heart, Sir Eglamour of Artoys, Sir Isumbras, the Seven Wise Masters, Charlemagne and Roland, &c., in his *Spec. Early English Metrical Romances*; of which J. O. Halliwell writes, in 1848 :— " Ellis did for ancient romance what Percy had previously accomplished for early poetry." In passing, we must not neglect to express the debt of gratitude due to the managers of the *E. E. Text Soc.*, for giving scholarly and trustworty prints of so many MSS., hitherto almost beyond reach. For *Orlando Inamorato* and *Orlando Furioso* we must go to Boiardo and Ariosto, or the translators, Sir John Harrington and W. Stewart Rose. Dunlop's *Hist. of Fiction* gives a slight notice of some of this ballad's heroes, including *Huon* of Bordeaux, the French *Livre de Jason*, Prince of the Myrmidons, the *Vie de Hercule*, the *Cléopâtre*, &c. Valentine and Orson is said to have been written in the reign of Charles VIII., and first printed at Lyons in 1495. SS. David, James, and Patrick, with the rest of the Seven Champions, like the Four Sons of Aymon, are of easy access. Cp. Warton.

ARTHUR O'BRADLEY.

(Merry Droll., Com., pp. 312, 395; *Antidote ag. Mel.*, 16).

Here is the five years' earlier Song of "Arthur o' Bradley," *(vide ante*, pp. 166—175) never before reprinted, we believe, and not mentioned by J. P. Collier, W. Chappell, &c., when they referred to "Saw ye not Pierce the Piper" of *Antidote* and *M. D., C.*, 1661. But ours is the earliest-known complete version [before 1642 ?] : —

A SONG. [p. 81.]

ALL you that desire to merry be,
   Come listen unto me,
And a story I shall tell,
Which of a Wedding befell,

Between *Arthur* of *Bradley*
And *Winifred* of *Madly*.
As *Arthur* upon a day
Met *Winifred* on the way,
He took her by the hand,
Desiring her to stand,
Saying I must to thee recite
A matter of [great] weight,
Of Love, that conquers Kings,
In grieved hearts so rings,
And if thou dost love thy Mother,
Love him that can love no other.
    Which is oh brave Arthur, &c.

For in the month of May,
Maidens they will say,
A May-pole we must have,   [∴ date before 1642.]
Your helping hand we crave.
And when it is set in the earth,
The maids bring Sullybubs forth;   [Syllabubs]
Not one will touch a sup,
Till I begin a cup.
For I am the end of all
Of them, both great and small.
Then tell me yea, or nay,
For I can no longer stay.
    With oh brave Arthur, &c.

Why truly *Arthur* [,] quoth she,
If you so minded be,
My good will I grant to you,
Or anything I can do.
One thing I will compell,
So ask my mothers good will.
Then from thee I never will flye,
Unto the day I do dye.
Then homeward they went with speed,
Where the mother they met indeed.
Well met fair Dame, quoth *Arthur*,
To move you I am come hither,

For I am come to crave,　　　　　　　　[p. 83.]
Your daughter for to have,
For I mean to make her my wife,
And to live with her all my life.
　　　With oh brave Arthur, &c.

The old woman shreek'd and cry'd,
And took her daughter aside,
How now daughter, quoth she,
Are you so forward indeed,
As for to marry he,
Without consent of me?
Thou never saw'st thirteen year,
Nor art not able I fear,
To take any over-sight,
To rule a mans house aright:
Why truly mother, quoth she,
You are mistaken in me;
If time do not decrease,
I am fifteen yeares at least.
　　　With oh brave Arthur, &c.

Then *Arthur* to them did walk,
And broke them of their talk.
I tell you Dame, quoth he,
I can have as good as thee;
For when death my father did call,
He then did leave me all
His barrels and his brooms,
And a dozen of wo[o]den spoones,
Dishes six or seven,
Besides an old spade, even
A brasse pot and whimble,
A pack-needle and thimble,
A pudding prick and reele,
And my mothers own sitting wheele;
And also there fell to my lot
A goodly mustard pot.
　　　With O brave Arthur, &c.

The old woman made a reply,
With courteous modesty,

If needs it must so be,
To the match I will agree.
For [when] death doth me call,
I then will leave her all;
For I have an earthen flaggon,
Besides a three-quart noggin,
With spickets and fossets five,
Besides an old bee-hive;
A wooden ladle and maile,
And a goodly old clouting paile;
Of a chaff bed I am well sped,
And there the Bride shall be wed,
And every night shall wear
A bolster stufft with haire,
A blanket for the Bride,
And a winding sheet beside,
And hemp, if he will it break,   [p. 85.]
New curtaines for to make.
To make all [well] too, I have
Stories gay and brave.
Of all the world so fine,
With oh brave eyes of mine,
    With oh brave Arthur, &c.

When *Arthur* his wench obtained,
And all his suits had gained,
A joyfull man was he,
As any that you could see.
Then homeward he went with speed,
Till he met with her indeed.
Two neighbours then did take
To bid guests for his sake;
For dishes and all such ware,
You need not take any care.
    With oh brave Arthur, &c.

To the Church they went apace,
And wisht they might have grace,
After the Parson to say,
And not stumble by the way;
For that was all their doubt,

That either of them should be out.
And when that they were wed,
And each of them well sped,
The Bridegroom home he ran,
And after him his man, [p. 86.]
And after him the Bride,
Full joyfull at the tyde,
As she was plac'd betwixt
Two yeomen of the Guests,
And he was neat and fine,
For he thought him at that time
Sufficient in every thing,
To wait upon a King.
But at the doore he did not miss
To give her a smacking kiss.
   With oh brave Arthur, &c.

   To dinner they quickly gat,
The Bride betwixt them sat,
The Cook to the Dresser did call,
The young men then run all,
And thought great dignity
To carry up Furmety.
Then came leaping *Lewis*,
And he call'd hard for Brewis;
Stay, quoth *Davy Rudding*,
Thou go'st too fast with th' pudding.
Then came *Sampson Seal*,
And he carry'd Mutton and Veal;
The old woman scolds full fast,
To the Cook she makes great hast,
And him she did controul,
And swore that the Porridge was cold.
   With oh brave, &c.

   My Masters a while be brief,
Who taketh up the Beef?
Then came *William Dickins*, [p 87.]
And carries the Snipes & Chickens.
Bartholomew brought up the Mustard,
Caster he carry'd the Custard.

D D

In comes *Roger Boore*,
He carry'd up Rabbets before :
Quoth *Roger*, I'le give thee a Cake,
If thou wilt carry the Drake.
[1] Speak not more nor less,
Nor of the greatest mess,
Nor how the Bride did carve,
Nor how the Groom did serve
    With oh brave Arthur, &c.

But when that they had din'd,
Then every man had wine ;
The maids they stood aloof,
While the young men made a proof,
Who had the nimblest heele,
Or who could dance so well,
Till *Hob* of the hill fell over,   [? oe'r]
And over him three or four.
Up he got at last,
And forward about he past ;
At *Rowland* he kicks and grins,
And he [? hit] *William* ore the shins ;
He takes not any offence,
But fleeres upon his wench.
The Piper he play'd [a] Fadding,
And they ran all a gadding.
    With oh brave Arthur [o' Bradley], &c.

("*Wits Merriment*," 1656, pp. 81-7.)

The often mentioned "Arthur o' Bradley's Wedding," a modern version attributed to Mr. Taylor, the actor and singer, is given, not only in *Songs and Ballads of the Peasantry*, &c., (p. 139 of R. Bell's Annot. ed.), collected by J. H. Dixon ; but also in Berger's *Red, White, and Blue Monster Songbook*, p, 394, where the music arranged by S. Hale is stated to be " at Walker's."

Pages 326, 402. *Why should we not laugh.?*

The reference to "Goldsmith's Hall" (see p. 363), where

a Roundhead Committee sate in 1647, and later, for the spoliation of Royalists' estates, levying of fines and acceptance of "Compounders" money, dates the song.

Pages 328, 402. *Now we are met.*

If we are to reckon the "twelve years together by the ears" from January 4, 1641-2, the abortive attempt of Charles I. to arrest at the House "the Five Members" (Pym, Hampden, Haslerig, Denzil Holles, and Strode), we may guess the date of this ballad to be 1653-4. Verse 14 mentions Oliver breaking the Long Parliament (20th April, 1653); and verses 15, 16 refer to the Little, or "Barebones Parliament" July 4, to 2nd December, 1653, (when power was resigned into the hands of Cromwell). Shortly after this, but certainly before Sept. 3rd, 1654 (when the next Parliament, more impracticable and persecuting, met), must be the true date of the ballad. "*Robin* the Fool" is "Robin Wisdom," Robert Andrews. "*Fair*" is Thomas Lord Fairfax the "Croysado-General." "Cowardly W—" is probably Philip, Lord Wharton, a Puritan, and Derby-House committee-man; of inferior renown to Atkins in unsavoury matters; but whose own regiment ran away at Edgehill: Wharton then took refuge in a saw-pit. President *Bradshaw* died 22nd Nov., 1659. Dr. Isaac DORISLAUS, Professor of History at Cambridge, and of Gresham College, apostatized from Charles I., and was sent as agent by the Commons to the Hague, where he was in June, 1649, assassinated by some cavaliers, falsely reported to be commissioned by the gallant Montrose (see the ballad "What though lamented, curst," &c., in King's Pamphlets, Brit. Mus).

"*Askew*," is "one Ascham a Scholar, who had been concerned in drawing up the King's Tryal, and had written a book," &c., (Clarendon. iii. 369, 1720). This Anthony Ascham, sent as Envoy to Spain from the Parliament in 1649, was slain at Madrid by some Irish officers, (Rapin:) of whom only one, a Protestant, was executed. See *Harl. Misc.* vi. 236-47. All which helped to cause the war with Spain in 1656.

Harry Marten's evil repute as to women, and lawyer Oliver St. John's building his house with stones plundered from Peterborough Cathedral, were common topics. "The women's war," often referred to as the "bodkin and thimble army," of 1647, was so called because the "Silly women," influenced by those who "crept into their houses," gave up their rings, silver bodkins, spoons and thimbles for support of Parliamentary troops.

Page 332, *line* 2, we should for *Our* read *Only*.

Page 348, line 10. "Old Lilly."

An allusion to William Lilly's predictive almanacks, shewing that this Catch was not much earlier in date than Hilton's book, 1652. Lilly was the original of Butler's "Cunning man, hight Sidrophel" in *Hudibras*, Part 2nd, Canto 3. Compare note, p. 353.

Page 361 (Appendix), *line* 5. For misprint *alterem*, read *alteram*.

Page 394 (Appendix), *New England, &c.*

References should be added to the *Rump* Coll., 1662, i. 95, and *Loyal Songs*, 1731, i. 92. "Isaack," is probably Isaac Pennington. Hampden and others were meditating this *journey to New England*, until stopped, most injudiciously, by an order in Council, dated April 6, 1638.

We here give our additional Note, on the "Sessions of the Poets," reserved from p. 376.

§ 3—SESSIONS OF POETS.

We believe that Sir John Suckling's Poem, sometimes called "A Sessions of Wit," was written in 1636-7; almost certainly before the death of Ben Jonson (6th August, 1637). Among its predecessors were Richard Barnfield's "Remembrance of some English Poets," 1598 (given in present volume, p. 273); and Michael Drayton's "Censure of the Poets," being a Letter in couplets, addressed to his friend Henry Reynolds; and the striking lines, "On the Time-Poets," pp. 5—7 of *Choyce Drollery*, 1656. The latter we have seen to be anonymous; but they were not impossibly by that very Henry Reynolds, friend of Drayton; although of this authorship no evidence has yet arisen. Of George Daniel's unprinted "Vindication of Poesie," 1636-47, we have given specimens on pp. 272, 280-1, and 331-2. Later than Suckling (who died in 1642), another author gave in print "The Great Assizes Holden in Parnassus by Apollo and his Assessors:" at which Sessions are arraigned Mercurius Britannicus, &c., Feb. 11th, 1644-5. This has been attributed to George Wither; most erroneously, as we believe. The mis-appropriation has arisen, probably, from the fact of Wither's name being earliest on the roll of Jurymen summoned:

"*Hee, who was called first in all the List,*
George Withers *hight, entitled Satyrist :*
Then *Cary,* May, *and* Davenant *were called forth,*
Renowned Poets all, and men of worth,
If wit may passe for worth : Then *Sylvester,*
Sands, Drayton, Beaumont, Fletcher, Massinger,
Shakespeare, and Heywood, *Poets good and free,*
Dramatick writers all, but the first three :
These were empanell'd all, and being sworne
A just and perfect verdict to return," &c. (p. 9.)

George Wither was quite capable of placing himself first on the list, in such a manner, we admit; but it is incredible to us that, if he had been the author, he could have described himself so insultingly as we find in the following lines, and elsewhere:—

> " he did protest
> That Wither *was a cruell Satyrist;*
> *And guilty of the same offence and crime,*
> *Whereof he was accused at this time:*
> *Therefore for him hee thought it fitter farre,*
> *To stand as a Delinquent at the barre,*
> *Then to bee now empanell'd in a Jury.*
> George Withers *then, with a Poetick fury,*
> *Began to bluster, but* Apollo's *frowne*
> *Made him forbeare, and lay his choler downe.*")
>
> (*Ibid,* p. 11.

Two much more sparkling and interesting "Sessions of Poets" afterwards appeared, to the tune of Ben Jonson's "Cook Laurel." The first of these begins:—

> Apollo, *concern'd to see the Transgressions*
>   *Our paltry Poets do daily commit,*
> *Gave orders once more to summon a Sessions,*
>   *Severely to punish th' Abuses of Wit.*
>
> Will d'Avenant *would fain have been Steward o' the Court,*
>   *To have fin'd and amerc'd each man at his will;*
> *But* Apollo, *it seems, had heard a Report,*
>   *That his choice of new Plays did show h' had no skill.*
>
> *Besides, some Criticks had ow'd him a spite,*
>   *And a little before had made the God fret,*
> *By letting him know the Laureat did write*
>   *That damnable Farce,* 'The House to be Let.'
>
> *Intelligence was brought, the Court being set*
>   *That a Play Tripartite was very near made;*
> *Where malicious* Matt. Clifford, *and spirituall* Spratt,
>   *Were join'd with their Duke, a Peer of the Trade,"* &c.

The author did not avow himself. It must have been written, we hold, in 1664-5. The second is variously attributed to John Wilmot, Earl of Rochester, and to George Villiers, Duke of Buckingham, being printed in the works of both. It begins:—

*" Since the Sons of the Muses grew num'rous aud loud,
For th' appeasing so factious and clam'rous a crowd,
Apollo thought fit in so weighty a cause,
T' establish a government, leader, and laws,"* &c.

Assembled near Parnassus, Dryden, Etherege, Wycherley, Shadwell, Nat Lee, Settle, Otway, Crowne, Mrs. Aphra Behn, Rawlins, Tom D'Urfey, and Betterton, are in the other verses sketched with point and vivacity; but in malicious satire. It was probably written in 1677. Clever as are these two later "Sessions," they do not equal Suckling's, in genial spirit and unforced cheerfulness.

We need not here linger over the whimsical Trial of Tom D'Urfey and Tom Brown (who squabbled between themselves, by the bye), in a still later "Sessions of the Poets Holden at the foot of Parnassus Hill, July the 9th, 1696: London, printed for E. Whitlock, near Stationers' Hall, 1696":—a mirthful squib, which does not lay claim to be called poetry. Nor need we do more than mention "A Trip to *Parnassus;* or, the Judgment of *Apollo* on Dramatic Authors and Performers. A Poem. London, 1788"—which deals with the two George Colmans, Macklin, Macnally, Lewis, &c. Coming to our own century, it is enough to particularize Leigh Hunt's "Feast of the Poets;" printed in his "Reflector," December, 1811, and afterwards much altered, generally with improvement (especially in the exclusion of the spiteful attack on Walter Scott). It begins—"*'Tother day as Apollo sat pitching his darts,*" &c. In 1837 Leigh Hunt wrote another such versical review, viz., "Blue-Stocking Revels; or, The Feast of the Violets." This was on the numerous "poetesses," but it cannot be deemed successful. Far superior to it is the clever and interesting "Fable for Critics," since written by James Russell Lowell in America.

Both as regards its own merit, and as being the parent of many others (none of which has surpassed, or even equalled it), Sir John Suckling's "Sessions of Poets" must always remain famous. We have not space remaining at command to annotate it with the fulness it deserves.

ADDITIONS AND CORRECTIONS.

The type-ornaments in *Choyce Drollery* reprint are merely substitutes for the ruder originals, and are not in *fac-simile*, as were the Initial Letters on pages 5 and 7 of our *Merry Drollery, Compleat* reprint.

Page 42, line 6, "a Lockeram Band:" Lockram, a cheap sort of linen, see J. O. Halliwell's valuable *Dictionary of Archaic and Provincial Words*, p. 525, edit. 1874. To this, and to the same author's 1876 edition of Archdeacon *Nares Glossary*, we refer readers for other words.

Page 73—77, 297, *Marchpine*, or *Marchpane*, biscuits often made in fantastic figures of birds or flowers, of sweetened almonds, &c. *Scettuall*, or *Setiwall*, the Garden Valerian. *Bausons*, i.e. badgers. *Cockers;* boots. Verse fifth omitted from *Choyce Drollery*, runs :—

"Her features all as fresh above,
 As is the grass that grows by *Dove,*
 And lythe as lass of *Kent;*
Her skin as soft as *Lemster* wool,
As white as snow on *Peakish Hull,*
 Or Swan that swims in *Trent.*"

A few typographical errors crept into sheet G (owing to an accident in the Editor's final collation with original). P. 81, line 2, read *Blacke*; line 20, Shaft ; p. 85, line 3, Unlesse; p. 86, line 5, Physitian; line 17, that Lawyer's; p. 87, line 9, That wil stick to the Laws; p. 88, line 8, O that's a companion; p. 90, first line, *basenesse;* line 23, nature; p. 91, line 13, add a comma after the word blot; p. 94, line 13, Scepter; p. 96, line 10, Of this; p. 97, line 15, For feare; p. 99 line 6, add a comma; p. 100, line 13, finde. These are all *single-letter* misprints.

Page 269, line 14, for *encreasing*, read *encreaseth ;* and end line 28 with a comma.

I. H. in line 35, are the initials of the author, "Iohn Higins."

Page 270, line 9, add the words—"It is by Sir Wm. Davenant, and entitled 'The Dying Lover.'"

Page 275, penultimate line, read *Poet-Beadle.* P. 277, l. 17, for 1698 read 1598.

Merry Drollery, 1670.

Page 281, line 20, for *liveth*, read *lives*; *claime*.

Page 289, after line 35, add—" Page 45, 'As I went to Totnam.' This is given with the music, in Tom D'Urfey's *Pills to purge Melancholy*, p. 180, of 1700 and 1719 (vol. iv.) editions; beginning " As I came from *Tottingham*.' The tune is named 'Abroad as I was walking. Page 52, *He that a Tinker;* Music by Dr. Jn. Wilson.

Page 330, after line 10, add—" *Fly, boy, fly:* Music by Simon Ives, in Playford's *Select Ayres*, 1659, p. 90."

The date of "The Zealous Puritan," *M.D.C.*, p. 95, was 1639. " He that intends," &c., *Ibid*, p. 342, is the *Vituperium Uxoris*, by John Cleveland, written before 1658 (*Poems*, 1661, p. 169).

"Love should take no wrong," in *Westminster-Drollery*, 1671, i. 90, dates back seventy years, to 1601: with music by Robert Jones, in his Second Book of Songs, Song 5.

Introduction to Merry Drollery (our second volume) p. xxii. lines 20, 21. Since writing the above, we have had the pleasure of reading the excellent " Memoir of Barbara, Duchess of Cleveland," and the "Althorp Memoirs," by G. Steinman Steinman, Esq., F. S. A., (printed for Private Circulation, 1871, 1869); by the former work, p. 22, we are led to discredit Mrs. Jameson's assertion that the night of May 29, 1660, was spent by Charles II. in the house of Sir Samuel Morland at Vauxhall. " This knight and friend of the King's *may* have had a residence in the parish of Lambeth before the Restoration, but as he was an Under Secretary of State at the time, it is more probable that he lived in London; and *as he did not obtain from the Crown a lease of Vauxhall mansion and grounds until April* 19, 1675, the foundations of a very improbable story, whoever originated it, are considerably shaken." Mr. Steinman inclines to believe the real place of meeting was Whitehall. He has given a list of Charles II.'s male companions in the Court at Bruges, with short biographies, in the *Archæologia*, xxxv. pp. 335-349. We knew not of this list when writing our Introduction to *Choyce Drollery*.

The Phœnix (emblematical of the Restoration) is adapted from Spenser's Works, 1611.

TABLE OF FIRST LINES
In "Merry Drollery," 1661, 1670, 1691
(Now first added.)

[The Songs and Poems *peculiar to the first edition*, 1661 (having been afterwards omitted), are here distinguished by being printed in Roman type. They are all contained *in the present volume*. Those that were added, in the later editions only, have no number attached to them in our first column of pages, viz. for 1661. The third edition, in 1691, was no more than a re-issue of the 1670 edition, with a fresh title-page to disguise it, in pretence of novelty (see p. 345, *ante*). The outside column refers to our Reprint of the "Drolleries;" but where the middle column is blank, as shewing the song was not repeated in 1670 and 1691, our Reprint-page belongs to the *present volume*. The "Reserved Pieces," given only in Supplement, bear the letter " R " (for the extra sheet, signed R*).—ED.]

FIRST LINES.	[In Editions]	1661	1670	1875
A Brewer may be a Burgess ...	ii.	70	252	252
A fig for Care, why should we			217	217
A Fox, a Fox, up gallants... ...		29	38	38
A Maiden of late, whose name ...		160	170	170
A Pox on the Jaylor, and on his			289	289
A Puritan of late		2		195
A Session was held the other day		68	72	72
A Story strange I will you tell ...	ii.	12	200	200
A young man of late...		27		201

Table of First Lines.

A young man that's in love ...		34	42	42
A young man walking all alone		32		204
After so many sad mishaps ...		112	118	118
After the pains of a desperate Lover			171	171
Ah, ah, come see what's		30	40	40
All in the Land of Essex		48	56	56
Am I mad, O noble Festus? ...	ii.	50	234	234
Amarillis *told her swain*			8	10
Among the Purifidian sect ...	ii.	103		243
Are you grown so melancholy? ...	ii.	101	286	286
Aske me no more why there appears		62	70	70
BACCHUS *I am, come from* ...		61	69	69
Be merry in sorrow		1[b]	6	8
Be not thou so foolish nice		61	69	69
Blind Fortune, if thou want'st ...		163	172	172
Bring forth your Cunny-skins ...	ii.	8	196	196
But since it was lately enacted ...	ii.	24	212	212
C*all for the Master, oh, this* ...			9	11
Call George *again, boy* ...	ii.	118	304	304
Calm was the evening, and clear			220	220
Calm was the evening, and clear			292	292
Cast your caps and cares aside ...		87	92	92
Come, Drawer, and fill us about	ii.	80	263	263
Come, Drawer, some wine ...	ii.	29		237
Come, Drawer, turn about the b.	ii.	86	268	268
Come, Drawer, come, fill us ...	ii.	3	190	190
Come, faith, let's frolick	ii.	65	246	246
Come, hither, my own sweet ...	ii.	106		247
Come, Imp Royal, come away ...	ii.	45	231	231
Come, Jack, *let's drink a pot of Ale*		45	52	52
Come, let us drink, the time invites		93	97	97

Table of First Lines.

Come, let's purge our brains ...		114	121	121
Come, my dainty Doxies, my Dove	ii.	44	230	230
Come, my Daphne, come away ...		86	91	91
Come, my delicate, bonny sweet ...		23	34	34
Cook Laurel would needs have ...	ii.	26	214	214
Discoveries of late have been	ii.	33		R^f
Doctors, lay by your irkesome		41	48	48
Fair Lady, for your New Year's	ii.	81		Rⁿ
Fetch me Ben Johnson's scull			293	293
From Essex Anabaptist Laws ...	ii.	38		241
From hunger and cold, who lives	ii.	9	197	197
From Mahomet and Paganisme		164	174	174
From the fair Lavinian shore ...			291	291
From what you call't Town ...		191	182	182
Full forty times over I have, &c.	ii.	61		Rⁱ
Gather your rosebuds while ...	ii.	11	199	199
Go, you tame Gallants, ...	ii.	57	242	242
God bless my good Lord Bishop...		166	176	176
Good Lord, what a pass is this ...		75	79	79
Had she not care enough			211	211
Hang Chastity! it is... ...		88		220
Have you observed the Wench ...	ii.	141	332	332
He is a fond Lover, that doateth	ii.	62		R^l
He that a happy life would lead	ii.	147	339	339
He that intends to take a wife ...	ii.	153	342	342
Heard you not lately of a man ...		169	180	180
Here's a health unto his Majesty			212	212
Hey, ho, have at all!...		168		R^e
Hold, quaff no more	ii.	19	210	210
How happy is the Prisoner ...		101	107	107
How poor is his spirit	ii.	48	232	232

I am a bonny Scot, Sir		119	127	127
I am a Rogue, and a stout one	ii.	16	204	204
I came unto a Puritan to woo ...		73	77	77
I doat, I doat, but am a sot ...	ii.	53	237	237
I dreamt my Love lay in her bed		11		197
I have reason to fly thee	ii.	97	281	281
I have the fairest Non-perel ...	ii.	99	283	283
I loved a maid—she loved not me	ii.	151		Rp
I marvel, Dick, that having been		46	54	54
I mean to speak of England's ...		85		218
I met with the Divel in the shape		103	109	109
I pray thee, Drunkard, get thee ...	ii.	119	306	306
I tell thee, Kit, where I have been			317	317
I went from England into France		64		213
If any one do want a House ...	ii.	64		Rm
If any so wise is, that Sack ...	ii.	157	348	348
If every woman were served in her		80	85	85
If none be offended with the scent	ii.	77	259	259
If that you will hear of a ditty ...	ii.	149		253
If thou wilt know how to chuse ...		21	32	32
If you will give ear	ii.	46		Rg
I'll go no more to the Old Exchange		126	134	134
I'll sing you a sonnet, that ne'er			66	66
I'll tell thee, Dick, where I have		97	101	101
I'll tell you a story, that never w.t.		123	131	131
In Eighty-eight, e'er I was born		77	82	82
In the merry month of May ...			99	99
It chanced not long ago, as I was	ii.	82	264	264
It was a man, and a jolly old man		95		222
Ladies, I do here present you ...	ii.	55	240	240
Lay by your pleading, Law...		118	125	125

Table of First Lines. 415

Lay by your pleading, Love lies a ii.	4	191	191
Let dogs and divels die	31	41	41
Let Souldiers fight for praise ... ii.	31	218	218
Let the Trumpet sound ... ... ii.	142	333	333
Let's call, and drink the cellar dry	130	138	138
Listen, lordings, to my story ... ii.	32		240
Mine own sweet honey bird ...	153		R^c
My bretheren all attend ...	91	95	95
My Lodging is on the cold ground		290	290
My Masters, give audience ... ... ii.	91	275	275
My Mistris is a shittle-cock ...	51	60	60
My Mistris is in Musick	154	163	163
My Mistris, whom in heart ...	107	113	113
Nay, out upon this fooling ...	79	84	84
Nay, prithee, don't fly me ...	25	36	36
Ne'er trouble thy self at the times		219	219
Nick Culpepper and William Lilly	56		190
No man Love's fiery passion ... ii.	1	187	187
No sooner were the doubtful people ii.	58	243	243
Now, gentlemen, if you will hear	18	29	29
Now I am married, Sir John ... ii.	96	280	280
Now, I confess, I am in love ...	1	5	7
Now Lambert's sunk, and gallant	12		198
Now thanks to the Powers below	156	166	166
Now that the Spring has filled ... ii.	110	296	296
Now we are met in a knot ... ... ii.	138	328	328
O that I could by any Chymick ii.	31		239
O the wily, wily Fox ... ... ii.	114	300	300
Of all the Crafts that I do know	7	17	17
Of all the rare juices		178	178
Of all the Recreations, which ...		146	146

Of all the Sciences beneath the Sun	ii. 129	319	319
Of all the Sports the world doth	ii. 111	296	296
Of all the Trades that ever I see	ii. 40	225	225
Of an old Souldier of the Queen's	20	31	31
Oliver, Oliver, *take up thy Crown*	ii. 72	254	254
Once was I sad, till I grew to be	2[b]	10	12
Pox take you, Mistris, I'll be gone	ii. 118	304	304
Pray, why should any man...	ii. 87	270	270
Riding to *London*, in *Dunstable*	14		200
Room for a Gamester... ...	ii. 10	197	197
Room for the best Poets heroick!	96	100	100
Saw you not Pierce *the piper* ...	ii. 124	312	312
She lay all naked in her bed...	ii. 115	300	300
She lay up to the navel bare ...	ii. 116		R°
She that will eat her breakfast ...	ii. 120	308	308
Shew a room, shew a room... ...	ii. 145	337	337
Sir Eglamore, *that valiant knight*	ii. 75	257	257
Some Christian people all give ear	81	87	87
Some wives are good, and some ...		302	302
Stay, shut the gate!	ii. 18	207	207
Sublimest discretions have club'd...		287	287
The Aphorisms of Galen ...	ii. 94	277	277
The best of Poets write of F.	141	153	153
The Hunt is up, the Hunt is up	20	30	30
The Proctors are two, and no more	105	111	111
The Spring is coming on	40	47	47
The thirsty Earth drinks up ...		22	22
The Turk *in linnen wraps*... ...	13	25	25
The Wise Men were but seven ...		232	232
The World's a bubble, and the life	104	110	110
There dwelt a Maid in the C. g.	37	46	46

There is a certain idle kind of cr.		140	152	152
There was a jovial Tinker		17	27	27
There was a Lady in this land ...		134		223
There was an old man had an acre		44	52	52
There was three birds that built		139		R^a
There was three Cooks in C ...	ii.	129	318	318
There's a lusty liquor which ...		132	140	140
There's many a blinking verse ...	ii.	35	221	221
Three merry Boys came out ...			220	220
Three merry Lads met at the Rose			143	143
'Tis not the Silver nor Gold ...		109	115	115
To friend and to foe		38	23	23
Tobacco that is wither'd quite ...		16	26	26
Tom *and* Will *were Shepherd* ...			149	149
Upon a certain time			146	R^b
Upon a Summer's day ...		148		230
Wake all you Dead, what ho!			151	151
Walking abroad in the m.		76	81	81
We Seamen are the honest boys ...		152	162	162
What an Ass is he, Waits, &c. ...	ii.	90	273	273
What Fortune had I, poor Maid	ii.	152	341	341
What is that you call a Maid. ...	ii.	68	249	249
What though the ill times do run		116	124	124
What though the times produce		161		R^d
When blind god Cupid, *all in an*	ii.	2	188	188
When first Mardike *was made* ...		4	12	12
When first the Scottish *war* ...		89	93	93
When I a Lady do intend to flatter	ii.	158	348	348
When I do travel in the night ...	ii.	73	255	255
When I'se came first to London	ii.	133	323	323
When Phœbus had drest	ii.	69	250	250

E E

When the chill Charokoe *blows*...	155	164	164
White bears have lately come ...	149	159	159
Why shonld a man care ... ... ii.	146	337	337
Why should we boast of Arthur ii.	122	309	309
Why should we not laugh ... ... ii.	136	326	326
Will you hear a strange thing ...	53	62	62
You Gods, that rule upon ... ii.	21		233
You talk of New England ... ii.	84	266	266
You that in love do mean to sport ii.	22		235

First Lines of the "Antidote" Songs:

GIVEN IN THIS VOLUME (AND NOT IN *M. D. C.*).

	[Present Reprint,] Page
A *Man of* Wales, *a little before* Easter...	157
An old house end	153
Bring out the [*c*]old *Chyne*	146
Come, come away to the Tavern, I say	150
Come hither, thou merriest of all the Nine	133
Come, let us cast dice who shall drink	151
Drink, drink, all you that think	158
Fly boy, fly boy, to the cellar's bottom	157
Good Symon, *how comes it*	154
Hang Sorrow, and cast away Care	152
Hang the Presbyter's *Gill*	144
He that a Tinker, a tinker will be	52
In love ? away ! you do me wrong	147
I's not come here to tauke of Prut...	141
Jog on, jog on the foot-path-way...	156
Let's cast away Care	152
'Mongst all the pleasant juices	150
My Lady and her Maid	152
Never let a man take heavily	151
Not drunken nor sober	113
Of all the birds that ever I see	155

E E 2

Old Poets Hypocrin *admire*	143
Once I a curious eye did fix	139
The parcht earth drinks the rain	157
The wit hath long beholden been	135
There was an old man at Walton Cross	151
This Ale, my bonny lads	155
'Tis Wine that inspires	145
Welcome, welcome, again to thy wit	159
What are we met? Come, let's see	156
Why should we boast of Arthur	129
Wilt thou be fat? I'le tell thee how	154
Wilt thou lend me thy mare	153
With an old song made by an old a. p.	125
You merry Poets, old boyes	149
Your mare is lame, she halts outright	153

HERE

HERE the Editor closes his willing toil, (after having added a *Table of First Lines*, and a *Finale*,) and offers a completed work to the friendly acceptance of Readers. They are no vague abstractions to him, but a crowd of well-distinguished faces, many among them being renowned scholars and genial critics. To approach them at all might be deemed temerity, were it not that such men are the least to be feared by an honest worker. On the other hand, it were easy for ill-natured persons to insinuate accusations against any one who meddles with Re-prints of *Facetiæ*. Blots and stains are upon such old books, which he has made no attempt to disguise or palliate. Let them bear their own blame. There are dullards and bigots in the world, nevertheless, who decry all antiquarian and historical research. A defence is unnecessary: "Let them rave!"

> *Fama di loro il mondo esser non lassa,*
> *Misericordia e giustizia gli sdegna,*
> *Non ragioniam di lor, ma guarda e passa.*

He thanks those who heartily welcomed the earlier Volumes, and trusts that no unworthy successor is to be found in the present Conclusion, which holds many rare verses. Hereafter may ensue another meeting. Our olden Dramatists and Poets open their cellars, full of such vintage as Dan Phœbus had warmed. Leaving these "*Drolleries of the Restoration*" behind him, as a Nest-Egg, the Editor bids his Readers cheerfully

FAREWELL!

FINALE.

FINALE.

" Laudator temporis acti" cantat :—

1.

CLOSED now the book, untrimmed the lamp,
   Flung wide the lattice-shutter;
The night-breeze strikes in, chill and damp,
   The fir-trees moan and mutter:
Lo, dawn is near! pale Student, thou
   No count of time hast reckon'd;
Go, seek a rest for weary brow
   From dreams of Charles the Second.

2.

Sad grows the world: those hours are past
   When, jovially convivial,
Choice Spirits met, and round them cast
   Such glow as made cares trivial;
When nights prolonged through following days
   Found night still closing o'er us,
While Youth and Age exchanged their lays,
   Or intertwined in chorus.

3.

Our gravest Pundits of the Bench,
   Most reverend Sirs of Pulpit,
Smiled at the praise of some coy wench,
   Or—if too warm—could gulp it.

Loyal to King, faithful to Church,
   And firm to Constitution,
No friend, no foe they left in lurch,
   Or sneaked to Revolution.

4.

There, many a sage Physician told
   Fresh facts of healing knowledge;
There, the dazed Bookworm could grow bold,
   And speak of pranks at College:
There, weary Pamphleteers forgot
   Faction, debates, and readers,
But helped to drain the clinking-pot
   With punning Special-pleaders.

5.

How oft some warrior, famed abroad
   For valour in campaigning,
Exchanged the thrust with foes he awed
   For hob-a-nob Champaigning!
While some Old Salt, an Admiral
   And Circumnavigator,
Joined in the revel at our call,
   Nor sheer'd-off three days later.

6.

Who lives to thrill with jest and song,
   Like those whose memories haunt us?—
Who never knew a night too long,
   Or head-ache that could daunt us.

The weaklings of a later day
    Win neither Mirth nor Thinking;
They mix, and spoil, both work and play:
    They've lost the art of Drinking!

7.

For me, I lonely grow, and shy,
    No one seems worth my courting;
Though girls have still a laughing eye,
    And tempt to May-day sporting:
For sillier youth, or richer Lord,
    Or some staid prig, and colder,
"Neat-handed Phillis" spreads the board,
    And Chloe bares her shoulder.

8.

In days gone by, light grew the task,
    For holidays were glorious;
It was the *talk* sublimed the flask,
    That now is deemed uproarious.
We've so much Methodistic cant,
    Abstainers' Total drivel,
And, worse, Utilitarian rant—
    One scarcely can keep civil.

9.

Our politics are insincere,
    For Statesmen cog and shuffle;
They hit not from the shoulder clear,
    But dodge, and spar with muffle.

How Bench and Bar sink steeped in mire,
    Avails not here recording:
While Prelates cannot now look higher
    Than to mere self-rewarding.

10.

Friends of old days, 'tis well you died
    Before, like me, you sickened
Amid the rottenness and pride
    That in this world have quickened:
You passed, ere yet your hopes grew dim,
    While Love and Friendship warmed you:
I look but to th' horizon's rim,
    For all that erst had charmed you.

11.

Not here, amid a lower crew,
    I seek to fill your places;
For men no more have hearts as true,
    Nor maids,—though fair their faces.
My thoughts flit back to earlier days,
    Where Pleasure's finger beckon'd,
Cheered with the Beauty, Love, and Lays
    That warmed our Charles the Second.

J. W. E.

Biblioth. Ashmol., Cantium, 1876.

[End of "The 'Drolleries' of the Restoration."]

Drollery Reprints.

Uniform with "Choice Drollery."
Published at 10s. 6d. to Subscribers, *now raised* to
21s; large paper, published at £1 1s, *now
raised* to £2 2s.

A RE-PRINT
OF THE
Westminster Drollery,
1671, 1672.

TO those who are already acquainted with the two parts of the *Westminster Drollery*, published in 1671 and 1672, it must have appeared strange that no attempt has hitherto been made to bring these delightful volumes within reach of the students of our early literature. The originals are of extreme rarity, a perfect copy seldom being attainable at any public sale, and then fetching a price that makes a book-hunter almost despair of its acquisition. So great a favourite was it in the Cavalier times, that most copies have been literally worn to pieces in the hands of its many admirers, as they chanted forth a merry stave from the pages. *There is no collection of songs surpassing it in the language,* and as representative of the lyrics of the first twelve years after the Restoration it is unequalled: by far the greater number are elsewhere unattainable.

The WESTMINSTER DROLLERIES are reprinted with the utmost fidelity, page for page, and line for line, not a word being altered, or a single letter departing from the original spelling.

DROLLERY RE-PRINTS.

NOW READY.

"*Merry Drollery, Complete,*"
1661, 1691.

ERRY DROLLERY, COMPLETE is not only amusing, but as an historical document is of great value. It is here reproduced, with the utmost exactitude, for students of our old literature, from the edition of 1691. The few rectifications of a corrupt text are invariably held within square brackets, when not reserved for the Appendix of Notes, Illustrations, and Emendations. Thirty-four Songs, additional, that appeared only in the 1661 edition, will be given separately; the intermediate edition of 1670 being also collated. A special Introduction has been prefixed, drawing attention to the political events of the time referred to, and some account of the authors of the Songs in this *Merry Drollery*.

The work is quite distinct in character from the *Westminster Drolleries*, 1671-72, but forms an indispensable companion to that ten-years-later volume. Twenty-five songs and poems, that had not appeared in the 1661 edition, were added to the after editions of *Merry Drollery;* but without important change to the book. It was essentially an offspring of the Restoration, the year 1660-61, and it thus gives us a genuine record of the Cavaliers in their festivity.

Whatever is offensive, therefore, is still of historical importance. Even the bitterness of sarcasm against the Rump Parliament, under whose rule so many families had long groaned; the personal invective, and unsparing ridicule of leading Republicans and Puritans; were such as not unnaturally had found favour during the recent Civil War and Usurpation. The preponderance of Songs in praise of Sack and loose revelry is not without significance. A few pieces of coarse humour, *double entendre*, and breaches of decorum attest the fact that already among the Cavaliers were spread immorality and licentiousness. The fault of an impaired discipline had borne evil fruit, beyond defeat in the field and exile from positions of power. Mockery and impurity had been welcomed as allies, during the warfare against bigotry, hypocrisy, and selfish ambition. We find, it is true, few of the sweeter graces of poetry in *Choice Drollery* and in *Merry Drollery;* but, instead, much that helps us to a sounder understanding of the social, military, and political life of those disturbed times immediately preceding the Restoration.

Of the more than two hundred pieces, contained in *Merry Drollery*, fully a third are elsewhere unattainable, and the rest are scarce. Among the numerous attractions we may mention the rare Song of "Love lies a bleeding" (p. 191), an earnest protest against the evils of the day; the revelations of intolerant military violence, such as The Power of the Sword (125), Mardyke (12), Pym's Anarchy (70), The Scotch War (93), The New Medley of the Country-man, Citizen, and Soldier (182), The Rebel Red-Coat (190), and "Cromwell's Coronation" (254), with the masterly description of Oliver's Routing the Rump (62). Several Anti-Puritan Songs about New England are here, and provincial descriptions of London (95, 275, 323). Rollicking staves meet us, as from the Vagabond (204), The Tinker of Turvey (27), The Jovial Loyallist, with the Answer to it, in a nobler strain, by one who sees the ruinous vileness of debauchery (pp. 207, 209); and a multitude of Bacchanalian Catches. The two songs on the Blacksmith (225, 319), and both of those on The Brewer (221, 252), referring to Cromwell, are here; as well as the ferocious exultation over the Regicides in a dialogue betwixt Tower-hill and Tyburn (131). More than a few of the spirited Mad-songs were favourites. Nor are absent such ditties as tell of gallantry, though few are of refined affection and exalted heroism. The absurd impossibilities of a Medicine for the Quartan Ague (277, cf. 170), the sly humour of the delightful "How to woo a Zealous Lady" (77), the stately description of a Cock-fight (242), the Praise of Chocolate (48), the Power of Money (115), and the innocent merriment of rare Arthur o' Bradley's Wedding (312), are certain to please. Added, are some of the choicest poems by Suckling, Cartwright, Ben Jonson, Alexander Brome, Fletcher, D'Avenant, Dryden, Bishop Corbet, and others. "The Cavalier's Complaint," with the Answer to it, has true dramatic force. The character of a Mistress (60), shows one of the seductive Dalilahs who were ever ready to betray. The lampoons on D'Avenant's "Gondibert" (100, 118) are memorials of unscrupulous ridicule from malicious wits. "News, that's No News" (159), with the grave buffoonery of "The Bow Goose" (153), and the account of a Fire on London Bridge (87), in the manner of pious balladmongers (the original of our modern "Three Children Sliding on the Ice"), are enough to make Heraclitus laugh. Some of the dialogues, such as "Resolved not to Part" (113), The Bull's Feather" (i.e. the Horn, p. 264), and that between a Hare and the hounds that are chasing him (296), lend variety to the volume; which contains, moreover, some whimsical stories in verse, (one being "A Merry Song" of a Husbandman whose wife gets him off a bad bargain, p. 17: compare p. 200), told in a manner that would have delighted Mat Prior in later days.

It is printed on Ribbed Toned paper, and the Impression is limited to 400 copies, fcap. 8vo. 10s. 6d.; and 50 copies large paper, demy 8vo. 21s. Subscribers' names should be sent at once to the Publisher,

ROBERT ROBERTS, BOSTON, LINCOLNSHIRE.

Every copy is numbered and sent out in the order of Subscription.

☞ This series of Re-prints from the rare *Drolleries* is now completed in Three Volumes (of which the first published was the *Westminster Drollery*): that number being sufficient to afford a correct picture of the times preceding and following the Restoration 1660, without repetition. The third volume contains "*Choice Drollery*," 1656, and all of the "*Antidote against Melancholy*," 1661, which has not been already included in the two previous volumes; with separate Notes, and Illustrations drawn from other contemporary Drolleries.

OPINIONS OF THE PRESS, &c.

"Strafford Lodge, Oatlands Park,
Surrey, Feb. 4, 1875.

DEAR SIR,
I received the "Westminster Drolleries" yesterday evening. I have spent nearly the whole of this day in reading it. I can but give unqualified praise to the editor, both for his extensive knowledge and for his admirable style. The printing and the paper do great credit to your press. . . . I enclose a post-office order to pay for my copy.

Yours truly,
Mr. Robert Roberts. WM. CHAPPELL."

From J. O. Halliwell, Esqre.

"No. 11, Tregunter Road, West Brompton,
London, S. W.,
DEAR SIR, 25th Feby. 1875.
I am charmed with the edition of the "Westminster Drollery." One half of the reprints of the present day are rendered nearly useless to exact students either by alterations or omissions, or by attempts to make eclectic texts out of more than one edition. By all means let us have introductions and notes, especially when as good as Mr. Ebsworth's, but it is essential for objects of reference that one edition only of the old text be accurately reproduced. The book is certainly admirably edited.

Yours truly,
To Mr. R. Roberts. J. O. PHILLIPPS."

From F. J. Furnivall, Esq.

"3, St. George's Square, Primrose Hill, London, N.W.,
2nd February, 1875.
MY DEAR SIR,
I have received the handsome large paper copy of your "Westminster Drolleries." I am very glad to see that the book is really *edited*, and that well, by a man so thoroughly up in the subject as Mr. Ebsworth.

Truly yours,
F. J. F."

From the Editor of the "Fuller's Worthies Library," "Wordsworth's Prose Works," &c.

"Park View, Blackburn,
Lancashire, 13th July, 1875.

DEAR SIR,
I got the "Westminster Drolleries" *at once*, and I will see after the "Merry Drollery" when published.

Go on and prosper. Mr. Ebsworth is a splendid fellow, evidently. Yours,

A. B. GROSART."

J. P. COLLIER, Esqre., has also written warmly commending the work, in private letters to the Editor, which he holds in especial honour.

From the "Academy," July 10th, 1875.

"It would be a curious though perhaps an unprofitable speculation, how far the 'Conservative reaction' has been reflected in our literature. . . . . Reprints are an important part of modern literature, and in them there is a perceptible relaxation of severity. Their interest is no longer mainly philological. Of late, the Restoration has been the favourite period for revival. Its dramatists are marching down upon us from Edinburgh, and the invasion is seconded by a royalist movement in Lincolnshire. A Boston publisher has begun a series of drolleries—intended, not for the general public, but for those students who can afford to pay handsomely for their predilection for the byways of letters.

"The Introduction is delightful reading, with quaint fancies here and there, as in the 'imagined limbo of unfinished books.' . . . . There is truth and pathos in his excuses for the royalist versifiers who 'snatched hastily, recklessly, at such pleasures as came within their reach, heedless of price or consequences.' We may not admit that they were 'outcasts without degradation,' but we can hardly help allowing that 'there is a manhood visible in their failures, a generosity in their profusion and unrest. They are not stainless, but they affect no concealment of faults. Our heart goes to the losing side, even when the loss has been in great part deserved.' .... The fact is, that in his contemplation of the follies and vices of 'that very distant time' he loses all apprehension of their grosser elements, and retains only an appreciation of their wit, their elegance, and their vivacity. Without offence be it said, in Lancelot's phrase, 'he does something smack, something grow to; he has a kind of taste,'—and so have we too, as we read him. These trite and ticklish themes he touches with so charming a liberality that his generous allowance is contagious. We feel in thoroughly honest company, and are ready to be heartily charitable along with him. For his is no unworthy tolerance of vice, still less any desire to polish its hardness into such factitious brilliancy as glistens in Grammont. It is a manly pity for human weakness, and an unwillingness to see, much less to pry into, human depravity. 'It would have been a joy for us to know that these songs were wholly speck must go hungry through many an orchard, even unobjectionable; but he who waits to eat of fruit without past the apples of the Hesperides.' .... The little book is well worth the attention of any one desirous to have a bird's-eye view of the Restoration 'Society.' Its scope is far wider than its title would indicate. The 'Drolleries' include not only the rollicking rouse of the staggering blades who 'love their humour well, boys,' the burlesque of the Olympian revels in 'Hunting the Hare,' the wild vagary of Tom of Bedlam, and the gibes of the Benedicks of that day against the holy estate, but lays of a delicate and airy beauty, a dirge or two of exquisite pathos, homely ditties awaking patriotic memories of the Armada and the Low Country wars, and 'loyal cantons' sung to the praise and glory of King Charles. The 'late and true story of a furious scold' might have enriched the budget of Autolycus, and Feste would have found here a store of 'love-songs,' and a few 'songs of good life.' The collection is of course highly miscellaneous. After the stately measure may come a jig with homely 'duck and nod,' or even a dissonant strain from the 'riot and ill-managed merriment' of Comus,

'Midnight shout, and revelry,
Tipsy dance, and jollity.'"

DROLLERY RE-PRINTS.

From the " Bookseller," March, 1875.

"If we wish to read the history of public opinion must read the songs of the times : and those who help to do this confer a real favour. Mr. Thomas Wright done enormous service in this way by his collections of political songs. Mr. Chappell has done better by giving us the music with them; but much remains to be done. On examining the volume before us, we are surprised to find so many really beautiful pieces, and so few of the coarse and vulgar. Even the latter will compare favourably with the songs in vogue amongst the fast men in the early part of the present century.

The "*Westminster Drolleries*" consist of two collections of poems and songs sung at Court and theatres, the first published in 1671, and the second in 1672. Now for the first time reprinted. The editor, Mr. J. Woodfall Ebsworth, has prefaced the volume with an interesting introduction . . . and, in an appendix of nearly eighty pages at the end, has collected a considerable amount of bibliographical and anecdotical literature. Altogether, *we think this may be pronounced the best edited of all the reprints of old literature*, which are now pretty numerous. A word of commendation must also be given to Mr. Roberts, of Boston, the publisher and printer—the volume is a credit to his press, and could have been produced in its all but perfect condition only by the most careful attention and watchful oversight."

From the "Athenæum," April 10*th,* 1875.

"Mr. Ebsworth has, we think, made out a fair case in his Introduction for reprinting the volume without excision. The book is not intended *virginibus puerisque*, but to convey to grown men a sufficient idea of the manners and ideas which pervaded all classes in society at the time of the reaction from the Puritan domination. . . . . Mr. Ebsworth's Introduction is well written. He speaks with zest of the pleasant aspects of the Restoration period, and has some words of praise to bestow upon the 'Merry Monarch' himself. . . . Let us add that his own "Prelude," "Entr' Acte," and "Finale" are fair specimens of versification."

www.ingramcontent.com/pod-product-compliance
Lightning Source LLC
Chambersburg PA
CBHW051852300426
44117CB00006B/367